A Hunter's Life among the Lions, El Animals
By Bayard Taylor

CHAPTER I

Having resolved to make a hunting expedition into the interior 'of Southern Africa, my first object was to seek out some experienced person, able to give me the necessary information as to what purchases I should require to make in the way of wagons and oxen, and as to my outfit in general, and I accordingly pitched upon an individual of the name of Murphy, a trader in the interior, who, I had reason to believe, was better acquainted than any other person in Grahamstown with the frontiers of the colony, and the adjoining territories of the Griqua and Bechuana tribes, situated beyond the Great Orange River. With this person I had already had the pleasure of becoming acquainted during the short time I was quartered in Grahamstown in the month of July, haying been introduced to him by another trader, a man from my own land of Moray, famous among the Dutch Boers about and beyond the frontiers. This man's name was Andrew Thompson, of Forres, one of three brothers, all of whom followed the same adventurous line of life, and were as steady, hard-working, and determined young men as might be met with throughout the colony.

As, in the course of the following pages, I may have occasion to allude to these traders, and others of a similar avocation, it will, perhaps, be as well to give the reader a sketch of the manner in which their occupation is conducted. Each trader is supposed to be the proprietor of one or two ox-wagons. These they "load up," from the large stores of the merchants in Grahamstown and Port Elizabeth, with every species of merchandise which the far-dwelling isolated Dutch Boers are likely to require. So supplied, they set out on their long journey, which usually occupies from six to eight months; at the end of which they return to the colony, enriched with immense droves of sleek oxen and fat weathers, selected from the numerous herds and flocks of the pastoral dwellers in the interior. The wagons of a trader generally contain every requisite for a farmer's establishment: groceries, hardware, bales of cloth and canvas, haberdashery, saddlery, crockery —in short, everything, from an awl for the Boer to mend his "feldt schoens" or country shoes, to a roll of cherry-colored or sky-blue ribbon to tie up the bonny brown locks of his fair davighters, whose beauty, like that of Skye terriers, I fear, in many cases, consists in their ugliness. They, however, sadly lack the "degagee" appearance of the Skye terrier, as their general air and gait might be more aptly likened to a yard of pump-water.

The price which a trader gives for a wagon is usually from d£40 to £60, and in war times often a thousand six dollars, or £75. The number of oxen which he usually obtains for it at the close of his journey is from forty to fifty, and these he is supposed to select himself. The value of the wagon is partly dependent on the character of the tent. Tents are of two kinds; the one being coarsely yet strongly constructed of green boughs fitting into iron staples along the sides of the wagon, and lashed together with strips of green hide so as to form a succession of arches overhead. These are kept in their position by means of long straight wands laid all along the outside of the arches, the whole frame-work being very strongly secured by the afore-mentioned strips of green hide. On the top of this are placed coarse Kaffir mats made of reeds, which act as a Scotchman (to use a sea-faring phrase) to keep the wagon-sail, which is of stout canvas, from chafing. The other variety of tent is of a less homely build, and is termed by the colonists a cap-tent wagon. It requires the hand of a skillful wagon-builder, and is much more elaborately finished, the wood, which supports and composes the tent being all neatly sawed and planed, and fastened together with iron rivets.

This description of wagon is preferred by the aristocracy among the Boers, as presenting a more distingue appearance, when they drive their fraus and children on a round of visits, which they are constantly doing, or when flocking to the "Nachmal," or communion, which happens three or four times in the year. The former, or common wand tent, however, possessed a great advantage over the cap tent, inasmuch as, in the first place, it is cheaper by £10, and, secondly, if broken in a capsize, which in Cape traveling is an affair of common occurrence, it is easily repaired on the spot; whereas the cap-tent wagon, if once upset, is irretrievably ruined.

When a trader arrives on a Boer's farm, he halts and walks up to the door to inquire where he is to "outspan," or unyoke the oxen, and also in what direction the oxen are to be driven to graze. At the door he is met by the baas, or master, generally pipe in mouth, who, cordially greeting him with one hand, raises his hat from his head with the other. The Boers lay great stress on this piece of etiquette, which has to be gone through with a whole string of juvenile Boers following in the rear, each incased in a very roomy pair of inexpressibles, and crowned with an immense broad rimmed tile, nearly half the size of its wearer. Permission to outspan being obtained, and a few complimentary speeches interchanged, the trader inquires of the Boer if he has any fat oxen to handle or barter, to which the Boer either at once replies in the negative, or more commonly says, "I do not know. What have you got on your wagon?" The trader answers, "I have got a little of everything, and all of the very best quality, and you shall have anything you require as low as a trader can possibly sell it. I shall presently unload a little for your inspection." The Boer politely says, " No, no, mynheer, you must not offload; it would grieve me that mynheer should exert himself so much;" to which the trader replies, "It is no trouble; we are accustomed to do it, and it is our business."

As the trader knows well from past experience that the Boer will be sure to endeavor to abate his prices, he makes a point of asking a little more than he intends to take, so as to be able to give in to the Boer's importunities, who, with a sly wink at his wife, congratulates himself on his shrewdness, and flatters himself that he has run a hard bargain.

When the trader has collected all his cattle, he drives them by steady marches of from twenty to thirty miles in the twenty-four hours, which are performed chiefly during the night, to Grahamstown or Beaufort, where he disposes of them to butchers. At the former place they are purchased for the use of the town, and by the government contractors for the supply of the troops. At Beaufort, which is on the high road to Cape Town, they are purchased for the supply of the Cape Town market. The payments for the cattle are seldom, if ever, made in hard cash, the poor trader having to content himself with approved bills, drawn at six and nine months, which in too many cases are never honored, the defaulter being found either bankrupt, or to have bolted for England or California. The life of a trader is hard and harassing, and he is often liable to very heavy losses by deaths from severe drought, distempers, and other causes ; also from the chances of war, oxen straying and being found no more, overstocked markets, and non-payments as above, besides the danger to which he is exposed from the attacks of wild beasts. During the time that he is engaged in driving his oxen, his rest is necessarily broken and disturbed, and, being compelled to watch his cattle every hour of the night, in all weathers, he is obliged always to have his clothes on, and to sleep when he can, after the manner of sea-captains in bad weather, who hang their nose on to a ratlin, and so take a nap. As an instance of the injury from chances of war, I may here allude to the severe losses sustained by my friend Mr. Peter Thompson, who, during the war which ravaged the colony in the years 1846 and 1847, was returning to Grahamstown with a large herd of some hundred fine oxen, the well-earned proceeds of a laborious and toilsome expedition, when he was attacked in De Bruin's Poort, a rugged and densely-wooded ravine, within one march of Grahamstown, by a band of the marauding Amaponda Kaffirs, armed with guns and assagais, who swept off the whole of his drove, he himself barely escaping with his life.

In years when the prices of cattle are low, these traders occasionally vary their line of march, and, forsaking the Boers for a season, they load up a suitable cargo, and direct their course for the Bechuana tribes, from whom they obtain ivory, karosses (skin cloaks), and ostrich feathers, along with various curiosities, for which they obtain a ready sale in the Grahamstown market, where good ivory averages from 45, to 4s. per pound. Karosses vary in price from £3 each, according to their size, kind, and quality. Ostrich feathers used to fetch from d£5 to £6 per pound, but, partly owing to the feathers being less worn by the votaries of fashion in London, and partly to the late disturbances throughout Europe, the prices have greatly fallen. The articles required for trading with the Bechuana tribes consist of beads of all sizes and colors, brass and copper wire, knives and hatchets, clothing for both sexes, ammunition, guns, young cows, and she-goats. The two latter the trader obtains in barter from the Boers, Griqua and Koranna tribes, more immediately adjacent to the colony. Some writers have erroneously stated that snuff and tobacco are a good circulating medium among the tribes in Southern Africa, but in the course of my experience I can scarcely remember having ever obtained the smallest article in barter for either, not even a drink of milk. The natives have certainly no objection to receive these articles when given gratuitously, but are far too wide awake to place any great value upon them.

On making inquiries, I had the pleasure to find that, contrary to my expectation, both Andrew Thompson and Murphy were still in Grahamstown, where I had left .them about three months before, when I marched thence into Caffraria with my regiment; and the latter, whom I found to be a confirmed tippler, was able in his few lucid moments to give me much valuable information relative to the preparations which I required to make in the way of purchasing oxen and wagons, engaging servants, &c., &c.; also various wrinkles as to the conducting of my establishment, the hours of marching, and the line of country which I had chalked out for my first expedition. Poor Murphy! he was as kind-hearted a creature as ever breathed.

From the 1st till the 22nd of October I was actively employed in making the necessary purchases and arrangements for my coming expedition, and in forwarding my affairs, in which Murphy, during his sober intervals, most willingly assisted me. As the reader will observe, my establishment at my first outset was on a much more limited scale than upon subsequent expeditions. This was partly owing to the uncertainty which I felt as to the success of my sporting undertakings, and the length of time which I might feel inclined to devote to this line of life. I was much in the dark as to what sport I might expect to realize, and what difficulties I should have to encounter, in the trip was about to make; the truth being that I could not find a single individual, cither among the natives or the military, who could in the smallest degree enlighten me on the subject.

The general impression among my military friends was, that any game which remained in the interior must have, ere then, retreated to such remote parts, far away in the territories of savage tribes, as to be utterly beyond the reach of any sportsman, however enterprising; and when they saw me bustling about, making my purchases, they used to say to me, "It is all nonsense your laying out your money in this way. Why don't you rather go home at once to your own country? We shall see you returning in a month or two, like those fellows who went on a shooting trip last year, with a coup-de-soleil and an attack of dysentery, utterly disgusted with the country, and selling off all these things on which you are now expending so much capital."

The shooting party here alluded to consisted of one officer of the 7th Dragoons, two of the 27th and others who, having obtained a few weeks' leave, and burning to distinguish themselves in a campaign against the ferae of Southern Africa, had hired a wagon and penetrated as far as the Thebus Mountain, where for a few days they enjoyed some good sport among the black wildebeest and springboks which abound on the plains surrounding that mountain; till, having broken the stocks of their rifles in falls from their horses while impetuously "jaging" the game, they returned to headquarters, one suffering from coup-de-soleil, and the rest from dysentery brought on by drinking bad water, they having been unfortunate in the lay beside which they had fixed their encampment.

Notwithstanding these friendly dissuasions on the part of my acquaintance, I continued to prosecute my affairs so unremittingly, that on the 22nd I considered my manifold arrangements complete, and, being much harassed and annoyed by the unavoidable delays to which I had been subjected, I was full of impatience to make a start. These delays were in a great measure occasioned by the weather, heavy and constant rains having fallen during the previous fourteen days, accompanied with a cold wind off the Southern Ocean. This, of necessity, materially interfered with and delayed me in my arrangements, and had also the effect of rendering the country perfectly unfit for locomotion, in many places cutting up the roads with rugged, impassable water-courses, and in low-lying districts converting them into deep, impracticable quagmires.

It will here be necessary to give a detailed account of my outfit, to put the reader at once in possession of the extent and nature of my establishment and camp equipage. My first object was, of course, to secure a traveling wagon, and I had the good fortune to obtain an excellent new cap-tent one, complete with all its gear ready for in spanning, from Mr. Ogilvie, of Grahamstown, for the sum of £60, which, as it eventually proved to be a right good one, was decidedly a bargain. I very soon, however, found out, as I extensively collected specimens of natural history, that one wagon was insufficient; and not long after, in the town of Colesberg, on the frontiers of the colony, I purchased a second, also a cap-tent wagon, with its necessary accompaniment, a span of oxen; and at a later period, as the reader will subsequently learn, I found it necessary to purchase a third, and became the proprietor of considerably more than a hundred draught oxen.

From an English farmer in the vicinity of Grahamstown I obtained a span of twelve excellent, well-trained, black, zuur-veldt oxen, which I judged suited for my work, they having been in the habit, with their late master, of bringing in very heavy loads of wood to the Grahamstown market. Their price was £o each; and as it is not unusual to see an ox, in the best of spans, knock up on long marches, by Murphy's advice I purchased two spare oxen of Mr. Thompson.

My stud of horses as yet consisted of but two, which had been my chargers in the regiment. These were "Sinon," a stallion which I had bought of Major Goodman of the 27th, and "The Cow," an excellent dark brown gelding which I had obtained from Colonel Somerset of "Ours." I did not think it wise to lay out more money in horse-flesh in Grahamstown, as I should shortly have to pass through the Hantam, where most of the Boers breed horses extensively, which are famed for their spirit and hardiness throughout the colony. I engaged four servants— namely, an Englishman called Long, as head-servant, a thorough Cockney, who, as I afterward learned, had formerly been a cab-driver in London, and whom I took into my service at Murphy's recommendation. Long being supposed to possess a certain degree of experience, having penetrated as far as the banks of the Orange River on a trading excursion on his own account; but his heart, as the event proved, inclined more to worship at the shrine of Venus than at that of Diana. A certain little dark-eyed damsel, who acted as laundress to the military, and who was employed all day in driving her mangle, seemed entirely to engross his thoughts. Long frequently observing that "there was that sweet little creature obliged to drive a mangle who ought rather to be sitting practicing at her 'pihanne.'"

My other three servants were natives. A wagon driver named Kleinboy, a stout, active

Hottentot, with the high cheek bones and woolly head of his race, and who was quite au fait at his department. Like many others of his countrymen, he was subject to fits of sulks, and much preferred reclining for hours under my wagons, or in the shade of a bush practicing on his violin, to looking after his master's work. My leader's name was Carollus: he was the third whom I had engaged in that capacity, the other two having absconded. He was a stout, powerful fellow, descended from the Mozambique races. He entered my service under cover of night, having absconded from Kingsley of "Ours," that gentleman, according to his assertion, being in the habit of administering a. little wholesome correction with the jambok, which, on further acquaintance with him, I had reason to believe he richly merited. My third native servant was Cobus, a Hottentot of light weight, the son of a veteran in my regiment. He 'listed in the capacity of after-rider, and proved to be first rate in his calling, being the best horseman I met with in South Africa. He also, like Kleinboy, was liable to fits of sulkiness, through which I eventually lost him; for on one occasion, finding it necessary to inflict on him a summary chastisement, he deserted from my service in consequence.

While I was laying in these stores, I once or twice amused myself by riding in quest of reebok in the rugged and precipitous high grounds lying immediately to the south of Grahamstown. On one of these occasions I was accompanied by my cousin, Colonel Campbell of the 91st (one of the bravest and most distinguished officers in the late Kaffir war, and, withal, about the best rifle-shot and keenest sportsman then in the colony), a brother of Captain Campbell of Skipness, the author of the "Old Forest-Ranger," a work highly approved among Indian Dimrods. The rheebok is a species of antelope generally found in all mountain districts throughout Southern Africa, from Table Mountain to the latitude of Kuruman or New Litakoo. Of the rheebok there are two varieties: the rhooye-rheebok, or red rheebuck; and the vaal-rheebok, or gray rheebuck. The range of the vaal-rheebok, to the northward, ceases in the latitude of the Long Mountains lying to the south of Kuruman; the other variety is met with as far north as the mountains in the territory of Sichely, chief of the Baquaines, about fifty miles to the north of the Kurrichane range. Both of these antelopes frequent high and rocky mountains. The manner of hunting them is alike; and, when properly pursued, I think more nearly resembles Scotch Highland deer-stalking than the pursuit of any other antelope.

CHAPTER II

On the 23rd of October, 1843, having completed my final arrangements, and collected and settled all out lying debts, the weather, which had been wet and stormy for many days past, assuming a more settled appearance, I resolved to "inspan" and "trek," which the reader will bear in mind mean to yoke and march. I accordingly communicated my intentions to my followers, and dispatched my leader Carollus to the neighboring mountains, where my cattle were supposed to be pasturing, to bring them up. He expended the greater part of the day in searching for them in vain about their wonted feeding-ground at length, late in the afternoon, lie chanced to meet a comrade, who informed him that the oxen he was seeking were safely lodged in the "skit-kraal" or pound, Colonel Somerset of "Ours" having detected them in the act of luxuriating in a field of green forage. This pleasing intelligence demanded my immediate attendance at the skit-kraal, where, by a dis-imbursement of 95, I obtained their release.

Having secured my oxen, my next business was to find my servants, who were all missing. Long, as I expected, was found gallantly assisting the dark-eyed heroine of the mangle, and Kleinboy and Cobus were discovered in a state of brutal intoxication, stretched on the greensward in front of one of the canteens, along with sundry other wagon-drivers and Hottentot Venuses, all in the same glorious condition, having expended on liquor the pay which they had extracted from me in advance on the plea of providing themselves with necessaries. Drunk as they were, Carollus, who was sober, managed to allure them to the wagons, and. Long assisting, the in-spanning commenced. As no man who has not visited the Cape can form any idea of the manner in which this daily operation is performed, its where he necessary to explain it, and to say a few more words concerning the structure of a wagon.

The Cape wagon is a large and powerful, yet loosely constructed vehicle, running on four wheels. Its extreme length is about eighteen feet, its breadth varying from three and a half to four feet; the depth of the sides is about two feet six inches in front, but higher toward the back of the wagon. All along the sides two rows of iron staples are riveted, in which are fastened the boughs forming the tent, which arches over the wagon to a height of five feet, with an awning of Caffre mat, and a strong canvas sail over all, with "fore-clap" and "after-clap," which is the colonial name for two broad canvas curtains, that form part and parcel of the sail, and hang in the front and rear of the wagon, reaching to within a few inches of the ground. In the front is placed a large chest occupying the extreme breadth of the wagon, on which the driver and two passengers of ordinary dimensions can sit abreast. This is called the fore-chest, and is secured from sliding forward by two buffalo rheims, or strips of dressed hide, placed across the front of it, and secured to the sides. A similar chest is fastened in like manner to the rear of the wagon, which is called the after-chest. Along the sides of the wagon and outside of it are two longer and narrower chests called side-chests. These are supported by two horizontal bars of hard wood riveted to the bottom of the wagon. The side-chests are very convenient for holding tools, and all manner of odds and ends too numerous to mention.

The wagon is steered by a pole, called the dissel-boom, to the end of which is fastened the trek-tow, a stout rope formed of raw buffalo-hide. It is pulled by a span, or team, consisting of twelve oxen, which draw the wagon by yokes fastened along the trek-tow at regular intervals by means of strips of raw hide. Passing through each end of the yoke, at distances of eighteen inches from one another, are two parallel bars of tough wood about eighteen inches in length; these are called yoke-skeys. In inspanning the yoke is placed on the back of the neck of the ox, with one of these skeys on either side, and toward the ends are notches in which is fixed the strap, made of twisted hide; this, passing under the neck of the animal, secures him in the yoke.

Besides these straps, each pair of oxen is strongly coupled by the buffalo rheims, which are used in catching and placing them in their proper order preparatory to inspanning them a rheim is a long strip of prepared hide with a noose at the end it is made either of ox or buffalo hide, and is about eight feet long. A wagon is also provided with a tar-bucket, two powerful iron chains which are called the rheim-chains, and a large iron drag called the rheim-schoen; also the invariable whip and jambok; the former consisting of a bamboo pole upward of twenty feet in length, with a thong of about twenty five feet, to the end of which is sewn with "rheim-pys," or strips of dressed steinbok-skin, the "after-slock," and to this again is fastened the "fore-slock," corresponding with the little whip-cord lash of the English coachman. The "fore-slock," about which the wagon-drivers are very particular, is about a yard in length, and is formed of a strip of the supple skin of some particular variety of antelope prepared in a peculiar manner. The skins of only a few species of antelopes are possessed of sufficient toughness for this purpose. Those most highly prized among the colonists are the skins of the hartebeest, koodoo, blesbok, and bushbuck; when none of these are to be obtained, they use the skin of a he-goat, which is very inferior. The colonial wagon driver wields this immense whip with great dexterity and grace. As he cracks it he produces a report nearly equal to that of a gun, and by this means he signals to his leader, who is perhaps herding the oxen at the distance of a mile, to bring them up when it is time to inspan.

The "jambok" is another instrument of persuasion, indispensable in the outfit of every Cape wagon. It is made of the thick tough hide either of the white rhinoceros or hippopotamus. Its length is from six to seven feet; its thickness at the handle is about an inch and a half, and it tapers gradually to the point. These "jamboks" are exceedingly tough and pliant, and are capable of inflicting most tremendous chastisement upon the thick hides of sulky and refractory oxen. Those manufactured from the skin of the hippopotamus are very much superior to those of the rhinoceros, being naturally of a much tougher quality. If properly prepared, one of these will last for many years. A smaller description of "jambok" is manufactured for the benefit of horses, and may be seen in the hands of every horseman in the colony.

When the leader brings up the oxen to the wagon to be inspanned, the wagon-driver, if possible, sends another Hottentot to his assistance, especially if any of the oxen in the span happen to be young or refractory. These, armed with a huge "jambok" in one hand, and a handful of stones in the other, one on either flank, with shouts, yells, and imprecations, urge forward the unwilling team toward the yokes, where the driver is standing with the twelve long buffalo rheims hanging on his left arm, pouring forth a volley of soothing terms, such as, "Ah! now, Scotland! You tramp there in front, exactly as you please; but I will yoke you further back, where I can reach you with facility.) This is said in allusion to "England's" having lately been in the habit of being yoked in the front of the team; and if it is very long, the driver cannot reach the leading oxen with his whip without descending from the box, and, therefore, when a fore-ox becomes lazy, he is yoked further back in the team, that he may have the full benefit of the persuasive "fore-slock."

While the driver's tongue is pouring forth this flow of Hottentot eloquence with amazing volubility, his hands and feet are employed with equal activity; the former, in throwing the open noose of the rheim, lasso-like, over the horns of each ox, and drawing it tight, round them as he catches him ; the latter in kicking the eyes and noses of those oxen which the jamboks and shouts of the leaders behind have driven too far in upon him. At this moment "Blauberg," who is an old offender, and who acquired in early youth the practice which he has never relinquished of bolting from the team at the moment of inspanning, being this day unusually lively, not having had any severe work for some weeks, suddenly springs round, notwithstanding Kleinboy, well aware of his propensities, has got his particular rheim firmly twisted round his hand; and having once got his tail where his head ought to have been, and thus deprived Kleinboy of all purchase over him, he bounds madly forward, heedless of a large sharp stone with which one of the leaders salutes him in the eye. By his forward career, Carollus is instantly dashed to the ground; and Kleinboy, who has pertinaciously grasped the rheim in the vain hope of retrieving the matter, is dragged several yards along the ground and eventually relinquishes the rheim, at the same time losing a good deal of the outer bark of his unfortunate hand. Away goes Blauberg in his headlong course, tearing frantically over hill and dale, his rheim flying from his horns like a streamer in the wind. His course lies right across the middle of the Cape-corps barracks, where about forty or fifty riflemen who are lounging about, parade being over, rush to intercept his course, preceded by a pack of mongrel curs of every shape and size, but in vain. Blauberg, heedless of a shower of sticks and stones hurled at his devoted head, charges through the midst of them, nor is he recovered for the space of about two hours.

The rest of the team, seeing the driver sprawling on the ground, as a matter of course follow Blauberg's example instantly wheeling to the right and left about, away they scamper, each selecting a course for himself, some with and others without the appendage of the streamers. The Hottentots, well aware that it will be useless to follow Blauberg in the usual way, as he would probably lead them a chase of four or five miles, now adopt the most approved method usually practiced in such cases. They accordingly drive out a small troop of tamer oxen, with which they proceed in quest of the truant. This troop they cunningly induce Mr. Blauberg to join, and eventually return with him to the wagon, the driver, with pouting lips and the sweat running down his brow, pouring forth a torrent of threatened vengeance against the offending Blauberg. The inspanning is then once more commenced as before; and Blauberg, being this time cautiously placed in a central position, well wedged up by the other oxen, whereby he is prevented from turning about, is lassoed with the strongest rheim, and firmly secured to the steady old ox who has purposely been driven up beside him. The twelve oxen are soon all securely yoked in their proper places; the leader has made up his "foretow," which is a long spare rheim attached round the horns of each of the fore or front oxen, by which he leads the team, and inspanning is reported to be accomplished.

I omitted to mention that the two fore-oxen, and the two after-oxen, which are yoked one on either side of the "dissel-boom" or pole, are always supposed to be the steadiest, most intelligent, and tractable in the team. The two fore-oxen in particular, to be right good ones, require a combination of excellences, as it is indispensable for the safety of the wagon that they thoroughly understand their duty. They are expected, unguided by reins, to hold the rarely trodden roads which occur throughout the remoter parts of the colony either by day or night; and so well trained are these sagacious animals, that it is not uncommon to meet with a pair of fore-oxen which will, of their own accord, hold the "spoor" or trade of a single wagon which has perhaps crossed a plain six months previously.

In dangerous ground, however—where the narrow road winds through stones and rocks, or along the brink of a precipice; or where the road is much intersected by water-courses, and bordered by the eternal hillocks raised by the white ants, which are of the consistence of a brick, being formed, during damp weather, of clay, which the sun afterward hardens; or where the "hardwarcke," or ant-bear, with his powerful claws, has undermined the road with enormous holes—the fore oxen, however trustworthy, should never be left to their own devices, but the leader should precede them, leading by the tow. This safe and highly necessary precaution is, however, rarely practiced by the ruffianly Hottentots if the "baas" or master is not present, these worthies preferring to sit still and smoke their pipes or play their violins during the march to performing their duty, thus frequently exposing their master's property to imminent peril. It is thus that more than half the capsizes, broken axle-trees, broken dissel-booms, and smashed cap-tents, daily occur throughout the colony. All being now in readiness, and some pots and spades, which the Hottentots, as a matter of course, had omitted to stow away in their proper places, being securely lashed on the trap and to the sides of the wagon, the illustrious Kleinboy brandishes his huge whip, and, cracking it with a report which loudly reverberates throughout the walls and houses of the Cape-corps barracks, shouts out, with stentorian lungs, "Trek, trek, you duivels! Rhure y'lla dar vor, you skellums! Ane spoor trap, you neuxels!"

Requiring to pick up several large parcels at the stores of some of the merchants in the town, we trekked down the main street of Grahamstown, and in passing the shops. of the butchers and bakers, laid in a large supply of bread and fresh meat for immediate use. Before we had proceeded far, some sharp-sighted Hottentots came running after us, calling out that a fountain of tiger's milk had started in the stern of the wagon; and on halting, we discovered that several loose cases of gin which I had purchased for immediate use, and which had not been properly stowed, had sprung leak. The Hottentots seemed to regret amazingly the loss of so much good liquor, and endeavored with their hands to catch it as it fell. Owing to the various delays which had occurred during the day, I did not get more than half a mile clear of Grahamstown when the sun went down; and there being then no moon, I deemed it expedient to halt for the night. We accordingly outspanned; and the Hottentots, having secured the oxen to the yokes, and picketed my two horses on the wheels, requested my permission to return to the town to take another farewell of their wives and sweet-hearts. This I did not deem altogether prudent; but knowing well that if withheld my consent they would go without it, I considered it best to comply with a good grace; and granting a general leave of absence, took on myself the charge of the castle which was destined to be my home during the next five years.

The Hottentots, strange to say, according to their promise, returned to the wagon during the night, and next morning, at earliest dawn of day, I roused them, and we inspanned. When this was accomplished, my head servant long not appearing, we marched without him; but we had only proceeded about three miles when he managed to overtake us, the road being hilly and very soft, owing to the recent rains. On coming up and recovering his breath, he expressed himself very much disgusted at my starting without him, when I took the liberty of explaining that I expected my servants to wait for me, and not that I should tarry for them. Our progress was considerably impeded by the bad state of the roads, and at ten A.M. we halted for breakfast beside a pool of rain-water, having performed a march of about nine miles. Here, having outspanned our oxen, we set about preparing our gipsy breakfast one collected sticks for the fires, another filled the kettles at the adjoining "vley," while Long and I were busied in spreading the table and dusting the beef-steaks with salt and pepper.

Having permitted the oxen to graze for a few hours, we again inspanned, holding the high road for Somerset; and about sundown we halted for the night on the farm of a Mr. Fichett, a great sheep-farmer, who race it me hospitably, and invited me to dine with him. Here I met Captain Codrington, who had lately sold out of the 7th Dragoons. Our march this day lay through a succession of low, undulating hills, richly clothed with a variety of grasses, herbs, and flowers, with here and there large patches of dwarfish evergreens. I had directed my Hottentots to kraal the oxen that night, with the intention of making an early start on the following morning, but the herd managed to lose them in the thick underwood. They were, however, recovered at an early hour on the following morning, and, having breakfasted, I was about to proceed, when Long, with a face worthy of his name, came up to me with a whole tissue of dire complaints about his personal inconveniences, the most galling of which appeared to be his having to sleep on the ground in the tent. On my friend's advancing these objections, I saw very plainly that he was not the man for my work, as the life before us was by no means likely to be one of luxury; so, having made over to him his impedimenta, and paid him his month's wages, I wished him a safe return to Grahamstown.

About mid-day I outspanned for two hours, to let the cattle graze; after which, having proceeded a few miles, we found the road so cut up that we were obliged to abandon it, and trek along the rugged hill-side, holding a course parallel to it. Marching in front, and sin lying up to my ankles in mud at every step, I endeavored to select the hardest ground, on which the wagon might follow. The ground now every moment became worse and worse; the panting oxen, straining every nerve to keep the wagon in motion, and halting every hundred yards to take breath. At length the wheels suddenly sank deep into the soil, and became immovably fixed, upon which we made loose our shovels and pickax, and worked hard for half an hour, clearing away the soil in front of and around the wheels; which being accomplished, we rigged out a fore-tow and extra yoke to inspan my two spare oxen, and then set our whole fourteen to draw, but they could not move the wagon an inch. We then lightened it of a part of the cargo, and after half an hour's further labor we had relieved it of upward of three 'thousand pounds; but still the oxen, notwithstanding the most unmerciful application of both whip and jambok, failed to move it.

A few minutes after this had occurred, another wagon meeting us from Somerset hove in sight, but shortly stuck fast within a quarter of a mile of us. Its owner, an Englishman, an Albany transport-rider or carrier, of the name of Leonard, now came up and requested me to lend him my oxen to assist him in his difficulties, which I did, he promising, in return, to help me out of mine; but it was not until unloaded of the entire cargo that they succeeded in extricating it; after which, with considerable trouble, they came up to us. We now hooked on to my wagon both spans, amounting to twenty-six strong oxen, the drivers standing one on either side, with their whips ready at the given signal to descend upon the devoted oxen. I myself, with one of the Hottentots, armed with the jamboks, stood by the after-oxen, upon whom, in a dilemma of this sort, much depends. Every man and beast being at their post, the usual cry of "Trek, trek!" resounded on all sides, accompanied by a torrent of unearthly yells and abusive epithets ; at the same time the whips were plied with energetic dexterity, and came down with startling reports on the backs of the oxen throughout all parts of the team. The twenty-six oxen, thus urged, at the same moment concentrated their energies, laying a mighty strain on the gear. In the present instance my gear did not escape; for, after battling with the oxen till the sun went down, and smashing the half of my rheiras, straps, and skeys, and splitting one of my yokes, we were obliged to drop it for the night. We cast loose the oxen, and, driving them up the hill-side, granted them their liberty until morning ; and leaving our broken gear, pickaxes, spades, and other utensils scattered about the ground in grand confusion, tired and worn out we kindled a fire, and set about cooking our dinner. Leonard and his servants declared that they had not tasted anything but a little biscuit and coffee during the last three days, the Dutchmen along their road being very unfriendly and inhospitable to the English transport-riders.

Next morning we awoke refreshed by sound slumbers; and having dispatched all the Hottentots, excepting one man, in quest of the oxen, Leonard and I were actively employed for two hours in digging out and of loading the wagon, after which Leonard and the Hottentot set about preparing the breakfast, while I proceeded to darn my worsted stockings, having had the good fortune to obtain some hanks of worsted from the wife of a Scotch sergeant in Grahamstown, after vainly seeking that article in the shops of all the haberdashers in the town. While we were thus employed, Captain Codrington and Mr. Fichett rode up to us, and seemed very much amused at our situation. Having drunk a cup of coffee with me, Fichett and Codrington returned home, previously engaging me to dine with them, as I had resolved to retrace my steps and try another line of country. About 11 A.M. the Hottentots returned with our oxen, when, with the united efforts of the teams, we succeeded in extricating my now lightened wagon. The two oxen I purchased from Thompson, though well-favored, proving indolent in a heavy pull, I exchanged them with Leonard for the liberty to pick any two out of his span, giving him a sovereign to boot. His team consisted of twelve tough little red Zoolah oxen, from the district of Natal, which, like the Albany cattle, are termed "Zuur-feldt." This colonial phrase is applied to all oxen bred and reared near the sea-coast, in districts where the majority of the grass is sour. Those from about the frontiers of the colony, or anywhere beyond the Orange River, are termed "Sweet-feldt" oxen.

We now reloaded my wagon, made all fast, and having put everything in order, Leonard and I journeyed together to Fichett's farm, where I once more took up my quarters for the night. While actively busied with my oxen, I saw today, for the first time, the honeybird. This extraordinary little bird, which is about the size of a chaffinch, and of a light gray color, will invariably lead a person following it to a wild-bees' nest. Chattering and twittering in a state of great excitement, it perches on a branch beside the traveler, endeavoring by various wiles to attract his attention; and having succeeded in doing so, it flies lightly forward in a wavy course in the direction of the bees' nest, alighting every now and then, and looking back to ascertain if the traveler is following it, all the time keeping up an incessant twitter. When at length it arrives at the hollow tree or deserted white-ants' hill which contains the honey, it for a moment hovers over the nest, pointing to it with its bill, and then takes up its position on a neighboring branch, anxiously awaiting its share of the spoil. When the honey is taken, which is accomplished by first stupefying the bees by burning grass at the entrance of their domicile, the honey-bird will often lead to a second and even to a third nest. The person thus following it ought to whistle. The savages in the interior, while in pursuit, have several charmed sentences which they use on the occasion. The wild bee of Southern Africa exactly corresponds with the domestic garden bee of England. They are very generally diffused throughout every part of Africa, beeswax forming a considerable part of the cargoes of ships trading to the Gold and Ivory Coasts, and the deadly district of Sierra Leone, on the western shores of Africa.

Interesting as the honey-bird is, and though sweet be the stores to which it leads, I have often had cause to wish it far enough, as, when following the warm "spoor" or track of elephants, I have often seen the savages, at moments of the utmost importance, resign the spoor of the beasts to attend to the summons of the bird. Sometimes, however, they are "sold," it being a well-known fact, both among the Hottentots and tribes of the interior, that they often lead the unwary pursuer to danger, sometimes guiding him to the mid-day retreat of a grizzly lion, or bringing him suddenly upon the den of the crouching panther. I remember on one occasion, about three years later, when weary with warring against the mighty elephants and hippopotaraoi which roam the vast forests and sport in the floods of the fair Limpopo, having mounted a pair of unwonted shot-barrels, I sought recreation in the humbler pursuit of quail-shooting. While thus employed, my attention was suddenly invited by a garrulous honeybird, which pertinaciously adhered to me for a considerable time, heedless of the reports made by my gun. Having bagged as many quails and partridges as I cared about shooting, I whistled lustily to the honeybird, and gave him chase after following him to a distance of upward of a mile, through the open glades adjoining the Limpopo, he led me to an unusually vast crocodile, who was lying with his entire body concealed, nothing but his horrid head being visible above the surface of the water, his eyes anxiously watching the movements of eight or ten large bull buffaloes, which, in seeking to quench their thirst in the waters of the river, were crackling through the dry reeds as they cautiously waded in the deep mud that a recent flood had deposited along the edge. Fortunately for the buffaloes, the depth of the mud prevented their reaching the stream, and thus the scaly monster of the river was disappointed of his prey.

CHAPTER III

My "trek-tow" having been destroyed during the recent struggles, I was glad to purchase a new one from a man named Mackenzie in Fichett's employ, which he supplied me, together with a strong thorn wood yoke, for £1. On leaving the farm we proceeded in an easterly course, and struck into a track which in a few hours led us into the high road leading from Grahamstown to Cradock. Having followed this road for several miles, we commenced descending through the De Bruin's Poort, where the road winds, in a deep, narrow, and rugged ravine, through dense ever-green underwood, in its descent to the lower ground adjacent to the banks of the Great Fish River. This port, or mountain pass, the terror of wagon-drivers, being at all times perilous to wagons, was in the present instance unusually dangerous and impassable, the recent heavy rains having entirely washed away the loose soil with which the colonists had been in the habit of embanking the permanent shelves and ridges of adamantine rock over which the wagons must necessarily pass, while they had, at the same time, undermined an immense number of large masses of rocks and stones which had hitherto occupied positions on the banks above, and which now lay scattered along the rocky way, presenting an apparently insurmountable barrier to our further progress.

As we were the first who had traveled this road since the late inundations, it had not undergone the slightest repair, which, to have done properly, would have required the labor of a week. Having halted the wagon, and descended into the ravine for an inspection, accompanied by Kleinboy, I at once pronounced it, in its present state, to be impassable. Kleinboy, however, well aware that he would not be called upon to pay for damages, seemed to entertain a different opinion, evidently preferring to run all risks to encountering the Herculean labors of rolling all these boulders to one side. Accordingly, having made up our minds to take the pass, we re-ascended to the wagon, and having rheimed or secured the two hind wheels by means of the drag-chains, Kleinboy took his position on the box, and the wagon commenced its perilous descent, I following in the firm expectation every moment of beholding its destruction. Jolting furiously along, it crashed and jumped from rock to rock; at one moment the starboard hind wheel resting on a projecting ledge of rock several feet in height, and the front wheel on the same side buried in a deep hollow, and next moment the larboard wheels suddenly elevated by a corresponding mass of rock on the opposite side, placing the wagon in such a position that it seemed as though another inch must inevitably decide its fate. I held my breath, doubting the possibility of its regaining the horizontal position. Righting again, however, with fearful violence, it was launched, tottering from side to side, down the steep stony descent, and eventually, much to my astonishment, the pass was won, and we entered upon the more practicable road beneath.

I could not help fancying how an English-built vehicle would have fared in a similar situation, and how a Brighton coachman would have opened his eyes could he have seen my Cape wagon in the act of descending this fine specimen of a colonial wagon-road, which I might aptly compare to the rugged mountain-bed of some Highland river. Having continued our journey till within an hour of sundown, we encamped for the night. The country through which we had passed was densely covered with one vast jungle of dwarfish evergreen shrubs and bushes, among which the speck-boom was predominant. This species of tree, which is one of the most abundant throughout the forests and jungles of Albany and Caffraria, is utterly unserviceable to man, as its pithy branches, even when dead, are unavailable for fuel. It is, however, interesting, as constituting a favorite food of the elephants which, about twenty-five years ago, frequented the whole of this country in large herds. The foot-paths formed through successive ages by the feet of these mighty animals are still discernible on the sides and in the necks of some of the forest-clad hills, and the skulls and larger bones of many are at this moment bleaching in some of the forest-kloofs or ravines adjacent to the sea in Lower Albany.

From time immemorial, these interesting and stupendous quadrupeds had maintained their ground throughout these their paternal domains, although they were constantly hunted, and numbers of them were slain, by the neighboring active and athletic warriors of the Amaponda tribes, on account of their flesh, the ivory so much prized among civilized nations being by them esteemed of no value, the only purpose to which they adapt it being the manufacture of rings and ornaments for their fingers and arms. These gallant fellows, armed only with their assagais or light javelins of their own manufacture, were in the constant habit of attacking the gigantic animals, and overpowering them with the accumulated showers of their weapons. At length, however, when the white lords of the creation pitched their camps on the shores of Southern Africa, a more determined and general warfare was waged against the elephants on account of their ivory, with the more destructive engines of ball and powder.

When the colonists first settled in Albany, they were in the habit of carrying on a very lucrative traffic with the chiefs of the neighboring Amaponda tribes, from whom they obtained large quantities of ivory in barter for beads, brass wire, and other articles of little value.

Throughout the jungles of Albany and Caffraria, but more particularly in the deep kloofs and valleys, many varieties of noble forest-trees are found of considerable size and great beauty, several of which are much prized by the colonists on account of their excellence for wagon-work and house-building ; of these I may enumerate the yellow-wood tree, the wild cedar, the stink-wood tree, and the black and the white iron-wood tree. The two latter are remarkable for toughness and durability, and are much used in the axle-trees of wagons. The primitive system of wooden axle-trees has of late years been superseded in some districts by patent iron ones; many, however, still use and prefer the old wooden axle-trees, because wagons having those made of iron, in steep descents, run too freely after the team, to the injury of the two after-oxen ; and, further, because a wooden axle, if broken, may be replaced in any remote part of the country; whereas a damaged iron axle-tree cannot be mended even by the skillful smiths through out the towns and villages of the colony. The iron axles are especially apt to be broken in cold frosty mornings during the winter, when a wagon, immediately after being set in motion,- has to pass through rough ground before the friction of the wheel has imparted to it a certain degree of heat.

On the following day a march of four hours brought us to the bank of the Great Fish River, having crossed an extensive open glade covered with several varieties of low shrubs and grasses and rough heather. Here, for the first time, I saw and shot the black Koran, an excellent game-bird, allied to the bustards, so abundant throughout South Africa. Its weight corresponds with that of our old cock grouse; its legs and neck are long like those of the ostrich; its breast and back are gray, and its wings black and white. They are everywhere to be met with where the country is at all level and open when disturbed, they take wing and fly over the plain in circles, much after the manner of the green plover or peewit, uttering a harsh grating cry. The best method of getting within range is to use a horse, and ride round them in a circle, gradually contracting it. To this open glade, whose name I have forgotten, the Nimrods about Grahamstown often resort, and indulge in the exciting sport of wild boar and porcupine hunting. This "chasse" is conducted on bright moonlight nights, with a gathering of rough strong dogs, the hunters being armed with a bayonet or spear, with which they dispatch the quarry when brought to bay.

I found the Great Fish River, as I had anticipated, still flooded and impassable to wagons. It was, however, ebbing rapidly, and apparently would be fordable on the morrow. During the previous heavy rains, which were said not to have been equaled for twenty seven years, it had risen to an immense height, and everywhere overflowed its banks. That part of the bank which formed the descent and ascent of the former wagon-road was, as a matter of course, entirely swept away, a steep wall on either side of the river remaining in its stead, flanked by a bank of deep and slimy mud. An immense deal of manual labor would consequently be necessary to form a road, by cutting down these walls, and clearing a channel through the mud, before a wagon could take the drift. Accordingly, the work being considerable, I thought the sooner we set about it the better; so, having cooked and partaken of a hot tiffin, we cast loose the pickaxes, spades, and shovels, stripped to our shirts, and, half wading, half swimming, succeeded in crossing the river, where, having labored hard till sundown, and constructed a famous piece of road, we considered our task on that side as completed. Early on the following morning we resumed our labors on our side of the river, and about 10 A.M. our path was finished. A party of Boers now hove in sight with three wagons, which they outspanned on the opposite bank, and drove their oxen into the neighboring hills to graze. Presently observing us preparing to inspan, they beckoned to me to hold a conference with them across the stream, the object of which was to endeavor to dissuade me from taking the drift until their oxen should return, under pretense of assisting us, but, in reality, fearing that we would stick fast, and that they should be forced to assist us, since, in the event of our was on sticking before their oxen came up, they would be unable to pass us until we were extricated. I saw the move with half an eye, and instantly ordered my men to inspan with all possible dispatch; when we got safely through the river and up the opposite bank, which was much more than I had anticipated.

About two P.M. we inspanned, and, having ascended a long and very steep hill, we entered upon a new line of country, of wide, undulating, open plains of rank, waving grass, dotted over with the mud-built habitations of white ants. We held on for three hours after sundown, and halted for the night at an uninhabited dilapidated mansion, in which we lighted a fire and cooked our dinner. Having secured our oxen on the yokes, instead of permitting them to graze during the night, we were enabled to march next morning some time before the break of day; and as the rising sun gradually unveiled the landscape, I had the pleasure of beholding for the first time several small herds of springboks scattered over the plain. This exquisite graceful and truly interesting antelope is very generally diffused throughout Southern Africa, and is more numerous there than any other variety; it is very nearly allied to the ariel gazelle of Northern Africa, and in its nature and habits reminded me of the saisin of India. A few herds of springboks are still to be met with on the plains in the district of. Somerset, on which I had now entered; but as this is one of the nearest districts to the abodes of men where this species remains, it is of course much hunted, and is annually becoming scarcer.

Owing to exposure to the sun while working at the Fish River drift on the preceding days, and also to having discarded coat, waistcoat, and neck cloth since leaving Grahamstown, my arms, neck, and shoulders were much swollen, and severely burned arid blistered, causing me much pain, and at night preventing me from sleeping. The kind-hearted no, or lady of the farm, commiserating my condition, and wishing to alleviate my pain, informed me that she had an excellent receipt for sunburn, which she had often successfully administered to her husband and sons. One of the chief ingredients of the promised balsam was green tea, which was to be reduced to powder, of which she directed me to send her a little by one of my servants. I do not know what the other components might have been, but I well know that, on applying the ointment to the raw and swollen parts, it stung mo as though it had been a mixture of salt and vinegar, giving me intense pain, and causing me to hop and dance about like one demented, and wish the Boer noe and her ointment in the realms of Pluto, to the infinite delight and merriment of my sympathizing Hottentots.

A peculiar expression in the eyes of these gentlemen, and their general demeanor, inclined me to think that their potations had consisted of some more generous beverage than water during the morning's march; and on examining one of my liquor cases, I found that I was minus a bottle and a half of gin since yesterday.

After breakfast we continued our march, when I was again tempted to saddle up and give chase to a troop of springboks, one of which I shot we continued our march until sundown, when we halted beside a pool of rain water. Here we found some young Boers and Hottentots, belonging to a neighboring farm, actively employed in digging out a nest of wild bees; several of them had their eyes nearly closed from the stings which they had received. The spoils of the "bike," however, repaid their pains by twenty pounds of honey. On approaching the nest, a large cluster of bees chose my sunburned arm as a place of rendezvous, from which I could not remove them until I had obtained a bunch of burning grass.

Cradock is a pretty little village, situated on the eastern bank of the Great Fish River, by which it is supplied with water and the gardens irrigated. It is inhabited by Dutch and English, and a goodly sprinkling of Hottentots, Mozambiques, and Fingoes. The principal street is wide, and adorned with shady trees on every side, among which I observed lots of peach trees covered with green fruit. The houses are largo and well built, generally of brick, some in the old Dutch and some in the English style. Each house has got a considerable garden attached to it: these are tastefully laid out, and contain all the vegetables most used in an English kitchen. Apples, pears, oranges, quinces, nectarines, and grapes abound. The vision is bounded on every side by barren, arid, rocky hills and mountains. I marched right through the town, and outspanned about a quarter of a mile beyond it, and after breakfast I re-entered the village on foot to purchase necessaries for myself and servants. Numbers of Dutch Boers, with their wives and families, were assembling to hold their Nachmahl or sacrament.

About 11 A.M. we inspanned, and continued oar journey about five miles, crossing the Goat Fish River twice, when I halted for some hours upon its bank on account of my oxen, the grass in the vicinity of the town having been very bare. This was the fifth and last time that we crossed the Great Fish River. Here about a dozen wagons passed us on their way to Cradock, containing Dutch Boers with their fraud and families. Several of these were horse-wagons, drawn by eight and ten horses in each wagon, harnessed two abreast, and drawing by straps across their breasts instead of collars. These straps are generally manufactured of the skin of the lion when it is to be obtained, that being reckoned by the Boers to be tougher and more enduring than any other. These long teams are well managed and dexterously driven by the Boers, one man holding the reins and another the whip. In the afternoon I again inspanned, and continued my march till sundown. The road since I left Cradock had improved, and was now fine and level, leading through a wide, open, undulating strath along the northeastern bank of the Fish River. The surrounding country presented in every direction endless chains of barren, stony mountains; the bold range of the Rhinaster Bergs standing forth in grand relief to the west war; not a tree to be seen, except a few thorny mimosas in some of the more favored hollows of the hills and along the banks of the river; the country covered with grass and heaths, dwarfish shrubs, and small thorny bushes.

In Cradock I engaged another Hottentot, named Jacob, in the capacity of after-rider. Having followed the course of the Fish River for a distance of about nine miles, our road inclined to the right in a more northerly direction, and we here bade that stream a final adieu. Two more marches through a succession of wide, undulating, sterile plains, bounded on all sides by bleak and barren mountains, brought us to the borders of the immense flats surrounding the Thebus Mountain.

Having followed along the eastern bank an insignificant little stream dignified by the appellation of the Brak River, I arrived at the farm of Mynheer Besta, a pleasant, hospitable Boer, and a field cornet of the district, which means a sort of resident magistrate. Here we halted to breakfast, and Besta, who is a keen sportsman, entertained me with various anecdotes and adventures which had occurred to him during the earlier days of his sporting career in Albany, where he had once resided. He informed me that the black wildebeest and springbok were extremely numerous on the plains immediately beyond his farm, which made me resolve to saddle up and go in quest of them as soon as I had breakfasted. The flesh of these animals forms one of the chief articles of food among the Boers and their servants who inhabit the districts in which they are abundant; and the skulls and horns of hundreds of black wildebeest and springbok were to be seen piled in heaps and scattered about the out-houses of the farm. Adjoining the house was a well-watered garden, with very green trees and corn in it, which formed a most pleasing contrast with the surrounding barren country.

Having directed my men to proceed to the next farm along the banks of the Brak River, I rode forth with Cobus and held a northerly course across the flats. I soon perceived herds of springbok in every direction, which, on ray following at a hard gallop, continued to join one another until the whole plain seemed alive with them. Upon our crossing a sort of ridge on the plain, I beheld the whole country, as far as my eye could reach, actually white with springboks, with here and there a herd of black gnoos or wildebeest, prancing and capering in every direction, whirling and lashing their white tails as they started off in long files on our approach. Having pursued them for many hours, and fired about a dozen shots at these and the springboks at distances of from four to six hundred yards, and only wounded one, which I lost, I turned my horse's head for the camp. The evening set in dark and lowering, with rattling thunder and vivid flashes of lightning on the surrounding hills. I accordingly rode hard for my wagon, which I just reached in time to escape a deluge of rain which lasted all night.

As I rode along in the intense and maddening excitement of the chase, I felt a glad feeling of unrestrained freedom, which was common to me during my career in Africa, and which I had seldom so fully experienced; and notwithstanding the many thorns which surrounded my roses during the many days and nights of toil and hardship which I afterward encountered, I shall ever refer to those times as by far the brightest and happiest of my life. On the following morning I rode through the Brak River to visit Mynheer Pocheter, with the intention of buying some horses from him, but he had none to dispose of I met the old fellow coming in from the "feldt," with his long single-barreled roer and enormous flint-lock, with the usual bullock's-horn power-flask dangling at his side. He had gone out with his Hottentot before the dawn of day, and taken up a position in a little neck in any seven part of the plain, through which the springbok's were in the habit of passing before sunrise. In places of this description the Boers build little watching-places with flat stones, from which they generally obtain a shot every morning and evening, and at such distances as to insure success To use their own words, "they secure a buck from these places, skot for skot," meaning a buck for every shot. On this occasion, however, our friend had been unfortunate, returning without venison, although I had heard the loud booming of his "roer" a short time previously. The report made by these unwieldy guns of the Boers, charged with a large handful of coarse gunpowder, is to be heard at an amazing distance through the calm atmosphere of these high table-lands; and during my stay on the flats adjoining Thebus Mountain, scarcely an hour elapsed at morning, noon, or eve, but the distant booming of some Dutchman's gun saluted the ear.

Mynheer Pocheter asked me in to take some breakfast with him, which I did, Cobus acting as interpreter, mine host not understanding a word of English, and not having at that time acquired the Dutch language, with which I not long afterward became thoroughly conversant.

After breakfast I took leave of Mynheer Pocheter, and having directed the wagon to strike out of the direct road to Colesberg, and hold across the country to the abode of a Boer named Hendric Strydom, where the game was represented to me as being extremely plentiful, I again rode forth, accompanied by Cobus, to wage war with the springboks. We pricked over the plain, holding an easterly course, and found, as yesterday, the springboks in thousands, with here and there a herd of black wildebeest. Finding that by jagging on the open plain I could not get within four or five hundred yards of them, I left my horses and after rider, and set off on foot to a low range of rocky hills, where I performed two difficult stalks upon a springbok and a wildebeest, both of which I wounded severely, but lost.

In the afternoon I came to a pool of mud; the little water it contained was almost boiling; I was, however, most thankful to find it, and tears of delight came into my eyes on discovering it. How trifling was this to the trials from thirst which I have often since undergone! Shortly after this I fell in with my servant, who, astonished at my long absence, had come in search of me with the horses. I was right glad to fall in with him, and, having got into the saddle, I rode hard across the plain for my wagon. On my way thither I took up a position behind a ridge, and directed Cobus to "jag" a herd of springbok toward me, which he did most successfully, sending upward of a hundred of them right in my teeth. I, however, was still unfortunate, firing both barrels into the herd without doing any apparent injury. On reaching my wagon, which I found outspanned at the desolate abode of Mynheer Hendric Strydom, I took a mighty draught of gin and water, and then walked, followed by my interpreter carrying a bottle of Hollands and glasses, to the door of Strydom, to cultivate the acquaintance of himself and frau, and wearing the garb of old Gaul, in which I generally hunted during my first expedition, to the intense surprise of the primitive Boers.

It is a strange thing that Boers are rather partial to Scotchmen, although they detest the sight of an Englishman. They have an idea that the Scotch, like themselves, were a nation conquered by the English, and that, consequently, we trek in the same yoke as themselves; and, further, a number of their ministers are Scotchmen. Hendric Strydom was a tall, sunburned, wild-looking creature, with light sandy hair, and a long, shaggy red beard. He was a keen hunter, and himself and household subsisted, in a great measure, by the proceeds of his long single-barreled "roer." His frau was rather a nice little woman, with a fresh color, and fine dark eyes and eyebrows, and displayed her good taste by taking a fancy to me; but perhaps the tea and coffee which she found I bestowed with a liberal hand might account for her partiality. These were Boers of the poorer order, and possessed but little of this world's goods. Their abode was in keeping with their means. It was a small mud cottage, with a roof which afforded scanty protection from the heavy periodical rains. The fire burned on the hearthstone, and a hole in the roof served at once for a window and chimney. The rafters and bare mud walls were adorned with a profusion of skins of wild animals, and endless festoons of "biltongue" or sun-dried flesh of game. Green fields or gardens there were none whatever; the wild Karroo plain stretched away from the house on all sides; and during the night the springboks and wildebeests pastured before the door.

The servants consisted of one old Bushman and his wife, and the whole of their worldly possessions were an old wagon, a span of oxen, a few milch cows, and a small herd of goats and sheep. Strydom's revenue seemed principally to be obtained by manufacturing ashes, with which he was in the habit of loading up his wagon and trekking many days' journey into other districts, where he sold them to richer Boers. These ashes are in great demand among all the Boers, as being an indispensable ingredient in the manufacture of soap. Every Boer in South Africa makes his own soap. There is a low, succulent, green bush from which the ashes are obtained, which is only found in certain districts, and in these desolate plains it was very abundant.

Strydom, having sympathized with me on my continued run of ill luck, remarked that it was quite a common thing when "jaging" on the principle which I had followed. He said that he was aware that in hunting on that system an immense amount of ammunition was expended with little profit, and that he, being a poor man, very rarely indulged in it; but that, if I would accompany him after I had taken my coffee, there being still about two hours of daylight, he would show me his method, and he thought it very probable that we should get a buck that evening. Accordingly, having partaken of coffee, Strydom and I stalked forth together across the wild and desolate-looking plain, followed by two Hottentots, large herds of graceful springboks pasturing on every side. It was a very beautiful thing altogether, and succeeded well. The whole herd came on slowly, right toward where I lay, until within a hundred yards, when I selected a fine fat buck, which I rolled over with a ball in the shoulder. This was the first fair shot that I had obtained at a springbok on these plains. I have always been reckoned by those who know my shooting to be a very fair rifle-shot, whether standing or running, but I do not profess to make sure work much beyond one hundred and ten paces, or thereabouts.

Two days before this, I brought down a Koran flying, with single ball. Our chances for this evening being now over, and night setting in, I returned to the farm with Strydom in high spirits.

CHAPTER IV

At an early hour on the morning of the 6th, while I was yet in bed, Hendric Strydom and his frau were standing over my fire, alongside of my wagon, with a welcome supply of sweet milk, and hurrying on the indolent Hottentots to prepare my breakfast, and rouse their slothful master, the earliest dawn being, as he affirmed, the best time to go after the springboks. On hearing their voices, I rose, and, having breakfasted, we shouldered our "roers," walked about a mile across the plain, and took up positions behind two very low bushes, about three hundred yards apart, and instructed our Hottentots to endeavor to drive the springboks toward us. We had two beats, but were unlucky both times, each of us wounding and losing a springbok. In the evening we went out again to hunt on the same principle, on a very wide flat to the west of his house, where we lay down behind very low bushes, in the middle of the bucks. We lay there on our breasts for two hours, with herds of springboks moving all round us, our Hottentots maneuvering in the distance. One small troop came within shot of me, when I sent my bullet spinning through a graceful doe, which bounded forward a hundred yards, and, staggering for a moment, fell over and expired. A little after this, I suddenly perceived a large pow or bustard walking on the plain before me. These birds are very wary and difficult to approach. I therefore resolved to have a shot at him, and lay like a piece of rock until he came within range, when I sent a bullet through him. He managed, however, to fly about a quarter of a mile, when he alighted; and ongoing up to the place half an hour after, I found him lying dead, with his head stuck into a bush of heath.

Strydom had two family shots, and brought down with each a well-conditioned buck. In high good humor with our success, we now proceeded to gralloch or disembowel the quarry;

after which, each of us shouldering a buck, we returned home in heavy marching order. On the following day I had the pleasure of beholding the first flight of locusts that I had seen since my arrival in the colony. We were standing in the middle of a plain of unlimited length, and about five miles across, when I observed them advancing.

On the morning of the 9th, Strydom and I having resolved over night to go in quest of a troop of ostriches which his Hottentot reported, frequenting the plains immediately adjacent to the Thebus Mountain, we started our Hottentots two hours before the dawn of day; and after an early breakfast we saddled up, and rode direct for the Thebus Mountain. This remarkable mountain, which I shall ever remember as the leading feature on the plains where I first really commenced my African hunting, is of peculiar shape, resembling a cone depressed at the apex, and surmounted by a round tower. It is also remarkable as being considerably higher than the surrounding mountains, with which the plains are bounded and intersected. As we rode along, a balmy freshness pervaded the morning air. We passed through herds of thousands of springboks, with small herds of wildebeest scattered among them. I fired two or three very long shots without success. Strydom, however, was more fortunate. He fired into a herd of about a hundred bucks at three hundred yards, and hit one fine old buck right in the middle of the forehead, the ball passing clean through his skull. We hid him in a hole in the ground, and covered him with bushes, and then rode on to our Hottentots, whom we found waiting beside a small fountain in a pass formed by a wide gap in a low range of hills, situated between two extensive plains which were thickly covered with game. I took up my position in a bush of rushes in the middle of the pass, and remained there for upward of eight hours, during which our boys were supposed to be endeavoring to drive the game toward us.

The Boer took up the best pass about a quarter of a mile to my right. Before we had been an hour at our passes, the boys drove up four beautiful ostriches, which came and stood within fifty yards of Strydom, but, alas! he was asleep. About this time I was busy trying to remember and practice a childish amusement which once delighted me as much as rifle-shooting—namely, making a cap of rushes, when, on suddenly lifting up my eyes, I saw standing within eighty yards of me about a dozen beautiful springboks, which were coming up to the pass behind me. I snatched up my rifle, and, lying flat on my breast, sent a bullet through the best buck in the troop, smashing his shoulder. He ran about fifty yards, and fell dead. I unfortunately left him lying exposed in the path, the consequence of which was that three other troops of springboks, which were coming up as he had come, were turned to the right about by his carcass.

It was now late in the day, so we made for home, taking up the buck which Strydom had shot in the morning. As we cantered along the flats, Strydom, tempted by a herd of springboks, which were drawn up together in a compact body, jumped off his horse, and, giving his ivory sight an elevation of several feet, let drive at them, the distance being about five hundred yards. As the troop bounded away, we could distinguish a light-colored object lying in the short heath, which he pronounced to be a springbok, and ongoing up we found one fine old doe lying dead, shot through the spine. This day, and every day since I arrived at these flats, I was astonished at the number of skeletons and well-bleached skulls with which the plains were covered. Thousands of skulls of springbok and wildebeest were strewed around wherever the hunter turned his eye. The sun was extremely powerful all day, but, being intent on the sport, I did not feel it until I found my legs burned; my dress, as usual, was the kilt, with a gray stalking-cap. On reaching home the following day, a large party of natives, belonging to the chief Moshesh, arrived on the farm. These poor men were traveling in quest of employment. Numbers of natives annually visit the colony, and work for the Boers, making stone enclosures for their cattle, and large dams or embankments across little streams in the mouths of valleys, for the purpose of collecting water in the rainy season for the supply of their flocks and herds during the protracted droughts of summer. They are paid for their labor with young cows or she-goats. The recent rains having washed away the embankment of a dam situated in a distant range of hills, on the borders of the farm, Strydom engaged these men to repair it. The vicinity of the dam being a favorite haunt for quaggas, and it being necessary that Strydom should go there on the morrow, we resolved to hunt in the neighboring district, in which were situated some high and rugged hills.

It was now quite dark, and it was hard to tell what sort of game we were going to fire at. Strydom, however, whispered to me that they were quaggas, and they certainly appeared to be such. His gun snapped three times at the wildebeest, upon which they all set off at a gallop. Strydom, who was riding my stallion, let go his bridle, when he ran in to fire, taking advantage of which the horse set off at a gallop after them I then mounted "The Cow," and after riding hard for about a mile I came up to them. They were now standing still, and the stallion was in the middle of them. I could make him out by his saddle; so, jumping off my horse in a state of intense excitement, I ran forward and fired both barrels of my two-grooved rifle into the quaggas, and heard the bullets tell loudly. They then started off, but the stallion was soon once more fighting in the middle of them. I was astonished and delighted to remark how my horse was able to take up their attention, so that they appeared heedless of the reports of my rifle.

In haste I commenced loading, but to my dismay I found that I had left my loading-rod with Hendric. Mounting "The Cow," I rode nearer to the quaggas, and was delighted to find that they allowed my horse to come within easy shot. It was now very dark, but I set off in the hope to fall in with Hendric on the wide plain, and galloped along, shouting with all my might, but in vain. I then rode across the plain for the hill to try to find some bush large enough to make a ramrod . In this, by the greatest chance, I succeeded, and, being provided with a knife, I cut a good ramrod, loaded my rifle, and rode off to seek the quaggas once more. I soon fell in with them, and, coming within shot, fired at them right and left, and heard both bullets tell, upon which they galloped across the plain, with the stallion still after them. One of them, however, was very hard hit, and soon dropped astern. The stallion remained to keep him company.

About this time the moon shone forth faintly. I galloped on after the troop, and presently coming up with them, rode on one side, and dismounting, and dropping on my knee, I sent a bullet through the shoulder of the last quagga; he staggered forward, fell to the ground with a heavy crash, and expired. The rest of the troop charged wildly around him, snorting and prancing like the wild horses in Mazeppa, and then set off at full speed across the plain. I did not wait to bleed the quagga, but mounting my horse, galloped on after the troop I could not, however, overtake them. I now returned, and endeavored to find the quagga which I had last shot; but, owing to the darkness, and to my having no mark to guide me on the plain, I failed to find him. I then set off to try for the quagga which had dropped astern with the stallion. Having searched some time in vain, I dismounted, and laid my head on the ground, when I made out two dark objects, which turned out to be what I sought.

I caught my stallion and rode home, intending to pay for the horses which I had killed and wounded; but on telling my story to Strydom, with which he seemed extremely amused, he told me not to say a word about it, as the owners of the horses were very avaricious, and would make me pay treble their value, and that, if I kept quiet, it would be supposed they had been killed either by lions or wild Bushmen. Strydom and I continued hunting springboks till the 17th, during which time we enjoyed a constant run of good luck, and so fascinating was the sport that I felt as though I never could tire of it. It was, indeed, a country where a person who loved rifle-shooting ought to have been content. Every morning, on opening my eyes, the first thing which I saw, without raising my head from the pillow, was herds of hundreds of springboks grazing before me on the plains. On the 17th, an old friend of Strydom's, a Boer from Magalisberg, outspanned on the farm. He had been to Grahamstown with a load of ivory, and was returning home with supplies of tea, coffee, clothing, &c., sufficient for two years' consumption.

Being anxious now to devote my attention more particularly to black wildebeests, of which I had not yet secured a specimen, I resolved to take leave of my friend Hendric Strydom, and proceed to the plains beyond the Thebus Mountain, where he informed me they abounded. Accordingly, about 9 P.M., having inspanned by moonlight, I took leave of my friend, having presented him with a coffee-mill and some crockery, to which his frau had taken a fancy, and also with a supply of coarse gunpowder, which is to a Boer a most acceptable gift. We held for the Thebus Mountain, steering across the open plains and following no track, with springboks and wildebeests whistling and bellowing on every side of us. About midnight we halted by a fountain near the pass where a few days before I had lain in ambush for eight hours, and as it was probable that the oxen would wander during the night, we secured them on the yokes. Two of my oxen and both my horses were reported missing when we left the farm, and I had left Cobus to seek for them.

In the afternoon of the next day my two servants joined me, bringing with them the lost oxen, but having failed to find the steeds. At night I took up a position in an old shooting-hole beside the vley, to watch for wildebeests. Several jackals, wildebeests, quaggas, and hyenas came to drink during the night, but, not being able to see the sight of my rifle, I did not fire. Here I remained until the bright star of morning had risen far above the horizon, and day was just beginning to dawn, when, gently raising my head and looking round, I saw, on one side of me, four wildebeests, and on the other side ten. They were coming to drink; slowly and suspiciously they approached the water, and, having convinced themselves that all was right they trotted, boldly up and commenced drinking. Selecting the finest bull, I fired, and sent a bullet through his shoulder, when, splashing through the water, he bounded madly forward, and, having run about a hundred yards, rolled over in the dewy grass. I did not show myself, other game being in sight, but lay still in the hole. In about an hour an old springbok fed up to within three hundred yards of me, and continued browsing there for a considerable time. As no more wildebeests seemed to be approaching, and as I was very hungry, I put up my sight and took a cool, calculating aim at him, and sent the ball through the middle of his shoulder. I then left my hole, and, having inspected the wildebeest bull, which was a noble specimen, I walked up to my wagon, and sent the boys to cut up the venison and preserve the head carefully.

On the following morning I woke as day dawned, and held for my hole beside the vley, but had not gone two hundred yards round the hillock when I saw an old springbok feeding, which I stalked, and broke his fore-leg. He went off toward the wagon, when the boys slipped "Ganger" (one of my greyhounds), who at once ran into him and pulled him down. Having lain about an hour at the vley, two old wildebeests approached up wind, and, suspecting the ground, described a wide semicircle, like our red deer. I wounded one of them, but he did not drop. I, however, managed to send a ball through the shoulder of the other when we ran several hundred yards, whisking his long white tail as if all was right, and suddenly rolled over in full career. His skin had a delicious smell of the grass and wild herbs on which these animals lie and feed. On proceeding to my wagon, I found all my men asleep. Having gralloched the wildebeest, we bore him bodily to the wagon on the "lechtezuit," which is a bar of hard wood used in greasing the wagon wheels, when I immediately set about curing the head, it being a very fine one.

On the following morning Cobus returned, having found my two horses. While taking my breakfast, I observed a gentleman approaching on horseback; this was Mr. Paterson, an officer of the 91st, a detachment of which was then quartered at Colesberg. Lieutenant Borrow, a brother officer of nine, had entrusted mo with the care of a rifle which he was sending to Mr. Paterson, and, as I had been a long time on the road, he had now come to look after it. He was a keen sportsman, and I had much pleasure in meeting so agreeable a person in the wilderness. Having joined me in my rough breakfast with a true hunter's appetite, we rode forth together to look for the wildebeest I had wounded in the morning, expecting to find him dead. On reaching the ground, we found five small herds of wildebeests charging about the plain, and for a long time could not discover the wounded one; at length I perceived an old bull with his head drooping, which I at once pronounced to be my friend. On observing him, we dismounted and watched him for a short time.

Paterson and I then made for the vley, and had not proceeded two hundred yards when, on looking back, I saw about thirty large vultures standing on the wildebeest, which in a very short space of time they would have devoured. On the morrow Paterson left me and rode back for Colesberg, having first extracted a promise that I would follow him within three days. I accordingly hunted until that time had expired, when I reluctantly inspanned and marched upon

Colesberg. Three Ions: marches brought us to the farm of a Boer named Penar, who had been recommended to me as having a good stamp of horses, and as being reasonable in his prices. I was, however, disappointed with his stud, and, finding him exorbitant in his prices, no business was transacted. The country continued much the same—wide Karroo plains, bounded by abrupt rocky mountains. One more long march brought us within five miles of Colesberg, where I halted for the night.

On the 27th, having taken an early breakfast, we trekked into Colesberg, where, having chosen a position for my camp, I outspanned and took up my quarters with Paterson. The village of Colesberg is so called from a conspicuous, lofty table-mountain in its immediate vicinity, which takes its name from a former governor of the colony. The town is situated in a confined hollow, surrounded on all sides by low rocky hills. The formation of these rocks is igneous, and the way in which they are distributed is very remarkable. Large and shapeless masses are heaped together and piled one above another, as if by the hand of some mighty giant of the olden times.

In the forenoon we had some rifle practice at a large granite stone above the town, which the privates of the 91st were wont to pepper on ball-practice days. On this occasion I saw some very good shooting by Campbell, Yarborough, Bailey, and Paterson, all officers of the 91st, and about the four best shots on the frontier. These four Nimrods had a short time previously boldly challenged any four Dutchmen of the Graf Reinet or Colesberg districts to shoot against them. The challenge was accepted by four Dutchmen, who, of course, got "jolly well licked."

After spending a few days very pleasantly with the until the end of March, at which time the horse distemper begins to subside, when I proposed starting on an elephant-hunting expedition into the more remote districts of the far interior. In Colesberg I purchased, by the kind recommendation of Captain Donovan, a second wagon of the cap-tent kind, which turned out to be an unusually good one. Its price was £50. I also purchased an excellent span of black and white oxen from a Dutch blacksmith in the town. From Donovan I bought a dark-brown horse, which I named Colesberg. His price was three hundred dollars, and he was well worth double that sum, for a better steed I never crossed. I purchased from a Boer in the town another horse, well known to the garrison by the sobriquet of the "Immense Brute." He was once the property of Captain Christie of the 91st. When, on one occasion, having wandered, an advertisement appeared in one of the frontier papers relative to an "immense brute" in the shape of a tall bay horse, the property of Captain Christie, &c., &c., and ever since he had been distinguished by this elegant appellation.

I engaged one more Plottentot, named John Stofolus, as driver to the new wagon. He was an active, stout little man, and very neat-handed at stuffing the heads of game, preserving specimens, or any other little job which I might give him to do. He was, however, extremely fond of fighting with his comrades, and was ever boasting of his own prowess; but when his courage was put to the proof in assisting me to hunt the more dangerous animals, he was found woefully deficient.

CHAPTER V

On the evening of the 2nd of December, with considerable difficulty I collected my drunken servants, my oxen and horses, and, taking leave of my kind entertainers, trekked out of Colesberg, steering west for the vast Karroo plains, where the gemsbok were said to be still abundant. It was agreed that Campbell should follow me on the second day to hunt springbok and black wild beast, in a district through which I was to travel; and Paterson had applied for a fortnight's leave, with the intention of joining me in the gemsbok country, and enjoying along with me, for a few days, the exciting sport of "jaging" that antelope. I did not proceed very far that evening, my men being intoxicated, and having several times very nearly capsized the wagons, I halted shortly after sundown, when, all the work with the oxen and horses falling upon me, and no fuel being at hand, I was obliged to content myself by dining on a handful of raw meal and a glass of gin and water. On the following day we performed two long marches, crossing the Sea-Cow River, and halted as it grew dark on a Boer's farm where the plains were covered with springbok. Here Campbell had instructed me to await his arrival, and next morning he was seen approaching the wagons, mounted on the "Immense Brute," and leading two others.

Having breakfasted, we started on horseback to "jag" springbok and wildebeest, ordering the wagons to proceed to a vley about four miles to the west. We galloped about the plains, loading and firing for about six hours. The game was very wild. I wounded three springboks and one wildebeest, but lost them all. Campbell shot two springboks. The first was entirely eaten by the vultures (notwithstanding the bushes with which we had covered him), and skinned as neatly as if done by the hand of man. The second had its leg broken by the ball, and was making off, when a jackal suddenly appeared on the bare plain, and, giving him chase, after a good course ran into him.

Next morning, having bathed and breakfasted, camp bell and I parted, he for Colesberg and I for the Karroo. I trekked on all day, and, having performed a march of twenty-five miles, halted at sundown on the farm of old Wessel, whom I found very drunk. My road lay through vast plains, intersected with ridges of stony hills. On these plains I found the game in herds exceeding anything I had yet seen—springbok in troops of at least ten thousand; also large bodies of quaggas, wildebeest, blesbok, and several ostriches. I had hoped to have purchased some horses from Wessel, but he was too drunk to transact any business, informing me that he was a Boer, and could not endure the sight of Englishmen, at the same time shoving me out of the house, much to the horror of his wife and daughters, who seemed rather nice people.

Two more days of hard marching, under a burning sun, brought me to the farm of Mynheer Stinkum, which I reached late on the evening of the 7th. He informed me that about fifteen miles to the west of his farm I should fall in with a Boer of the wandering tribe who would direct me to a remote vley in the Karroo, a good many miles beyond his encampment, to which ho advised me at once to proceed and hunt in its vicinity. He represented that district as not having been recently disturbed by hunters, and doubted not but I should find gemsbok and other varieties of game abundant

It being now summer, flies prevailed in fearful swarms in the abodes of the Boers, attracted thither by the smell of meat and milk. On entering Stinkum's house, I found the walls of his large sitting-room actually black with these disgusting insects. They are a cruel plague to the settlers in Southern Africa, and it often requires considerable ingenuity to eat one's dinner or drink a cup of coffee without consuming a number of them. When food is served up, two or three Hottentots or Bush-girls are always in attendance with fans made of ostrich feathers, which they keep continually waving over the food till the repast is finished.

This morning I purchased a handsome chestnut pony from a Boer named Duprey, a field cornet, from whom I obtained an egg of the bustard of the largest species for my collection, oology being a subject in which for many years of my life I had taken great interest, having in my possession one of the finest collections in Great Britain, amassed with much toil and danger. I have descended most of the loftiest precipices in the central Highlands of Scotland, and along the sea-shore, with a rope round my waist, in quest of the eggs of the various eagles and falcons which have their eyries in those almost inaccessible situations. Among Stinkum's stud was a handsome brown gelding, to which I took a great fancy; and after consulting for some time with his wife, he made up his mind to part with him The lowest price was to be £18.

Four of my oxen being footsore and unable to proceed, I left them in charge of old Sweirs, and in the cool of the evening I inspanned, and, having proceeded about five miles through an extremely wild and desolate looking country, on clearing a neck in a range of low, rocky hills I came full in view of the vley or pool of water beside which I had been directed to encamp. The breadth of this vley was about three hundred yards. One side of it was grassy, and patronized by several flocks of Egyptian wild geese, a species of barnacle, wild ducks, egrets, and cranes. The other side was bare, and here the game drank, and the margin of the water was trampled by the feet of wild animals like an English horse-pond. There being no trees beside which to form our camp, we drew up our wagons among some low bushes, about four hundred yards from the vley. When the sun went down I selected the three horses which were to carry myself and two after-riders in the chase of the unicorn on the following morning, and directed my boys to give them a liberal supply of forage to eat during the night.

On the 10th of December, everything having been made ready overnight, I took coffee, saddled up, and started an hour before day-dawn, accompanied by Cobus and Jacob as after-riders, leading a spare horse with my pack-saddle. We held a southwesterly course, and at length reached the base of a little hillock slightly elevated above the surrounding scenery. Here dismounted, and, having ascended to the summit, examined the country all around minutely with my spyglass, but could not see anything like the onyx. I was in the act of putting up my glass again, when, to my intense delight, I perceived, feeding within four hundred yards, in a hollow between two hillocks, a glorious herd of about five-and-twenty of the long-wished for gemsbok, with a fine old ball feeding at a little distance by himself, their long, sharp horns glancing in the morning sun like the cheese-toasters of a troop of dragoons. I scarcely allowed myself a moment to feast my eyes on the thrilling sight before me, when I returned to my boys, and with them concerted a plan to circumvent them.

We agreed that Jacob and I should endeavor to ride by a circuitous course a long way to windward of the herd, and that Cobus should then give chase and drive them toward us. The wind was westerly, but the district to which this herd seemed to belong unfortunately lay to the northward. Jacob and I rode steadily on, occasionally looking behind us, and, presently taking up a commanding position, strained our eyes in the direction of the gemsboks, in the full expectation of seeing them flying toward us. After waiting a consider, able time and nothing appearing, I felt convinced that we were wrong, and in this conjecture I judged well. A slight inequality in the plain had concealed from our view the retreating herd, which had started in a northerly course. Cobus had long since dashed into the Herd, and was at that moment flying across the plains after them, I knew not in what direction. After galloping athwart the boundless plains in a state bordering on distraction, I gave it up, and, accompanied by Jacob, returned to the wagons in anything but a placid frame of mind.

About two hours after, Cobus reached the wagon, having ridden the old bull to a stand-still. The old fellow had lain down repeatedly toward the end of the chase, and at length could proceed no further, and Cobus, after waiting some time and seeing no signs of his master, had reluctantly left him. In the height of the day the sun was intensely powerful; I felt much disgusted at my want of luck in my first attempt, and, burning with anxiety for another trial, I resolved to take the field again in the afternoon, more especially as we had not a pound of flesh in camp. Between 3 and 4 P.M. I again sallied forth with the same after riders leading a spare horse. "We cantered across plains to the northeast, and soon fell in with ostriches and quaggas, and, after riding a few miles through rather bushy ground, a large herd of hartebeest cantered across our path, and these were presently joined by two or three herds of quaggas and wildebeests, which kept retreating as we advanced, their course being marked by clouds of red dust.

While I was thus engaged, Cobus was shifting his saddle from the "Immense Brute" to the gray, which being accomplished, I ordered him to renew the chase and try to ride down the old bull for me. We fastened the "Immense Brute" to a bush beside the dead gemsbok, and then, mounting the horse which Jacob had been riding, I followed on as best I might. On gaining the first ridge, I perceived the troop of oryx about two miles ahead of me, ascending another ridge at the extremity of the plain, and Cobus riding hard for them about a mile astern, but rapidly gaining on them. Oryx and boy soon disappeared over the distant ridge, the boy still far behind.

The country here changed from grass and bushes to extreme sterility; the whole ground was undermined with the holes of colonies of meercat or mouse-hunts. This burrowed ground, which is common throughout these parts, was extremely distressing to our horses, the soil giving way at every step, and my steed soon began to flag. On gaining the distant ridge a wide plain lay before me. I looked in every direction, straining my eyes to catch a glimpse of Cobus and the oryx, but they were nowhere to be seen. At length, after riding about two miles further in the direction which he seemed to hold when I had last seen him, I detected his white shirt on a ridge a long way to my right, and on coming up to him I found that he had ridden the old bull to a stand-still: the old fellow was actually lying panting beside a green bush. I thought him one of the most lovely animals I had ever beheld, and I could have gazed for hours at him; but I was now many miles from my wagons, without a chance of water, and dying of thirst, so I speedily finished the poor oryx, and having carefully cut off the head, commenced skinning him.

It was now late—too late to take home the cow oryx that night; the bull was much too far from my camp to think of saving any part of the flesh. I therefore sent off Cobus to the wagons to fetch water and bread, desiring him to meet me at a spot where the cow gemsbok was lying, where I resolved to sleep, to protect her from hyenas and jackals; but before Jacob and I had accomplished the skinning, and secured the skin and the head upon the horse, night had set in. My thirst was now fearful, and becoming more and more raging. I would have given any thing I possessed for a bottle of water. In the hope of meeting Cobus, Jacob and I rode slowly forward, and endeavored to find out the place; but darkness coming on, and there being no feature in the desert to guide me, I lost my way entirely, and after wandering for several hours in the dark, and firing blank shots at intervals, we lay down in the open plain to sleep till morning, having tied our horse to a thorny bush beside where we lay. I felt very cold all night, but my thirst continued raging. My clothes consisted of a shirt and a pair of knee-breeches. My bed was the bull's hide laid over a thorny bush, which imparted to my tough mattress the elasticity of a feather bed. Having slept about two hours, I awoke, and found that our horses had absconded; after which I slept little. Day dawned, and I rose; and on looking about, neither Jacob nor I had the most remote idea of the ground we were on, nor of the position of our camp.

Within a few hundred yards of us was a small hill, which we ascended and looked about, but could not in the least recognize the ground. I, however, ascertained the points of the compass and the position of my camp by placing my left hand toward the rising sun. I was then returning to the spot where I had slept, when suddenly I perceived, standing within three hundred yards of me, the horse which I had fastened beside the cow oryx on the preceding evening, and ongoing up I found both all right. I immediately saddled the horse and rode hard for camp, ordering Jacob to commence skinning the cow, and promising to send him water and bread as soon as I reached the wagons.

On the 14th we went out on foot after a troop of ostriches, one of which we wounded, and came home much exhausted. The very ground was as hot as the side of a stove. The following day we were visited by a party of Boers from the neighboring encampments, who had come to see how we were getting on. Finding our brandy good, they made themselves very agreeable, and sat for many hours conversing with us. The leading subject of conversation was gemsbok and lion shooting, and the slaying and capturing of whole tribes of marauding Bushmen in by-gone days. They informed us that when they first occupied these districts the game was far more abundant, and eland and koodoos were plentiful. Their herds of cattle were constantly attacked and plundered by the vindictive wild Bushmen. The Boers informed us that in a country to the southwest of our actual position, a tribe of these natives for many years were in the habit of practicing raids with impunity upon the herds of the farmers in the Raw-feldt, assisted by a vast and impracticable desert which intervened between their country and the more fertile pastoral districts. They seemed to prefer extremely dry seasons for these incursions, their object in this being that their pursuers, who of course followed on horseback while they were always on foot, should not obtain water for their horses. Their own wants in this respect they provided form the following curious manner. They had regular stages at long intervals in a direct line across the desert, where, assisted by their wives, they concealed water in ostrich eggs, which they brought from amazing distances, and these spots, being marked by some slight inequality in the ground, they could discover either by day or night from their perfect knowledge of the country.

CHAPTER VI

At an early hour on the morning of the 16th Paterson and I again took the field, accompanied by our three after-riders, and, having ridden several miles in a northerly direction, we started an oryx, to which Paterson and his after-rider gave immediate chase. I then rode in an easterly direction, and shortly fell in with a fine old cow oryx, which we instantly charged. She stole away at a killing pace, her black tail streaming in the wind, and her long, sharp horns laid well back over her shoulders. Aware of her danger, and anxious to gain the desert, she put forth her utmost speed, and strained across the bushy plain. She led us a tearing chase of upward of five miles in a northerly course, Cobus sticking well into her, and I falling far behind. After a sharp burst of about three miles, Cobus and the gray disappeared over a ridge about half a mile ahead of me I here mounted a fresh horse, which had been led by Jacob, and followed. On gaining the ridge, I perceived the gray disappearing over another ridge a fearfully long way ahead. When I reached this point I commanded an extremely extensive prospect, but no living object was visible on the desolate plain.

While deliberating in which direction to ride, I suddenly heard a pistol shot some distance to my left, which I knew to be Cobus's signal that the oryx was at bay. Having ridden half a mile, I discovered Cobus dismounted in a hollow, and no oryx in view. Pie had succeeded in riding the quarry to a stand, and I not immediately appearing, he very injudiciously had at once lost sight of the buck and left it. Having upbraided Cobus in no measured terras for his stupidity, I sought to retrieve the fortunes of the day by riding in the direction in which he had left the oryx. The ground here was uneven, and interspersed with low hillocks. We extended our front, and rode on up wind, and, having crossed two or three ridges, I discovered a troop of bucks a long way ahead. Having made for these, they turned out to be hartebeests. At this moment I perceived three magnificent oryx a short distance to my left. On observing his, they cantered along the ridge toward a fourth oryx, which I at once perceived to be "embossed with foam and dark with soil," and knew to be the antelope sought for. Once more we charged her. Our horses had now considerably recovered their wind, but the poor oryx was much distressed; and after a chase of half a mile, I jumped off my horse and sent a bullet through her ribs, which brought her to a stand, when I finished her with the other barrel.

On my way home I came across Paterson's after rider, "jaging" a troop of seven gemsbok, but fearfully to leeward, his illustrious master being nowhere in sight. An hour after I reached the camp Paterson came in, in a towering rage, having been unlucky in both his chases. I now dispatched one of my wagons to bring home my oryx. It returned about twelve o'clock that night, carrying the skin of my genbok and also a magnificent old blue wildebeest (the brindled gnoo), which the Hottentots had obtained in an extraordinary manner. Pie was found with one of his fore legs caught over his horn, so that he could not run, and they hamstrung him and cut his throat. He had probably managed to get himself into this awkward attitude while fighting with some of his fellows. The vultures had consumed all the flesh of the gemsbok, and likewise torn my blanket with which I had covered her.

On the following day, all our steeds being very much done up, Paterson and I visited the neighboring Boers to endeavor to buy and hire some horses. I bought one clipper of Mynheer Gous for £25, and called him "Grouse," and Paterson succeeded in hiring one, and with these, on the following day, we continued our campaign against the gemsboks. Paterson's after-rider not being well up to his work, I lent him Cobus, and on this occasion his perseverance was rewarded by a noble gemsbok, which he rode down and slew, and also a fine bull blue wildebeest, which last animal is rather rare in these parts. We had one more day together, after which, much to my regret, Paterson was obliged to take leave of me and start for Colesberg, his leave of absence having expired. One of his horses being foot-sore, I purchased him, in the hope of his soon recovering, which after a few days' rest he did I called him "Paterson," after his old master. My stud now consisted of eight horses; but three of them were missing, and I dispatched Jacob in quest of them, who returned on the third day bringing them with him, having followed the spoor upward of fifty miles.

In the evening two of the Hottentots walked in to camp, bending under a burden of ostrich eggs, having discovered a nest containing five-and-thirty. Their manner of carrying them amused me. Having divested themselves of their leather "crackers," which in colonial phrase means trousers, they had secured the ankles with rheimpys, and, having thus converted them into bags, they had crammed them with as many ostrich eggs as they would contain. They left about half of the number behind concealed in the sand, for which they returned on the following morning. While encamped at this vley we fell in with several nests of ostriches, and here I first ascertained a singular propensity peculiar to these birds. If a person discovers the nest and does not at once remove the eggs, on returning he will most probably find them all smashed. This the old birds almost invariably do, even when the intruder has not handled the eggs or so much as ridden within five yards of them.

A favorite method adopted by the wild Bushman for approaching the ostrich and other varieties of game is to clothe himself in the skin of one of these birds, in which, taking care of the wind, he stalks about the plain, cunningly imitating the gait and motions of the ostrich until within range, when, with a well-directed poisoned arrow from his tiny bow, he can generally seal the fate of any of the ordinary varieties of game. These insignificant-looking arrows are about two feet six inches in length; they consist of a slender reed, with a sharp bone head, thoroughly poisoned with a composition, of which the principal ingredients are obtained sometimes from a succulent herb, having thick leaves, yielding a poisonous milky juice, and sometimes from the jaws of snakes. The bow barely exceeds three feet in length; its string is of twisted sinews. When a Bushman finds an ostrich's nest, he ensconces himself in it, and there awaits the return of the old birds, by which means he generally secures the pair. It is by means of these little arrows that the majority of the fine plumes are obtained which grace the heads of the fair throughout the civilized world.

Having covered him with bushes, we rode on, and shortly came upon an immense, compact herd of several thousand "trekking" springboks, which were exceedingly tame, and in the middle of them stood two oryx. These we managed for the first time to drive in a southerly direction, being that in which the camp, lay; and, after a sharp and rather circular burst, I headed the finer, and bowled her over. She proved to be a young cow about three years old. Having disemboweled her, and prepared her for the pack-saddle with a cotdeau-de'chasse, by splitting the brisket, passing the knife along the gristly bones on ono side of it, and breaking the ribs well known to the hunter join the vertebrae, whereby the animal can more easily be balanced on the packsaddle, we succeeded with great difficulty in placing her on "Sunday," and rode slowly for the place where we had left the porcupine. We placed him on the oryx, and secured him with a rheim, but we had not proceeded far when some of the quills pricked the steed, upon which he commenced bucking and prancing in the most frantic manner, which of course made matters ten times worse, causing the porcupine to beat the devil's tattoo on his back. The gemsbok's head, also, which, being a poor one, I had not cut off, unfortunately got adrift, and kept dangling about his haunches, the sharp horns striking his belly at every spring. He broke loose from Jacob, who led him, and set off across the country at a terrific pace, eventually smashing the pack-saddle, but still failing to disengage himself from the gerasbok, whose hind and fore feet, being fastened together, slipped round under his belly, impeding his motions, and in this condition he was eventually secured, being considerably lacerated about the haunches by the horns of the oryx.

Next day Cobus and I fell in with the finest bull oryx I had yet met, which, after a severe chase, we rode into and slew. For some evenings previous a large bright comet had appeared in the southwest, having a tearing, fiery tail, which strange meteor, to the best of my recollection, shone brightly in the clear firmament for five or six weeks. We lived well, but lonely. My camp abounded with every delicacy—tongues, brains, marrow-bones, kidneys, rich soup, with the most delicious venison in the world, &c., &c., and a constant supply of ostrich eggs. The 20th was cool and cloudy, being the first day that the sky had been overcast once I had left the Thebus Flats.

In the afternoon I resolved to ride far into the oryx country, sleep under a bush, and hunt them on the following morning. I accordingly left my wagons about 3 P.M., with my two after-riders and a spare horse, and rode about fifteen miles in a northerly course, when we secured our horses to a bush, to leeward of which we slept. On my way thither I dismounted on an arid plain to breathe our steeds and dig up some bulbs of the water-root for immediate consumption, my thirst being very severe. While cantering along we passed several troops of hartebecsts and ostriches, and late in the day I observed a small troop of oryx.

On the 26th I raised my head from my saddle about 1 o'clock A.M., imagining the day was dawning, and, having reused my after-riders, we proceeded to saddle our horses; but I soon perceived that the bright moon, across which a bank of clouds was at that moment passing, had deceived me, and accordingly we off-saddled, and in a few minutes I was once more asleep. Toward morning, a smart shower of rain, suddenly falling on my face, broke in abruptly on my slumbers, when we once more arose, and, when day dawned, we saddled up, and held a northerly course. We found the fresh tracks of hyenas not more than fifteen yards from our horses. Within a hundred yards of our bush we at once discovered the spoor of an old bull gemsbok which had fed past us during the night and we had proceeded but a short distance when we discovered a herd of seven noble oryx within a quarter of a mile of us, pasturing in a low hollow; upon which I directed Cobus to ride round and "jag" them up to me, while I took up a position in front. The oryx presently charged past me; but Cobus had started after an old bull which I did not see, and which he rode to a stand. The ball passed within inches of his ear, and raised the dust about fifty yards in advance of him; and I had the mortification of Laving to content myself with watching his lessening form as he retreated across the boundless waste. Faint and weary, and intensely mortified at the issue of my long-continued chase, my lips cracking, and my tongue and throat parched with raging thirst, I threw my bridle on my arm, and led my weary steed homeward, and I inwardly wished that, instead of my being a man of fourteen stone weight, nature had formed me of the most Liliputian dimensions. I was now a fearful long way from my camp; hills that in the morning were blue before me, were now equally blue far, far behind me; "Grouse" could scarcely walk along with me, nor did he ever recover that morning's work.

Upon my return I observed Jacob making for me, landing a free horse, of which I stood not a little in need; he stated that he had seen an oryx standing at a distance on the plain, which bore the appearance of being wounded. We then made for this oryx, and on my overhauling her with my spy-glass I saw plainly that she was badly hit. On my cantering up to her she ran but a short distance, when she. gave in, and, facing about, stood at bay. I foolishly approached her without firing, and very nearly paid dearly for my folly; for, lowering her sharp horns, she made a desperate rush toward me, and would inevitably have run me through had not her strength at this moment failed her, when she staggered forward and fell to the ground.

On the following day the waters of my vley sank into the earth and disappeared: the water for some days past had become very "brack," making myself and my people very unwell.

On the 28th I had the satisfaction of beholding, for the first time, what I had often heard the Boers alludeto—viz., a "trek-bokken," or grand migration of spring-Doks. This was, I think, the most extraordinary and striking scene, as connected with beasts of the chase, that I have ever beheld. For about two hours before the day dawned I had been lying awake in my wagon, listening to the grunting of the bucks within two hundred yards of me, imagining that some large herd of springboks was feeding beside my camp; but on my rising when it was clear, and looking about me; I beheld the ground to the northward of my camp actually covered with a dense living mass of springboks, marching slowly and steadily along, extending from an opening in a long range of hills on the west, through which they continued pouring, like the flood of some great river, to a ridge about a mile to the northeast, over which they disappeared. The breadth of the ground they covered might have been somewhere about half a mile. I stood upon the fore crest of my wagon for nearly two hours, lost in wonder at the novel and wonderful scene which was passing before me, and had some difficulty in convincing myself that it was reality which I beheld, and not the wild and exaggerated picture of a hunter's dream. During this time their vast legions continued streaming through the neck in the hills in one unbroken compact phalanx. At length I saddled up, and rode into the middle of them with my rifle and after-riders, and fired into the ranks until fourteen had fallen, when I cried "Enough." We then retraced our steps to secure from the ever-voracious vultures the venison which lay strewed along my gory track. Having collected the springboks at different bushes, and concealed them with brushwood, we returned to camp, where I partook of coffee while my men were inspanning.

A person anxious to kill many springboks might have bagged thirty or forty that morning. I never, in all my subsequent career, fell in with so dense a herd of these antelopes, nor found them allow me to ride so near them. Having inspanned, we proceeded with the wagons to take up the fallen game, which being accomplished, we held for the small periodical stream beside which the wandering Boers were encamped, that point being in my line of march for Beer Vley. Vast and surprising as was the herd of springboks which I had that morning witnessed, it was infinitely surpassed by what I beheld on the march from my vley to old Sweirs's camp; for, on our clearing the low range of hills through which the springboks had been pouring, I beheld the boundless plains, and even the hill sides which stretched away on every side of me, thickly covered, not with "herds," bat with "one vast herd" of springboks; far as the eye could strain the landscape was alive with them, until they softened down into a dim red mass of living creatures.

To endeavor to form any idea of the amount of antelopes which I that day beheld were vain; but I have, nevertheless, no hesitation in stating that some hundreds of thousands of springboks were that morning within the compass of my vision. On reaching the encampment of the Boers, I out-spanned, and set about cutting up and salting my venison the Boers had likewise been out with their "roers," and shot as many as they could carry home. Old Sweirs acknowledged that it was a very fair "trek-bokken," but observed that it was not many when compared with what he had seen. "You this morning," he remarked, "behold only one flat covered with springboks, but I give you my word that I have bidden a long day's journey over a succession of flats covered with them, as far as I could see, as thick as sheep standing in a fold." I spent the following two days with the Boers. Each morning and evening we rode out and hunted the springboks, killing as many as we could bring home.

On the morrow I removed my encampment about eight or nine miles further down the vley, being obliged, from the broken and uneven nature of the ground, to march in a semicircular course, holding along the outside of the vley. I drew up my wagons on the plain close to the bank of a dry channel, with a fine large pool of running water in my vicinity. This was the finest place that can be described to shoot springboks, and also to select extraordinary specimens on account of their horns, which I was anxious to do. The country, on every side, was covered with immense herds of these antelopes, and they all seemed to have an inclination to come and feed close along the side of the watercourse beside which we lay. This channel being about ten feet deep, and extending throughout the entire length of the plain, I had only to study the wind, and could walk up within easy shot of any herd, and select what buck I pleased.

Here I remained for several days, enjoying brilliant sport, both oryx and springboks giving me each day excellent shots. Here, also, I shot my first ostrich, a fine old cock. It was a very long shot; I gave my rifle several feet of elevation, yet nevertheless the ball struck him on the leg, breaking it below the knee, when he fell and was unable to rise. The power possessed by an ostrich in his leg can hardly be imagined. The thigh is very muscular, and resembles that of a horse more than that of a bird. In the act of dying, he lashed out and caught me a severe blow on my leg, which laid me prostrate.

CHAPTER VII

On the 9th I considered I had sufficiently long enjoyed the sweets of Beer Vley; and accordingly, the wagons being properly packed, I inspanned in the afternoon, and trekked to the south. On the following morning we inspanned at the dawn of day, and retraced our steps to the Rhinoceros Pool. The heat^ continued most oppressive, the wind still northerly. We were infested with myriads of common flies, which proved a constant annoyance, filling tent and wagons to such a degree that it was impossible to sit in them. I rode out in the morning of the 11th, accompanied by an after-rider, and shot two springboks, which we bore to camp secured on our horses behind our saddles by passing the buckles of the girths on each side through the fore and hind legs of the antelopes, having first performed an incision between the bone and the sinews with the couteau-de-chasse according to colonial usage.

The Boers had informed me of a small fountain one march in advance, where they recommended me to hunt for a short time, and this place I intended to be my next encampment. On the morrow we inspanned at earliest dawn, and trekked about ten miles in a northeasterly course across a barren, extensive plain, steering parallel with the country frequented by the oryx. "We drew up our wagons at a place where some Boers had been encamped during the winter months. Here we found a well with nothing but mud in it. I set to work with the spade and cleaned it out, and presently had good water for myself and people. I dispatched one of my Hottentots on horseback to seek for water in advance for the horses and oxen. He shortly returned, and reported another deserted Boer encampment about a mile ahead, at which there was a stronger fountain, but considerably choked with mud. Having breakfasted, I removed my wagons thither, and encamped."

In the afternoon I saddled up, and started with my two after-riders and a spare horse, with the intention of sleeping in the oryx country, and hunting next day. We rode north through sandy plains and hollows on which large herds of gnoos and springboks were grazing. Just as the sun descended we started a nine old bull oryx. We discovered him in a bushy hollow; after a sharp burst Cobus managed to turn him, when, by heading him, I got within range, and finished him with a couple of shots. It was now dark; having off saddled our horses, we knee-haltered them, and allowed them to graze for an hour; after which, having secured them to a neighboring bush, we lay down to sleep on the hard ground. My pillow was the neck of the old bull; the jackals sang his coronach. On the 13th I shot a fine old steinbok, and on nearing my encampment I discovered two different vleys containing water. Upon reaching my camp I found a funny little fellow in the shape of the Bushboy before alluded to awaiting my arrival. My Hottentots had detected his black, woolly head protruding from the reeds adjoining the fountain, and had captured him. I presented him with a suit of new clothes and a glass of spirits, and we immediately became and have ever since continued the best of friends.

In the afternoon I rode to one of the vleys, accompanied by two of my men, bearing pickaxes and spades and my bedding. We dug a shooting-hole on the usual principle, about three feet deep and eight in diameter, on the lee side of the largest vley. In this hole I used to take my station every night—the jackals and hyenas growling around me—and await the coming of the dawn to get a sight of the game that came to drink. In this manner I enjoyed excellent sport among the wildebeests and quaggas until the 17th, when, through want of water for my oxen, I was compelled to march for the Great Orange River, which was the nearest water, being distant upward of thirty miles. We inspanned in the afternoon, and, having performed a march of twelve miles, holding a northeasterly course, I outspanned for a couple of hours to allow my oxen to graze; after which I again inspanned, and trekked about twelve miles further by moonlight, when we halted till the day dawned, making fast the horses and oxen. The country here assumed a less sterile appearance than that which I had occupied during the last five weeks, being ornamented with a few ancient trees, bearing a leaf resembling that of the willow, and called by the Dutch "clean wood;" there were also a few dwarfish thorny trees of a species of mimosa.

On the 18th we inspanned at the dawn of day, and after a march of about four hours, through a wild and uninhabited country, we suddenly found ourselves on the bank of the magnificent Orange River. This queen of African rivers forms a leading feature in the geography of Southern Africa. Its length, I believe, is somewhere about a thousand miles. It rises in the east, in the Vitbergen mountain range, a little to the northward of the latitude of Port Natal, and, flowing westward, is joined by the fair Vaal River about fifty miles below the spot where I had now arrived; thence it continues its course westward, and falls into the South Atlantic about five hundred miles to the north of the Cape of Good Hope. We made the river at a place called Davinar's Drift or ford, beside which was a comfortable Dutch farm. The owner was a young Boer from the Cape district, and had obtained his present enviable position by marrying a fat old widow. Their chief riches consisted of sheep and goats, of which they possessed enormous flocks, which were in very fine condition, the country being suitable for pasturing these animals. Large herds of trekking springboks were feeding in sight of the homestead. I had passed several herds on my morning's march, and had shot three, which were in good order.

The Boers, contrary to my expectation, reported the river fordable, though I had been informed that it was very large. Before venturing to cross we were occupied for upward of an hour in raising the goods liable to be damaged by water, by means of a platform consisting of green willow boughs, with which we filled the bottom of the wagons, and then replaced the cargo. The descent on our side was extremely steep, and we found it necessary to rheim, viz., to secure, by means of the drag-chains, both hind wheels of each wagon. The drift was extremely rough, and jolted the wagons about sadly. We, however, got safely through, and, having proceeded about half a mile up the opposite bank, encamped. No person who has not contemplated a magnificent river under similar circumstances can form a side of the pleasure I felt in reaching this oasis of the desert. For many weeks past our lot had been cast in the arid plains of the parched karroo, where there had often been barely sufficient water for our cattle to drink, with cloudless skies and an intense burning sun over our heads, and no tree nor bush of any description whose friendly shade might shelter us from the power of its rays. Here, "of the sudden," a majestic river rolled before our delighted eyes, whose fertile banks were adorned with groves clad in everlasting verdure. At the spot where we crossed, the river reminded me of the appearance exhibited by certain parts of the River Spey in summer during a spate. The breadth of the Orange River, however, is in general about three hundred yards. The whole of the banks are ornamented with a rich fringe of weeping willows, whose branches dip into the stream, and also of many other trees and bushes, whose blossoms and pleasing foliage yielded the most delicious balmy perfume. Numerous flocks of the feathered tribe by their beautiful plumage and melodious notes increased the charm of this lovely scene.

At 1 P.M. on the following day I inspanned and trekked north to the salt-pan, which we reached in the dark. The general character of the country became richer after crossing the Orange River. The plains were adorned with a more luxuriant coating of grass and in greater profusion; and the small karroo bushes were replaced by others of fairer growth, and of a different variety. Most of these yielded a strong aromatic perfume, but more particularly when the ground had been refreshed by a shower of rain, on which occasions the African wilderness diffuses a perfume so exquisite and balmy, that no person that has not experienced its delights can form an idea of it. Our march lay through an extensive undulating country. We passed several troops of hartebeests and springboks, and saw for the first time one sassayby, a large antelope allied to the hartebeest, and of a purple color. Mountain ranges bounded the view on every side, and I could discover by means of my spy-glass that strips of forests of mimosa stretched along their bases. The salt-pan to which we had come was of an oval shape, and about a quarter of a mile in diameter.

It was a low basin whose sides sloped gently down, but the middle was a dead level of fine sand. Upon this sand, throughout the greater part of the pan, lay a thick layer of good coarse salt, varying from one to four inches in depth. Heavy rains fill the pan or basin with water, and, the dry season succeeding, the water disappears, and large deposits of salt are found. These pans or salt-licks are met with in several parts of South Africa. Those which mainly supply the colony with good salt are situated between Utenage and Algoa Bay; they are of considerable extent, and yield a surprising quantity. Ostriches and almost every variety of ante lope frequent these pans for the purpose of licking the brack or salt ground, to which they are very partial. The pan which we had reached was formerly visited by Boers and Griquas for the purpose of obtaining salt, but had of late years been abandoned for others yielding it of a better quality. The country around was consequently undisturbed; and, being utterly uninhabited, was lonely, and as still as the grave.

On the morning of the 21st I left my wagons encamped beside the salt-pan, and, having proceeded about half a mile in a northerly direction along a seldom-trodden wagon-track, I discovered a fountain of excellent water, but very strongly impregnated with saltpeter. This fountain I afterward learned is termed by the Boers "Cruit Vonteyn," or Powder Fountain, its waters resembling the washings of a gun-barrel; but the Griquas more elegantly call it "Stink Vonteyn." At breakfast-time I was joined by a party of ruffian Griquas, who were proceeding with a dilapidated-looking wagon, which had no sail, to hunt hartebeests and blue wildebeests in the vicinity of a small fountain to the northeast, where game was reported abundant. They were accompanied by several wild-looking, naked Bushmen attendants, whom they had captured when young, and domesticated. These drove their shooting-horses loose behind the wagon, grazing as they went along. I also observed a couple of milk cows with calves among their loose oxen, a healthy luxury without which that race of people seldom proceed on a journey.

Another tribe of men in every way similar to these Griquas inhabit an extensive and fertile country immediately to the east of their territory. These men term themselves Bastards. Their chief's name is Adam Kok. The name of their capital is Philipolis, a small village about thirty miles to the north of Colesberg, Their country is bounded on the south by the Great Orange River, and is about the most desirable district in Southern Africa for farming purposes, there being abundance of fountains throughout its whole extent capable of being led out to irrigate the land, without which no gardens can be formed, nor wheat grown, in that country. Rich pasture is abundant. Cattle and sheep thrive and breed remarkably well; goats also an animal valuable to the South African settler, but for which only certain districts are suitable, are here very prolific. The goat in many districts is subject to a disease called by the Boers "brunt sickta," or burnt sick ness, owing to the animals afflicted with it exhibiting lie appearance of having been burned. It is incurable and if the animals infected are not speedily killed or put out of the way, the contagion rapidly spreads, and it is not uncommon for a farmer to lose his entire flock with it. I have known seasons when the three latter animals were so generally affected by it that the vast plains throughout which they are found were covered with hundreds of skulls and skeletons of those that had died therefrom. One of the chief recommendations of the Bastards' country is its admirable suitableness for breeding horses. Large herds of these may be seen throughout their country pasturing high on the mountain sides, or scattered in troops over its grassy plains. The deadly distemper so prevalent along the frontiers of the colony is here of comparatively rare occurrence. In the far interior, however, it is so virulent during five or six months of the year that it is often impossible to save a single horse, and through its ravages I was annually in the habit of losing the greater part of my stud.

The chiefs of the Griquas and Bastards are in close alliance with the English government, which protects them from the attacks of the rebel Dutch Boers. These, well aware of the excellent qualities of the Bastards' country, are possessed with a strong desire to appropriate it. The language spoken by both these tribes is Dutch. They have, in general, embraced the Christian religion, and several worthy missionaries have, for several years past, devoted their lives to the improvement of their temporal and eternal condition. The dress worn by the men consists of home-made leather jacket, waistcoat, and trowsers, feldtchoens, or home-made shoes, a Malay handkerchief tied round the head, and on Sundays and other great occasions a shirt and a neckcloth. The females wear a close-fitting corset reaching to the small of the waist, below which they sport a petticoat like the women of other countries. These petticoats are sometimes made of stuffs of British manufacture, and at other times of soft leather prepared by themselves. Their headdress consists of two handkerchiefs, one of black silk, the other of a striped red and green color, usually termed Malay handkerchiefs. They are very fond of beads of every size and color, which they hang in large necklaces round their necks. They have one description of bead peculiar to themselves and to the tribes extending along the banks of the Great Orange River to its junction with the sea. This bead is formed of the root of a bush found near the mouth of the Orange River, and possesses a sweet and peculiar perfume.

When this party of Griquas came up to me, being anxious to see as much as possible of the natives of those parts which I traversed, I invited them to halt and drink coffee with me, an invitation which a Griqua was never yet known to decline. They informed me that, in the mountain ranges to the northeast, koodoo were to be met with and they invited me to accompany them on their chasse. When breakfast was finished they sent their wagon in advance, with instructions to wait for their arrival at the fountain, where they intended to pitch their camp ; and, having saddled up, we all set forward and rode east to hunt koodoos and hartebeests, or any other game we might fall in with. After riding three or four miles, on approaching the base of the hills we entered an ancient forest of mimosas, every tree being a study for an artist. There was also a considerable under-cover of various sweet-smelling shrubs and bushes. Here steinbok and duyker were abundant. This venerable forest extended all around the bases of various ranges of rocky hills, which stretched in different directions through these plains. Close in, at the foot of one of the hills, we discovered a Bushman residence, consisting of three small huts, each about four feet high, and about eight in diameter. They were formed of boughs of trees, thatched over with rank grass drawn up by the roots. The natives, as usual, had fled on our approach, and no living creature was to be seen. I entered each of the hats, and found lots of well "braid" (or dressed) skins of all the wild beasts of these parts. All their dishes were made either of ostrich eggs or of the shells of land tortoises, and these were ranged round the floor on one side of the hut. Most of the ostrich egg-shells contained water.

We crossed the hills by a stony neck and having proceeded some distance through several well-wooded glades and hollows in the table-land of the hills, we suddenly looked forth upon a noble prospect. A wide grassy plain, covered with picturesque mimosas and detached clumps of ever-green bushes, stretched away from the bases of the hills on which we stood. Beyond, the landscape was shut in by the bold and abrupt forms of rugged mountain ranges, which were colored with a softened blue tint. Having descended into this line picturesque plain, we held north, riding parallel with the hilly chain. Presently, my comrades adopting a course which did not strike me as the most likely to fall in with game, I chose a line of march for myself, and, following along under the mountain chain, I soon lost sight of them, and saw them no more that day. On this occasion I had taken the field without any after rider. Having ridden about a mile further, I started a doe koodoo, the first I had seen, and shortly after I started another, with a young one, which I determined to secure, there being no flesh in our camp. Having pursued it a short distance, I came suddenly upon a troop of koodoos, consisting of three bucks and several does. Two of the bucks were old fellows, and carried magnificent, wide-set, long, spiral horns.

I had ridden about a mile, when I suddenly perceived a gallant herd of nine old oryxes cantering toward me, all of them carrying horns of immense length and beauty, surpassing anything I had hitherto seen. They were preceded by four beautifully-striped zebras, the first I had met with, and followed by two brilliant red hartebeests. In half a minute I was flying along within sixty yards of the troop of oryxes, carefully studying the horns of each, and at a loss to decide which was the finest, they were all so very handsome. As I swept along I deplored my folly in having taken the field without my after-riders; I nevertheless entertained hopes of success, as these antelopes had evidently been followed by the Griquas from whom I parted. They led me a long and severe chase along the skirts of the hill, the wind fortunately blowing right across them. After riding hard for several miles I felt my horse very much distressed, and was on the point of giving up the pursuit, when I observed one old bull make a momentary halt under a mimosa, evidently very much blown. This gave me fresh hope; I resolved to follow him as long as my horse could go, and once more I gave chase with renewed speed. I was soon riding opposite to him, within sixty yards, with the hill on the other side, and by a desperate effort I managed to cut him off from his comrades, and turn his head down the wind.

This noble oryx carried the finest horns I had met with, and I had, moreover, the satisfaction of knowing that he was the finest in the herd. Having off-saddled and knee-haltered my horse, I commenced cutting off the head of the oryx, which I accomplished with some trouble, the skin at the neck being an inch in thickness. I then broke thorny branches from a neighboring mimosa, which I heaped over the carcass, to protect it from the vultures. This being accomplished, I returned to camp, carrying the head on the pommel of the saddle before me, and my rifle over my shoulder. On occasions like this, I have often felt that I should have been the better for a third hand for the management of my steed. At an early hour on the following morning I left my wagons, accompanied by two after riders, to look for koodoos, and secure the skin of the oryx of the preceding day. Contrary to my expectations, the hyenas had not discovered him. The flesh, however, owing to the heat of the weather, was unserviceable. I rode with my boys deployed into line along the likely part of the old mimosa forest, hoping to fall in with koodoos. Here I shot two fine old steinboks, with very good horns, and these I carefully preserved for my collection. By firing I lost a chance of koodoos, as I presently discovered fresh spoor of a troop of these antelopes, which my shots had disturbed.

On the 23rd I stood up in my hole at dawn of day, and, having donned my old gray kilt and Badenoch brogues, took up the spoor of the herd of brindled gnoos. After I had proceeded a short distance I perceived the head of the old bull looking at me over a small rise on the bushy plain. The head disappeared, and I heard a loud noise of tramping, as of an animal endeavoring to gallop upon three legs. On gaining this rise I again saw the handsome head, with its strangely hooked, fair-set horns, gazing at me from the long grass some hundred yards in advance. He had lain down. I held as though I intended to go past him; but before I neared him he sprang to his feet, and endeavored to make off from me. Poor old bull! I at once perceived that it was all over with him. He was very faint from loss of blood, and one fore leg was broken in the shoulder. He made a tottering run of about a hundred yards, and again lay down, never more to rise. I walked up to within eighty yards of him, and sent a bullet through his heart. Receiving the ball, he rolled over on his side, and expired without a groan. I then made for my wagons, and dispatched men with a span or team of oxen to slip the wildebeest to camp. He afforded us a welcome supply of excellent flesh, as he was in fine condition. I breakfasted on an ostrich egg, Kleinboy having found a nest the preceding day. He had, unfortunately, taken only eight of the eggs out of the nest, foolishly leaving the other twelve, which on his return he found smashed by the old birds, according to their usual custom.

CHAPTER VIII

On the evening of the 24th we inspanned, and, leaving "Stink Wonteyn," marched upon the Vaal River, distant about twenty-five miles. Our road lay through soft sand, rendering the work very severe for the oxen. About 2 A.M. on the following morning we reached the fair Vaal River by fine moonlight. Having sent mounted men through the stream to ascertain its depth, and finding a passage practicable, I resolved at once to cross it—a rule generally adopted by all experienced in the country, among whom a general maxim prevails never to defer the passage of a river if at all fordable when they reach it. Endless are the stories related by South African travelers, who, by failing to adopt this plan, have been compelled to remain for weeks, and even months, on the banks of its various rivers. The current here being very powerful, I mounted the leaders of my teams, and in a few minutes my long double line of oxen was stoutly stemming the rapid stream, which reached half way up their sides. We got both the wagons across in safety. The water had just reached the bottom of my cargoes, but did not damage anything. The bank on the further side was extremely steep and stony, and required every ox to exert himself to the utmost. The river here is very beautiful; broad and rapid streams are succeeded by long, deep, and tranquil pools, termed by the natives "zekoe ychots," signifying sea-cow or hippopotamus' holes, these vast and wondrous amphibious animals having, not many years since, been plentiful along the entire length of the Vaal River. The hippopotamus, however, like the elephant, is of a very shy and secluded disposition, and rapidly disappears before the approach of civilization.

I drew up my wagons on a commanding open position on the northern bank of the stream. The margin of the Vaal, like the Orange River, is richly clad with dense groves of various evergreen trees, among which drooping willows predominate, whose long waving fringes dip gracefully into the limpid waters as they glide along in their seaward course. All along the banks of both these rivers huge trunks of trees are strewn, having been borne thither by the mighty floods to which they are annually subject. A short distance above my position was a beautiful island, adorned with trees of the richest verdure.

About 3 P.M. I rode northeast to look for roan antelopes, which, next to the eland, are the largest in the world, and, being incapable of great speed, may at times be ridden into with a good horse. I was accompanied by Cobus and Jacob. We found the country covered with bushes, of which the majority were of a most impracticable description, reminding me of a kill devil, an implement used in angling, they being covered with thorns on the fish-hook principle. This variety of mimosa is waggishly termed by the Boers "yacht um bige," or wait-a-bit thorns, as they continually solicit the passing traveler not to be in a hurry; if he disregards which request, the probability is that he leaves a part of his shirt or trowsers in their possession. Here and there were hills covered with sharp adamantine rocks, throughout which, however, there was abundance of excellent grass and fine green bushes. In short, it was just the country to suit the taste of the rock-loving koodoos. Having proceeded some miles, we discovered fresh spoor of a troop of them at the foot of one of the ranges of rocky hills. We then crossed the ridge, still finding spoor, and the country becoming more and more likely.

Suddenly, on raising our eyes, we saw standing on the hill-side, within three hundred yards of us, five buck koodoos, four of which were tearing old fellows carrying extremely fine horns; and majestic as they were, the elevated position which they occupied imparted to them a still more striking appearance. We galloped toward them, on which they bounded higher up the rocky hill, and stood for a few seconds looking at us.

On the 26th we arose at earliest dawn, and having packed the trophies of the koodoo and a part of his flesh upon my spare horse, I dispatched Jacob with him to camp, while Cobus and I held northeast to seek for roan antelope. I sought that day and the two following for these antelopes, but saw no traces of them.

On the morning of the 30th I inspanned, and trekked some miles further up the northern bank of the Vaal, and encamped opposite where the Rict or Reed River joins it. The stream here is extremely beautiful, being about a hundred and fifty yards in breadth, with sloping banks richly adorned with shady evergreen groves, and fringed with lofty reeds—a never-failing prognosticator of a sleepless night, a virulent species of mosquito being always abundant where reeds are met with. Several large bustards were stalking on a small bushy flat as we drew up the wagons. I went after these, and made a fine off-hand shot at an old cock at a hundred and fifty yards. Here I lost Cobus and Jacob, my two Hottentot after-riders. Returning from the bustards to my wagons, where I expected to find my breakfast waiting me, I discovered these two worthies, whose duty it was to be preparing it, quietly reclining under the shade of a mimosa, and enjoying the soothing influence of their short clay pipes. Being now beyond the pale of magisterial law, I deemed that a little wholesome correction might prove beneficial, which I accordingly administered. This so disgusted these high-minded youths, that after breakfast they embraced the opportunity of my bathing to abscond from my service. I imagined that they had sneaked into the bushes, and would soon return. I, however, saw no more of them until several months after, when I met them at Colesberg, which place they had reached, assisted by the Bastards, through whose country they had passed. Cobus, though a first-rate after rider, was a great scamp and mischief-maker; and I learned from my remaining people that it was by his persuasion Jacob had left me.

In the forenoon, the sun being extremely powerful, I built for myself a bower under an old willow beside the river. In this bower I made my bed, and might have had a sound sleep by way of a change, had not the mosquitoes and midges assaulted me throughout the whole night, so that I hardly closed my eyes. The 31st was a charming cool day, the sky beautifully overcast. Having enjoyed a good swim in the waters of the Vaal, I breakfasted, after which I saddled up, and rode north to seek for roan antelope. I was accompanied by Carollus, the native of Mozambique, who was much too heavy to act as after-rider, and by the little Bushboy named Ruyter, who had joined me on the plains of the karroo. This Bushboy, although he had learned to ride among the Boers, had an indifferent seat on horseback, and would never push his horse to overtake any antelope if the ground were at all rough.

Having explored the country to a considerable distance, in the course of which we fell in with four sassabies and a troop of hartebeests, I resolved to make for home, as the darkening sky and distant thunder to the southward threatened a heavy storm. I had not long, however, determined on returning, when the wind, which had been out of the north, suddenly veered round, and blew hard from the south. In less than half an hour the rain descended in torrents, the wind blew extremely cold, and the rain beat right in my face; the peals of thunder were most appalling, the most fearful, I think, I had ever heard, the forked lightning dancing' above and around me with such vividness as to pain my eyes I thought every moment would be my last. I shifted my saddle from "Sunday" to "The Cow," and we pricked along at a smart pace. We were entering a thicket of thorny bushes, when a very large gray-looking antelope stood up under one of them. I could not see his head, but I at once knew that it was the long-sought-for roan antelope, or bastard gemsbok. Carollus quickly handed me my little Moore rifle, secure from the pelting storm in one of Mr. Hugh Snowie's patent water-proof covers.

I felt extremely cold. I had lost my shirt in the chase, and all that was left me was my shoes and leather knee breeches. I nevertheless took some time to inspect the beautiful and rare antelope which I had been fortunate enough to capture. He proved to be a first-rate specimen his horns were extremely rough and finely knotted. I now proceeded to cut off his head and "gral loched" him, all of which I accomplished before my followers came up. They stumbled on me by chance having lost sight of me in the denseness of the storm, Having shifted my saddle from "The Cow" to "Colesberg," I ordered them to follow, and I rode hard for camp, which was distant many miles. At sunset the storm ceased, and my boys arrived with the head. The following day was the 1st of February. In the morning I dispatched two men to bring home the skin of the roan antelope and a supply of the venison, which was in high condition. Strange to say, they found the buck all safe, having escaped the attacks both of hyenas and vultures.

My meal-bag was reported almost empty; and this being a dangerous country for the horse-sickness, a distemper which rages during February, March, and April, I resolved to re-cross the Vaal River, and bend my course for the land of blesboks, a large and beautiful violet-colored antelope, which is found, together with black wildebeests and springboks, in countless thousands on the vast green plains of short sour grass situated about a hundred and fifty miles to the eastward of my then position. My purpose was to amuse myself hunting in these parts until the beginning of April, when the most dangerous period of the horse-sickness would be past, and after that to revisit Colesberg, where I intended to store the specimens of natural history which I had already accumulated, and, having refitted and laid in a store of supplies, to start for the remote districts of the far interior in quest of elephant, rhinoceros, giraffe, buffalo, eland, and other varieties of large and interesting game to be found in those secluded regions.

On the afternoon of the 3rd of February we inspanned, and retraced our steps to the drift, which we reached in the dark I, however, crossed the river, and encamped on the opposite bank. On the following day marched to a small kraal of Griquas, in hope of obtaining some corn. Our march was a heavy one, through a sandy country adorned in parts with very ancient-looking picturesque trees of the "camel-dorn" species. From the site of these kraals I obtained a distant view of both the Vaal and Orange River. I found these Griquas very importunate, flocking round my wagons and begging for tea, coffee, tobacco, gunpowder, &c. Some if these ruffians formed a plot to make me give up the Bushboy who had entered my service, but, on my threatening them with the vengeance of government if they interfered with any men in my service, they relinquished the idea. On the morrow it was ascertained that the oxen, having missed the fountain, had wandered very far in search of water they were recovered more than half way back to the Vaal River. I purchased eight "emirs" or measures of wheat from one of the Griquas, and also a couple of goats for slaughter. In the afternoon we inspanned, and trekked to "Stink Vonteyn," already mentioned.

In the forenoon I observed the base of an extensive range of hills to the northward, concealed for miles, as if by thick clouds or mist, which steadily advanced toward us, holding a southerly course. This was a flight of countless myriads of locusts, in my opinion one of the most remarkable phenomena that a traveler can behold. They resembled very much a fall of snow, when it gently descends in large light flakes. The sound caused by their wings reminded me of the rustling of the summer breeze among the trees of the forest. In the afternoon I hunted in a mountain range to the westward of the salt-pan, named by the Boers and Bastards "Saut-pan's berg;" and in the evening I visited the old Bushman's hut, whom I found at home with a litter of very small Bush-children: these he signified to me were his grandchildren. I lay down to sleep beneath an aged mimosa in their vicinity, and about midnight the wind set in from off the Southern Ocean, and, having no covering but my shirt, I felt it piercingly cold, Sleep was out of the question, and I was right glad when I heard the sparrow's chirp announcing the dawn of day.

On reaching my wagons I breakfasted, after which wo inspanned and trekked east along a very rarely trodden old wagon-track, making for a small mountain situated on the borders of a large pan, which lay in a broad hollow in the center of an extensive open tract of undulating country. Here the entire country was of a soft, sandy character, and utterly uninhabited; the plains were covered with long, rough heath and other low scrubby bushes, intermingled with much sweet grass. Ranges of hills of goodly height and considerable extent intersected the plains, and bounded the view at various distances on every side. Ancient forests of picturesque and venerable mimosas, interspersed with high, gray-leaved bushes, detached and in groups, stretched along the bases of these mountain-ranges, their breadth extending about a mile into the surrounding extensive campaign country. We reached the small fountain in the dark, our road leading through the saltpan, where we halted for an hour for the purpose of collecting salt. We had little difficulty in filling two large sacks with it.

The next day, as we crossed a vast plain, a flight of locusts passed over our heads during upward of half an hour, flying so thick as to darken the sun; they reached in dense clouds as far as we could see, and maintained an elevation of from six to three or four hundred feet above the level of the plain. Woe to the vegetation of the country on which they alight! In the afternoon two mounted Boers were observed leading a spare horse and following on our track. While they were yet afar off, Ruyter, the little Bushboy, recognized them as old acquaintances, and pronounced one of them to be the brother of the master from whom he had absconded. I at once guessed the object of their visit, and was right in my conjecture. By some clew they had ascertained that the boy was in my possession, and were now following me in the hope of recovering him. Accordingly, when they rode up and requested me to halt the wagons for a conference, I received them very gruffly, and replied that, the water being distant, I had no time for conferences until I should arrive there. Having repeated their request, and finding that I paid them no regard, they took up a position in the rear, and followed my wagons to the halting-place.

On the morning of the 12th I rode northeast with attendants, and after proceeding several miles through an open country we entered a beautiful forest of camcel dorn trees, and rode along beneath a range of steep rocky hills. The country gave me the idea of extreme antiquity, where the hand of man had wrought no change since the Creation. In a finely-wooded broad valley or opening among the hills, we fell in with a magnificent herd of about sixty blue wildebeests. As they cantered across the grassy sward, tossing their fierce-looking, ponderous heads, their shaggy manes and long, black, bushy tails streaming in the breeze, they presented an appearance at once striking and imposing; and to a stranger they conveyed rather the idea of buffaloes than anything belonging to the antelope tribe, to which, indeed, wildebeests, both black and white, are but remotely allied, notwithstanding the classification of naturalists.

About midnight on the 16th, weary with tossing on my restless couch, I arose, and taking my two-grooved rifle, a pillow, and a blanket, I held for my shooting hole beside the fountain. The remainder of the night was very cool, with a southerly breeze. At dawn I looked from my hole, and, seeing no game approaching, I rolled my blanket tight around me and tried to sleep. In this manner I had lain for about half an hour, when I was suddenly startled by a large, heavy animal galloping past within six feet of me. I at once knew that it must be either some beast which had been coming to drink and had got my wind, or one hunted, which, according to the custom of deer and the larger antelopes, had rushed for refuge to the water in its distress. In the latter conjecture I was right; for, on cautiously peeping through the stones which surrounded my hole, I had the pleasure to behold a fine bull brindled gnoo dash into the waters of the fountain within forty yards of me, and stand at bay, followed by four tearing, fierce looking wild dogs.

I could not help feeling very reluctant to fire at the jolly hounds. The whole affair reminded me so very forcibly of many gallant courses I had enjoyed in the Scottish deer-forests with my own noble deer-hounds, that I could not divest myself of the idea that those now before me deserved a better recompense for the masterly manner in which they were pursuing their desperate game. One hound, in particular, bore a strong expression of dear old Factor in his face, a trusty stag-hound bred by myself, whose deeds, though not renowned in verse like Ossian's Oscar and Luath, were perhaps little inferior either in speed or prowess to those lamed in ancient song.

Having summoned my men, and with considerable difficulty dragged the ponderous carcass of the old bull out of the water, we found that he had been cruelly lacerated by the hounds. It appeared to me that they had endeavored to hamstring him. His hind legs, haunches, and belly were dreadfully torn; he had lost half his tail, and was otherwise mutilated. Poor old bull! I could not help commiserating his fate. It is melancholy to reflect that, in accordance with the laws of nature, such scenes of pain must ever be occurring; one species, whether inhabiting earth, air, or ocean, being produced to become the prey of another. At night I watched the water, with fairish moonlight, and shot a large spotted hyena.

I continued here hunting hartebeests until the 21st, when I inspanned at an early hour, and trekked due east till sundown, when I halted near a small fountain of fine water, having performed a march of about twenty five miles. Our road lay through a wild, uninhabited country, producing sweet grass in abundance, but destitute of water. On the morning of the 22nd, having breakfasted, I rode southwest, with after-riders, and found the game abundant, but wild and shy, having been recently hunted by Boers.

CHAPTER IX

We inspanned before the dawn of day on the 23rd of February, and after steering east and by north for a distance of about twelve miles, we found ourselves on the southern bank of the Riet River, where we outspanned. Along the banks, both above and below me, several families of the nomad Boers were encamped with their tents and wagons. Their overgrown flocks and herds were grazing on the plains and grassy hill sides around. Five of these Boers presently came up to my wagons, and drank coffee with me. They seemed much amused with the details of my sporting adventures, which I was now able to give them in broken Dutch, in which language, from lately hearing no other spoken, I was daily becoming more proficient. On learning that I had not as yet enjoyed any blesbok shooting, they said they were certain I should be delighted with the sport. The borders of the country inhabited by the blesboks they stated to be about four days distant in a northeasterly direction, and that, on reaching it, I should fall in with those antelopes in countless herds, along with black wildebeest, springbok, and ether game. The Boers supplied me liberally with milk. In the height of the day we all bathed in the Riet River, and in the afternoon I continued my journey eastward. The breadth of the Riet River "Sere is about thirty yards. It rises about one hundred miles to the eastward, and, flowing westerly, joins the Vaal River opposite Campbellsdorp.

On the third day after making the Riet River we crossed below a very picturesque waterfall, and resumed our march along its northern bank. The day was cool and pleasant, the sky overcast; the hot days of summer were now past, and the weather was most enjoyable. Continuing my march in the afternoon, I left the Riet River on my right, and held on through an open, sandy country richly covered with abundance of sweet grass, and intersected by mountain ranges of very considerable extent. At sunset I encamped beside a Boer's farm, who received me hospitably, and asked me to dine with him. During dinner, according to the custom of the Boers, he pestered me with a thousand questions, such as. What was my nation? Where was I from? Where was I bound for? Why I traveled about alone in such a manner? Where was my farm? Were my father and mother living? How many brothers and sisters I had? Was I married? And had I never been married in the whole course of my life? On my replying in the negative to this last question, the Boer seemed petrified with astonishment, and the family gazed at one another in utter amazement. On the farm was a fine specimen of the African wild boar, which was perfectly tame, and took vegetables from the hands of the children.

Notwithstanding this cold reception, on returning to the house I soon managed to get into their good graces, and took dinner with them. During dinner the conversation turned on politics, when a keen discussion arose concerning the present administration of the government. This being at all times a disagreeable subject, I thought it time to change the conversation to sporting subjects, in which the Boers always take intense interest. I accordingly mentioned to one of the young ladies who sat next to me that I had in my wagon a large work containing engravings of all the most interesting animals in the world, on which she instantly expressed a strong desire to see it. I then produced my "Museum of Animated Nature," which never failed to enchant the Boers, and it put an end to all political discussions, shooting and wild animals engrossing the conversation during the rest of the evening. These Boers informed me that I should see herds of blesboks on the following day. They also stated that lions frequented the bushy mountain ranges which look down upon the plains frequented by the blesboks, and they mentioned that a considerable party of Boers had mustered that day upon a farm a few miles in advance, to hunt a troop of lions which had killed some horses on the preceding day.

At an early hour on the following morning a young Boer rode up to the farm, and informed us that the party who had been lion-hunting on the preceding day had bagged two fuse lions, a male and female. As the farm lay directly in my line of march, I mounted Colesberg, and, directing my followers to follow with the wagons, I rode hard for the farm, to inspect the noble game. On my way thither I met a horse-wagon, drawn by eight horses, containing some of the party who had mustered for the battue. Arriving on the farm, I found the Hon and lioness laid out on the grass in front of the house, and the Boers' Hottentots busy skinning them. Both lions were riddled with balls, and their heads were shot all to pieces. This is generally the way in which the Boers serve their lions after they have killed them, fearing to approach, though dead, until they have expended a further supply of ammunition. A Hottentot is then ordered to approach and throw a stone at him; the Boers then ask if he is dead, and on the Hottentot replying, "Like so, baas," he is ordered to pull him by the tail before the hunters will venture to approach My little Bushman informed me that he had often been out lion-hunting during his captivity with the Boers. On one of these occasions, a Boer, who had dismounted from, his horse to fire, was dashed to the ground by the lion before he could regain his saddle.

The Boer on whose farm I had arrived was a tall, powerful, manly-looking fellow. He informed me that he was a Dane. He was in great distress about two favorite dogs which the lions had killed during the attack on the preceding day. Three more were badly wounded, and their recovery seemed doubtful. He confirmed the reports of an impending war between the Boers and Griquas, which I had previously heard, and he asked me if I was not afraid, in times of war, to remain hunting, with only a few followers, in the wilderness. Being anxious to commence my operations against the blesboks, I resumed my march shortly after mid-day. On taking leave, the Dane presented me with some meal and a couple of loaves of bread, a luxury to which I had been an utter stranger for many months, and which, together with vegetables, I may further add, I hardly ever tasted during the five hunting expeditions which I performed in Southern Africa. Another short march in a northeasterly direction brought me to the western borders of the boundless regions inhabited by the blesboks. I drew up my wagons beside a vley of rain water, in open country, the plains before me being adorned with herds of black wildebeest, springbok, and blesbok.

The blesbok, in his manners and habits, very much resembles the springbok, which, however, it greatly exceeds in size, being as large as an English fallow-deer. It is one of the true antelopes, and all its movements and paces partake of the grace and elegance peculiar to that species. Its color is similar to that of the sassayby, its skin being beautifully painted with every shade of purple, violet, and brown. Its belly is of the purest white, and a broad white band, or "blaze," adorns the entire length of its face. Blesboks differ from springboks in the determined and invariable manner in which they scour the plains, right in the wind's eye, and also in the manner in which they carry their noses close along the ground. Throughout the greater part of the year they are very wary and difficult of approach, but more especially when the does have young ones. At that season, when one herd is disturbed, and takes away up the wind, every other herd in view follows them; and the alarm extending for miles and miles down the wind, to endless herds beyond the vision of the hunter, a continued stream of blesboks may often be seen scouring up wind for upward of an hour, and covering the landscape as far as the eye can see. The springboks, which in equal numbers frequent the same ground, do not, in general, adopt the same decided course as the blesboks, but take away in every direction across the plains, sometimes with flying bounds, beautifully exhibiting the long, snowy-white hair with which their backs are adorned, and at others walking slowly and carelessly out of the hunter's way, scarcely deigning to look at him, with an air of perfect independence, as if aware of their own matchless speed.

The black wildebeests, which also thickly cover the entire length and breadth of the blesbok country, in herds averaging from twenty to fifty, have no regular course, like the blesboks. Unless driven by a large field of hunters, they do not leave their ground, although disturbed. Wheeling about in endless circles, and performing the most extraordinary variety of intricate evolutions, the shaggy herds of these eccentric and fierce looking animals are forever capering and gamboling round the hunter on every side. While he is riding hard to obtain a family shot of a herd in front of him, other herds are charging downwind on his right and left, and, having described a number of circular movements, they take up positions upon the very ground across which the hunter rode only a few minutes before.

Singly, and in small troops of four or five individuals, the old bull wildebeests may be seen stationed at intervals throughout the plains, standing motionless during a whole forenoon, coolly watching with a philosophic eye the movements of the other game, eternally uttering a loud snorting noise, and also a short, sharp cry which is peculiar to them. When the hunter approaches these old bulls, they commence whisking their long white tails in a most eccentric manner; then springing suddenly into the air, they begin prancing and capering, and pursue each other in circles at their utmost speed. Suddenly they all pull up together to overhaul the intruder, when two of the bulls will often commence fighting in the most violent manner, dropping on their knees at every shock ; then quickly wheeling about, they kick up their heels, whirl their tails with a fantastic flourish, and scour across the plain enveloped in a cloud of dust.

Throughout the greater part of the plains frequented by blesboks, numbers of the sun-baked hills or mounds of clay formed by the white ants occur. The average height of the ant-hills, in these districts, is from two to three feet. They are generally distant from one another from one to three hundred yards, being more or less thickly placed in different parts. These ant hills are of the greatest service to the hunter, enabling him with facility to conceal himself on the otherwise open plain. By means of them I was enabled to hide, and select out of the herds the bucks and bulls carrying the finest heads, for my collection.

On the 28th, having breakfasted, I rode forth with two after-riders to try for blesboks, and took up positions on the plain, lying flat on my breast behind anthills, while my after-riders, one of whom led my horse, endeavored to move them toward me. We found the blesboks abundant, but extremely wary. I wounded several, but did not bag one. I, however, shot two springboks, which were fat, and whose flesh we stood much in need of. I had several chances of wildebeests, but I had resolved not to fire at them.

The following day was the 1st of March. After an early breakfast I again took the field, with my after riders and a spare horse. There was thunder and lightning on all sides, and I expected the day would set in wet: it all passed over, however, with a few showers, and the weather was delightfully cool. I lay behind ant-hills, while my men, extending to the right and left, endeavored to drive the game toward me. Late in the day I bagged a fine old blesbolc : it was a family shot, running at two hundred yards. I also shot a springbok, and mortally wounded another; both were very long shots.

The blesbok is one of the finest antelopes in the world, and is allowed to be the swiftest buck in Africa. He, nevertheless, attains very high condition, and at this period was exceedingly fat. I was surprised and delighted, with the exquisite manner in which his beautiful colors are blended together. Nothing can exceed the beauty of this animal. Like most other African antelopes, his skin emitted a most delicious and powerful perfume of flowers and sweet-smelling herbs. A secretion issues from between his hoofs which has likewise a pleasing perfume.

On the following day I hunted to the northeast of my camp, and made a fine shot at a blesbok, knocking him over at a hundred and fifty yards. Returning to camp in a low-lying grassy vley, I started a herd of "vlacke vareke," or wild hogs. The herd consisted of seven half-grown young ones and three old ones, one of which carried a pair of enormous tusks, projecting eight or nine inches beyond his lip. Being well mounted and the ground favorable, I at once gave chase, and was soon at their heels. My horse was "The Gray." I selected the old boar for my prey, and immediately separated him from his comrades. After two miles of sharp galloping, we commenced ascending a considerable acclivity, when I managed to close with him, and succeeded in turning his head toward my camp. He now reduced his pace to a trot, and regarded me with a most malicious eye, his mouth a mass of foam. He was entirely in my power, as I had only to spring from my horse and bowl him over. I felt certain of him, but resolved not to shoot as long as his course lay in the direction of the wagons. At length, surprised at the resolute manner in which he held for my camp, I headed him; when, to my astonishment, he did not in the slightest swerve from his course, but trotted along behind my horse like a dog following me. This at once roused my suspicions, and I felt certain that the cunning old fellow was making for some retreat, so I resolved to dismount and finish him. Just, however, as I had come to this resolution, I suddenly found myself in a labyrinth of enormous holes, the burrows of the ant-bear. In front of one of these the wild boar pulled up, and, charging stern foremost into it, disappeared from my disappointed eyes, and I saw him no more. I rode home for my men; and returning, we collected grass and bushes, and endeavored to smoke him out, but without success.

On the 7th we inspanned at dawn of day, and trekked east about ten miles, encamping beside a small, isolated farm-house, which had been lately vacated by some Boer, owing to the impending war with the Griquas. Here we found plenty of old cow-dung for fuel; an article which, throughout the whole of the blesbok country, is very scarce, there often being great difficulty in obtaining sufficient fuel to boil the kettle for coffee. Beside the farm-house were two strong springs of excellent water, in which cresses flourished. Game was abundant on all sides, wildebeests and springboks pasturing within a few hundred yards of the door as we drove up. Below the fountains was a small garden, in which I found a welcome supply of onions and other vegetables.

On the 12th I bagged two bull wildebeests and two springboks to the northward of my camp. In the evening I took my pillow and "komberse," or skin blanket, to the margin of a neighboring vley, where I had observed doe blesboks drink. Of these I had not yet secured a single specimen, which I was very anxious to do, as they likewise carry fine horns, which, though not so thick as those of the males, are more gracefully formed. Shortly after I had lain down, two porcupines came grunting up to me, and stood within six feet of where I lay. About midnight an old wildebeest came and stood within ten yards of me, but I was too lazy to fire at him. All night I heard some creature moving in the cracked earth beneath my pillow; but, believing it to be a mouse, I did not feel much concerned about the matter. I could not, however, divest myself of a painful feeling that it might be a snake, and wrapped my blanket tight round my body. Awaking at an early hour the following morning, I forgot to look for the tenant who had spent the night beneath my pillow. No blesbok appearing, I stalked an old springbok through the rushes and shot him. Having concealed him, I held for camp, and dispatched two men to bring home the venison and my bedding.

On the 15th I had a very good day's sport. As the day dawned I peeped from my hole, and saw troops of blesboks feeding on every side of me, but none came within range. I shot one springbok, and, having concealed him in the rushes, walked to camp. After breakfast I took the field with Kleinboy and the Bushman, and rode north to try for blesboks. While lying behind an ant-hill on the bare plain, a herd of about thirty wildebeests came thundering down upon me, and the leading bull nearly jumped over me. Into one of these I fired; he got the ball too far back, however, and made off, but was found by one of my men the following day. Presently Kleinboy rode up, and stated that while he was driving the blesboks he had observed an old stag hartebeest standing in the shade of some tall green bushes in the adjacent range of hills. I resolved to stalk him in the most approved Highland fashion; so, having made an accurate survey of the ground with my spy-glass, I rode within a quarter of a mile of him, and then proceeded to creep in upon him on my hands and knees. In this manner I got within sixty yards of him, where I lay flat on-my breast for several minutes until lie should give me his broadside. Presently he walked forth from the cover of the bush beneath which he had been standing, when I sent a ball in at his right shoulder, which rested on the skin in his left haunch. Wheeling about, he bounded over an adjacent ridge and was out of sight in a moment. On gaining this ridge, I was just in time to see the noble hartebeest stagger for a moment, and then subside into the long grass in a hollow below me. He was a princely old stag, carrying splendid horns and a beautiful coat of new hair.

I had not slept long when my light dreams were influenced by strange sounds. I dreamed that lions were rushing about in quest of me, and, the sounds increasing, I awoke with a sudden start, uttering a loud shriek. I could not for several seconds remember in what part of the world I was, or anything connected with my present position. I heard the rushing of light feet as of a pack of wolves close on every side of me, accompanied by the most unearthly sounds. On raising my head, to my utter horror I saw on every side nothing but savage wild dogs, chattering and growling. On my right and on my left, and within a few paces of me, stood two lines of these ferocious-looking animals, cocking their ears and stretching their necks to have a look at me; while two large troops, in which there were at least forty of them, kept dashing backward and forward across my wand within a few yards of me, chattering and growling with the most extraordinary volubility. Another troop of wild dogs were fighting over the wildebeest I had shot, which they had begun to devour. On beholding them, I expected no other fate than to be instantly torn to pieces and consumed. I felt my blood curdling along my cheeks and my hair bristling on my head. However, I had presence of mind to consider that the human voice and a determined bearing might overawe them, and accordingly, springing to ray feet, I stepped on to the little ledge surrounding the hole, where, drawing myself up to my full height, I waved my large blanket with both hands, at the same time addressing my savage assembly in a loud and solemn manner. This had the desired effect the wild dogs removed to a more respectful distance, barking at me something like collies. Upon this I snatched up my rifle and commenced loading, and before this was accomplished the entire pack had passed away and did not return.

These had not been gone many minutes when twelve or fifteen large hyenas were hard at work on the wildebeest. I fired two shots at them at different times during the night, but none fell to my shots. Heedless of me, they continued their banquet, and long before morning nothing was left of the wildebeest save a few of the larger bones. On the two following mornings I was annoyed by a cunning old bull wildebeest, which, having discovered my retreat, kept sentry over me, and successively drove away every troop of his fellows that approached my vley to drink. He kept feeding just out of rifle-range, and not only warned his comrades of their danger by fixing his eye on my place of concealment and snorting loudly, but when this failed he drove the other wildebeests from me in the most determined manner, like a collie dog driving sheep. Before leaving my hole, however, on the second morning, had my revenge. A troop of cows, heedless of his warnings, approached the vley.

The male lion is adorned with a long, rank, shaggy mane, which in some instances almost sweeps the ground. The color of these manes varies, some being very dark, and others of a golden yellow. This appearance has given rise to a prevailing opinion among the Boers that there are two distinct varieties of lions, which they distinguish by the respective names of "Schwart fore life" and "Chiel fore life:" this idea, however, is erroneous. The color of the lion's mane is generally influenced by his age. He attains his mane and the third year of his existence. I have remarked that at first it is of a yellowish color; in the prime of life it is blackest, and when he has numbered many years, but still is in the full enjoyment of his power, it assumes a yellowish-gray, pepper-and-salt sort of color. These old fellows are cunning and dangerous, and most to be dreaded. The females are utterly destitute of a mane, being covered with a short, thick, glossy coat of tawny hair. The manes and coats, of lions frequenting open-lying districts utterly destitute of trees, such as the borders of the great Kalahari desert, are more rank and handsome than those inhabiting forest districts.

One of the most striking things connected with the lion is his voice, which is extremely grand and peculiarly striking. It consists at times of a low, deep moaning, repeated five or six times, ending in faintly audible sighs; at other times he startles the forest with loud, deep-toned, solemn roars, repeated five or six times in quick succession, each increasing in loudness to the third or fourth, when his voice dies away in five or six low, muffled sounds, very much resembling distant thunder. At times, and not unfrequently, a troop may be heard roaring in concert, one assuming the lead, and two, three, or four more regularly taking up their parts, like persons singing a catch. Like our Scottish stags at the rutting season, they roar loudest in cold, frosty nights; but on no occasions are their voices to be heard in such perfection, or so intensely powerful, as when two or three strange troops of lions approach a fountain to drink at the same time. When this occurs, every member of each troop sounds a bold roar of defiance at the opposite parties; and when one roars, all roar together, and each seems to vie with his comrades in the intensity and power of his voice. The power and grandeur of these nocturnal forest concerts is inconceivably striking and pleasing to the hunter's ear.

Among Indian Ninirods, a certain class of royal tigers is dignified with the appellation of "man-eaters." These are tigers which, having once tasted human flesh, show a .predilection for the same, and such characters are very naturally famed and dreaded among the natives. Elderly gentlemen of similar tastes and habits are occasionally met with among the lions in the interior of South Africa, and the danger of such neighbors may be easily imagined. I account for lions first acquiring this taste in the following manner: the Bechuana tribes of the far interior do not bury their dead, but unceremoniously carry them forth, and leave them lying exposed in the forest or on the plain, a prey to the lion and hya3na, or the jackal and vulture; and I can readily imagine that a lion, having thus once tasted human flesh would have little hesitation, when opportunity presented itself, of springing upon and carrying off the unwary traveler or "Bechuana" inhabiting his country. Be this as it may, man-eaters occur; and on my fourth hunting expedition, a horrible tragedy was acted one dark night in my little lonely camp by one of these formidable characters, which deprived me, in the far wilderness, of my most valuable servant. In winding up these few observations on the lion, which I trust will not have been tiresome to the reader, I may remark that lion-hunting, under any circumstances, ia decidedly a dangerous pursuit. It may nevertheless be followed, to a certain extent, with comparative safety by those who have naturally a turn for that sort of thing. A recklessness of death, p3rfect coolness and self-possession, an acquaintance with the disposition and manners of lions, and a tolerable knowledge of the use of the rifle, are indispensable to him who would shine in the overpoweringly exciting pastime of hunting this justly celebrated king of beasts.

CHAPTER X

On the 22nd of March I rode south to a distant farm, for the double purpose of obtaining some corn or meal, and of hearing the news of the impending war between the Boers and Griquas. On reaching the farm, I found that a large party of Boers were here encamped together they had mustered for mutual protection. Their tents and wagons were drawn up on every side of the farm-house, forming a very lively appearance. The Boers informed me that all their countrymen, and also the Griquas, were thus packed together in "lagers" or encampments, and that hostilities were about to commence. They remonstrated with no on v/hat they were pleased to term my madness, in living alone in an isolated position in such sharp times, and invited me to place myself for protection under their banner. I endeavored to persuade them to get up a party to hunt the lion; but this they declined to do, remarking that "a lion (like Johnnie Gordon's bagpipes) was not to be played with." Returning to my camp, I bowled over a springbok at one hundred and fifty yards. On the 23rd, having breakfasted, I rode north, with after riders, to try for blesboks. It was a cool day, with a strong easterly breeze, and we found the game extremely wild. As we proceeded, vast herds kept streaming up on the wind, darkening the plain before us in countless thousands. About two miles north of the bushy mountain where I had heard the lion roar, far in the vast level plain, were some bushy mimosa trees. Within a few hundred yards of these we discovered an old bull wildebeest, newly killed by a lion and half eaten. His large and striking foot-prints were deeply imbedded in the sand, and so fresh that they seemed to have been imprinted only a few minutes before. Moreover, there was not a single vulture near the carcass. We therefore felt convinced that the lion must be lying somewhere near us, having hidden himself on our approach. We searched for some time in the adjacent hollows, where the grass was very rank, but in vain. We had not lain down an hour when the sky to leeward became black as pitch. Presently the most vivid flashes of lightning followed one another in quick succession, accompanied by terrific peals of thunder. The wind, which, during the day, had been out of the northeast, now, as is usual on such occasions, veered right round, and came whistling up from the southwest, where the tempest was brewing; and in a few minutes more it was upon us in all its fury, the rain descending in torrents on our devoted heads, while vivid flashes of lightning momentarily illumined, with the brilliancy of day, the darkness that reigned around. In a very few minutes the whole plain was a sheet of water, and every atom of my clothes and bedding was thoroughly saturated. My three rifles had excellent holsters, and with the help of two sheep skins, which I used instead of saddle-cloths, I kept their quite dry. In two hours the tempest had passed away, but light rain fell till morning, until which time I lay on the wet ground, soaked to the skin. About midnight we heard the lion roar a mile or so to the northward, and a little before the day dawned I again heard him in the direction of the carcass which we had found on the preceding day. Soon after this I gave the word to march. We then a rose and saddled our horses. I found my trowsers lying in a pool of water, so I converted a blanket into a long kilt by strapping it round my waist with my shooting-belt. The costume of my followers was equally unique. We held for the north end of the lion's mountain at a sharp pace, which we gained before it was clear enough to see surrounding objects. As the light broke in upon us we reduced our pace, and rode slowly up the middle of the vast level plain toward the carcass of the wildebeest, with large herds of wildebeests, springbok, blesbok, and quaggas on every ride of us, which were this day as tame as they had been wild on the previous one. This is generally the case after a storm.

Now, then, for it, neck or nothing I She is within sixty yards of us, and she keeps advancing. We turned the horses' tails to her. I knelt on one side, and, taking a steady aim at her breast, let fly. The ball cracked loudly on her tawny hide, and crippled her in the shoulder, upon which she charged with an appalling roar, and in the twinkling of an eye she was in the midst of us. At this moment Stofolus's rifle exploded in his hand, and Kleinboy, whom I had ordered to stand ready by me, danced about like a duck in a gale of wind. The lioness sprang upon Colesberg, and fearfully lacerated his ribs and haunches with her horrid teeth and claws; the worst wound was on his haunch, which exhibited a sickening, yawning gash, more than twelve inches long, almost laying bare the very bone. I was very cool and steady, and did not feel in the least degree nervous, having fortunately great confidence in my own shooting; but I must confess, when the whole affair was over, I felt that it was a very awful situation, and attended with extreme peril, as I had no friend with me on whom I could rely.

When the lioness sprang on Colesberg, I stood out from the horses, ready with my second barrel for the first chance she should give me of a clear shot. This she quickly did; for, seemingly satisfied with the revenge she had now taken, she quitted Colesberg, and, slewing her tail to one side, trotted sulkily past within a few paces of me, taking one step to the left. I pitched my rifle to my shoulder, and in another second the lioness was stretched on the plain a lifeless corpse. In the struggles of death she half turned on her back, and stretched her neck and forearms convulsively, when she fell back to her former position; her mighty arms hung powerless by her side, her lower jaw fell, blood streamed from her mouth, and she expired. At the moment I fired my second shot, Stofolus, who hardly knew whether he was alive or dead, allowed the three horses to escape. These galloped frantically across the plain, on which he and Kleinboy instantly started after them, leaving me standing alone and unarmed within a few paces of the lioness, which they, from their anxiety to be out of the way, evidently considered quite capable of doing further mischief.

Such is ever the case with these worthies, and with nearly all the natives of South Africa. No reliance can be placed on them. They will to a certainty forsake their master in the most dastardly manner in the hour of peril, and leave him in the lurch. A stranger, however, hearing these fellows recounting their own gallant adventures, when sitting in the evening along with their comrades round a blazing fire, or under the influence of their adored "Cape smoke" or native brandy, might fancy them to be the bravest of the brave. Having skinned the lioness and cut off her head, we placed her trophies upon Beauty and held for camp. Before we had proceeded a hundred yards from the carcass, upward of sixty vultures, whom the lioness had often fed, were feasting on her remains.

We led poor Colesberg slowly home, where, having washed his wounds and carefully stitched them together, I ordered the cold water cure to be adopted. Under this treatment his wounds rapidly healed, and he eventually recovered. The sky remained overcast throughout the day. When the shades of evening set in, terror seemed to have taken possession of the minds of my followers, and they swore that the mate of the lioness, on finding her bones, would follow on our spoor and revenge her death. Under this impression, they refused to remain about the wagons or in the tent after the sun went down; and having cut down the rafters and cupboards of the Boer's house for fuel, they kindled a large fire in the kitchen, where they took up their quarters for the night.

I continued hunting here until the 29th, when I deemed it high time to return to Colesberg, for the purpose of packing and storing my curiosities, increasing my establishment, and refitting generally, preparatory to starting for the distant land of elephants in the far forests of the interior. The distemper or horse sickness, which rages in those parts during the summer months, might be expected shortly to be past; there was, therefore, not much time to lose. The morning was spent in stowing the wagons, greasing the wheels, securing the pots, gridirons, spades, &c;, and overhauling the yokes, rheims, straps, and other gear, preparatory to inspanning, and in the afternoon we inspanned, and, turning our faces to the south, marched upon Colesberg.

On the 31st I continued my march, and on the evening of the 2nd of April I reached Philipolis, a missionary station, and the chief town of the Bastards' country. My road had led between the encampments of the contending parties. Troops of mounted Boers had been scouring the country in every direction, plundering all they could lay their hands on, and sweeping off the cattle and horses of the Bastards. Halting at an encampment of Bastards on the preceding day, I was much amused by their taking me for a missionary. My costume was not very clerical, consisting of a dirty .shirt and an old Gordon tartan kilt. From a Bastard in the vicinity of Philipolis I obtained two large rough dogs in exchange for three pounds of coffee and a little tea. The names of these dogs were "Bles" and "Flam." Bles was of an extremely fierce and savage disposition. On the evening of the 3rd we encamped on the northern bank of the mighty Orange River, at a place called "Boata's Drift," which is nearly opposite Colesberg. Our march had been through a succession of mountains, covered with excellent pasture to their summits. It had rained heavily throughout the day. After inspecting the drift or ford on the following morning, we calculated that the river was too high for the wagons to cross; and by sending a man over on horseback, according to the most approved custom, we ascertained that a passage for the wagons was impracticable. I accordingly instructed my men to proceed to Nerval's Punt, situated a long march higher up the river, there to cross and join me in Colesberg on the evening of the following day; and having breakfasted, I saddled "The Immense Brute," and, taking the ford high up, managed to cross the river in safety, the current having twice taken my horse off his legs. In two hours I entered the village of. Colesberg, where I found the officers of the 91st and all my other friends in great force."

At half past twelve the men mustered on the parade ground, and marched out of the village for Alleman's Drift. Paterson politely requested me to occupy his quarters as long as I remained in Colesberg, and not to spare his cellar, which contained most excellent wine. On the following day, while actively employed in forwarding my affairs, a friend informed me that all my oxen were safely lodged in the skit-kraal or pound, from which I released them, after a deal of trouble and annoyance, by a small pecuniary disbursement. In the evening the village was agitated by a report that a skirmish had taken place between the Boers and Bastards, in which several had fallen on both sides, and that it was the intention of the Boers to pillage Colesberg.

On the 15th, in company with Messrs. Gibbon and Draper, two merchants of Colesbeig, I rode out to visit my friends of the 91st, who were encamped at Alleman's Drift, on the south side of the river. At this spot the Orange River and the surrounding scenery are very beautiful, reminding me of Highland scenery. At one bold sweep of the river the waters are hemmed in by stupendous granite rocks, which cause a deep and sweeping rapid. Below are long deep pools, enclosed by banks adorned with drooping willows and everlasting verdure. I found my friends the military employed, according to the most approved system I the army, luxuriating in brandy and cheroots. The privates, availing themselves of the proximity of the river, were enjoying the recreations of angling and dragging the river with nets. They captured lots of mullet and barbel, averaging from one to four pounds in weight.

On the forenoon of the 16th I rode through the river to visit a gentleman of the name of Bain, who was then living on one of Mr. Fossey's farms. Mr. Bain had made several trips into the interior, and gave me much valuable information and dazzling accounts of the sport I might expect. He recommended my trekking down the Orange River to a drift near Rhama, and thence proceeding by Campbellsdorp to Kuruman, a missionary station distant from Colesberg about two hundred and fifty miles, where I should obtain a Bechuana interpreter, and all necessary information from the resident missionary. On the following day, having taken leave of my kind friends and brother sportsmen, I rode into Colesberg. Here I had the pleasure of meeting two Nimrods, Messrs. Murray and Oswell, proceeding, like myself, on a hunting expedition into the far interior—the former a keen salmon-fisher from the banks of Tay, the latter a civilian in the Honorable East India Company's service. During my stay in Colesberg I was actively employed storing my collection and refitting. All my specimens were carefully sown up in canvas, and nailed down in cases; and perishable articles, such as skins and stuffed heads, were hermetically sealed, being carefully soldered up in tin cases by old Mr. Privet, the tinsmith, one of the leading members of the community of Colesberg.

I covered my wagons with new sails, and had the wheels and iron-work carefully overhauled by the black smith. I purchased from various parties several excellent horses and trek-oxen, and increased my kennel of dogs to twelve stout, rough, serviceable-looking curs. From Mr. Williams of the commissariat I purchased a largo elephant-gun, carrying four to the pound. I engaged two additional Hottentots, named Johannus and Kleinfeldt, and replenished my supplies in every department; and on the 22nd, everything being ready, I resolved, if possible, to get under way that afternoon. With inconceivable trouble, I managed to collect all my runaway men, dogs, oxen, and horses together; and, after much bustle and angry altercation with my inebriated and swarthy crew, my caravan was in motion, and started on its distant journey. We were followed by the female acquaintances of our Hottentots, screaming, yelling, and cursing at their men, at the same time catching up handfuls of red dust, which they tossed into the air with true Hottentot action. Having no hair fortunately to rend, they contented themselves with scratching their woolly pates and rending their petticoats, which they soon reduced to tatters.

On the fourth day I reached Salt-pan's Drift, which I crossed with considerable difficulty, the wagons repeatedly sticking fast in the deep sand. The opposite bank was extremely steep, and required an hour's cutting with our pickaxes and shovels. We passed the farms of several Boers, from whom I purchased three excellent dogs, named "Wolf," "Prince," and "Bonteberg." On one of these farms were half a dozen ostriches, which the Boer endeavored to persuade me to purchase. Continuing our march, on the 28th we passed through the Griqua kraal named Rhama. In the morning, on proceeding to rouse my men, I discovered Kleinboy very coolly smoking his pipe over my loose, dilapidated powder-casks; upon which I seized the culprit, and handled him rather roughly. This so disgusted my friend that he dashed his pipe on the ground with true Hottentot action, and swore he would go no farther with me. The appearance, however, of a fine fat sheep, which I purchased a few minutes after from a Griqua, induced Mr. Kleinboy to alter his mind on the subject, and he sulkily returned to his duty. On the 4th of May Ave made the fair Vaal River, which we crossed at my old drift. Here a party of Korannas rode up to the wagons, mounted on pack-oxen.

On the third day after leaving Campbellsdorp we reached Daniel's Kuil, a kraal of Griquas under Waterboer. The country through which we passed was level and uninteresting, no hill nor landmark relieving the ocean-like expanse and sameness of the scene in any direction. In parts the country was covered as far as I could see with a species of bush, averaging about nine feet in height, having a gray leaf and bunches of small gray blossoms, yielding a very sweet and powerful aromatic perfume. In the evening we continued our march to Kramer's Fonteyn, a very powerful fountain, whose waters issue hot from the earth, as if they were mixed with boiling water. Leaving Kramer's Fonteyn on the 9th, we held for Roning, a very distant water on the road to Kuruman. Toward midnight my men commenced driving furiously, and I ascertained that they were under the influence of liquor, which I imagined they had obtained from the Griquas. On ordering them to halt and outspan, Mr. Kleinboy only drove the harder, so that I found it necessary to send him flying off the box. A short time after I had been asleep I was wakened by a commotion among my cattle, and found that my men had commenced inspanning the oxen, stating that they intended to proceed no further, but to return with the wagons to the colony. Finding monstrance vain, I had recourse to my double-barreled rifle, upon which my followers for the moment relinquished their intention of inspanning, and, retiring to the shelter of a neighboring bush, they shortly fell asleep. I kept sentry over the wagons during the remainder of the night, with my rifle in my hand and a hatchet by my side. At dawn of day on the following morning I roused my ruffans, and ordered them to inspan, which orders they mechanically obeyed swearing, however, that this was the last time they would inspan my oxen.

Having proceeded about ten miles, we arrived at Roning this was a vley of fine spring water, about six hundred yards in length, densely covered with lofty reeds from twelve to fifteen feet high. This place is said never to be without lions. Here was spoor of zebras and hartebeests. In the afternoon I observed that my men were again in liquor. I had at first imagined that the

Griquas had supplied them with brandy; but, upon examining my liquor-case, I discovered that one had been broken into, and two bottles of brandy stolen. This was a second night of anxiety and trouble. I kept watch over my goods and cattle, with my rifle in my hand, till morning. The night was piercingly cold, and in the morning the ground was white with hoar-frost, and a thick coating of ice covered the pools of water. At mid-day on the 11th we left Roning, and continued our march to Kuruman, halting at sundown without water.

Mr. Moffat informed me that a missionary named Dr. Livingstone, who was married to his eldest daughter, had lately established a missionary station among the Bakatlas at Mabotsa, in the vale of Bakatla, about fourteen days' journey to the northeast. Thither he recommended me at once to proceed, as few of the larger varieties of game could now be expected to be found to the southward of Bakatla. He represented to me that my falling in with elephants, even throughout the vast forests in the country immediately beyond Bakatla, was very uncertain, and recommended me, if I was determined to have good elephant-shooting, to endeavor to push on to the remote and endless forests beyond the mountains of Bamangwato, in the territory of Sicomy, the great and paramount chief of the extensive country of the Bamangwato. There would also be a probability of obtaining ivory in barter from Sicomy, he being reported to possess large quantities of that valuable commodity. By Mr. Moffat's assistance I engaged a Bechuana in the capacity of interpreter in the Dutch and Sichuana languages. From Mr. Hume I purchased a supply of wheat; and on the following day I set all my people to work on a mill of Mr. Moffat's to reduce this wheat to flour.

On the 15th I took leave of my friends at Kuruman, and continued my journey in a northeasterly course through a heavy sandy country of boundless level plains, stretching away on every side, covered with rank yellow grass, which, waving in the breeze, imparted the idea of endless fields of ripe corn. At sundown we crossed the Matluarin River, an insignificant stream, and encamped on its northern bank. On the march we saw a few blue wildebeests and ostriches. At dawn of day on the following morning we pursued our journey through the same description of country, varied, however, with detached clumps of thorny mimosas. On the march we crossed a swarm of locusts, resting for the night on the grass and bushes. They lay so thick that the wagons could have been filled with them in a very short time, covering the large bushes just as a swarm of young bees covers the branch on which it pitches. Locusts afford fattening and wholesome food to man, birds, and all sorts of beasts; cows and horses, lions, jackals, hyenas, antelopes, elephants, &c., devour them. We met a party of Batlapis carrying heavy burdens of them on their backs. Our hungry dogs made a fine feast on them. The cold frosty night had rendered them unable to take wing until the sun should restore their powers. As it was difficult to obtain sufficient food for my dogs, I and Isaac took a large blanket, which we spread under a hush, whose branches were bent to the ground with the mass of locusts which covered it; and having shaken the branches, in an instant I had more locusts than I could carry on my back these we roasted for ourselves and dogs.

Soon after the sun was up, on looking behind me, I beheld the locusts stretching to the west in vast clouds, resembling smoke; but the wind, soon after veering round, brought them back to us, and they flew over our heads, for some time actually darkening the sun. In the evening I continued my march by moonlight, and halted within a few miles of Motito, an extensive kraal of the Batlapis, a tribe of Bechuanas. The nights were piercing cold, the grass being every morning covered with white frost.

CHAPTER XI

At an early hour on the 17th I outspanned at Motito, where I was kindly received by Monsieur Loga and Mr. Edwards, the former a French missionary stationed at Motito, and the latter an English missionary from Mabotza. Another French missionary, named Monsieur Lemue, belonging to the station, was absent. The women at Motito wear heavier ornaments of beads than any with whom I am acquainted. As I have now reached the southern borders of that vast tract of Southern Africa inhabited by the numerous tribes of the Bechuanas, it will be necessary, before proceeding further, to give a sketch of their manners and customs. They arc a lively and intelligent race of people, and remarkable for their good humor they are well formed, if not starved in infancy. They possess pleasing features, and very fine eyes and teeth; their hair is short and woolly; the color of their complexion is of a light copper. The various tribes live in kraals, or villages, of various sizes, along with their respective chiefs. Their wigwams are built in a circular form, and thatched with long grass; the floor and wall, inside and out, are plastered with a compound of clay and cow-dung. The entrances arc about three feet high and two feet broad. Each wigwam is surrounded with a hedge of wickerwork, while one grand hedge of wait-a-bit thorns surrounds the entire kraal, protecting the inmates from lions and other animals.

The dress of the men consists of a kaross, or skin cloak, which hangs gracefully from their shoulders; and another garment, termed tsecha, which encircles their loins, and is likewise made of skin. On their feet they wear a simple sandal formed of the skin of the buffalo or camelopard. On their legs and arms they carry ornaments of brass and copper of different patterns, which are manufactured by themselves. The men also wear a few ornaments of beads round their necks and on their arms. Around their necks, besides beads, they carry a variety of other appendages, the majority of which are believed to possess a powerful charm to preserve them from evil. One of these is a small hollow bone, through which they blow when in peril; another is a set of dice, formed of ivory, which they rattle in their hands and cast on the ground to ascertain if they are to be lucky in any enterprise in which they may be about to engage ; also a host of bits of root and bark which are medicinal. Around their necks, arms, waists, and ankles they wear large and cumbrous coils of beads of a variety of colors, tastefully arranged in different patterns. The women chiefly employ their time in cultivating their fields and gardens, in which they rear corn, pumpkins, and water-melons, and likewise in harvesting their crops and grinding their corn. Both men and women go bareheaded they anoint their heads with "sibelo," a shining composition, being a mixture of fat and a gray sparkling ore, having the appearance of mica. Some of the tribes besmear their bodies with a mixture of fat and red clay, imparting to them the appearance of Red Indians. Most of the tribes possess cattle; these are attended to and milked solely by the men, a woman being never allowed to set foot within the cattle-kraal. Polygamy is allowed, and any man may keep as many wives as he pleases the wife, however, has in the first instance to be purchased. Among tribes possessed of cattle, the price of a wife is ten head of cattle; but among the poorer tribes a who may be obtained for a few spades with which they cultivate their fields. These spades, which are manufactured by themselves, are fastened in the end of a long shaft, and are used as our laborers use the hoe. Rows of women may be seen digging together in the fields singing songs, to which they keep time with their spades.

The name of the chief at Motito was Motchuara, a subordinate of the great chief Mahura. He was very anxious that I should remain a day with him, for the purpose of trading in ostrich feathers and karosses; but, being anxious to push forward, I resumed my march in the afternoon, and trekked on till near midnight, when I encamped in an extensive forest of gray and ancient-looking cameel-dorn trees. These were the finest I had yet seen in Africa, each tree assuming a wide-spreading and picturesque appearance. They were detached and in groups, like oaks in an English deer-park. Many of them were inhabited by whole colonies of the social grosbeak, a bird with whose wonderful habitations the branches were loaded. These remarkable birds, which are about the size and appearance of the British green-finch, construct their nests and live socially together under one common roof, the whole fabric being formed of dry grass, and exhibiting at a short distance the appearance of a haycock stuck up in the tree. The entrances to the nests are from beneath. They are built side by side, and when seen from below resemble a honey-dim.

At dawn of day on the following morning we continued our march through the venerable cameel-dorn forest. The road was extremely heavy, consisting of left, loose sand. Having proceeded about six miles, emerging from the forest, we entered once more on a wide-spreading open country, covered in some parts with bushes, and in others only with grass. Another hour brought us to Little Chooi, a large salt-pan, where we obtained water for ourselves and cattle from a deep pit made by men. In sight were a few zebras, ostriches, and springboks. In the forenoon a number of cattle, belonging to Mahura, came to drink at the pit. Some of these carried enormous wide-spreading horns. Mahura and his tribe possess immense herds of cattle, the majority of which they "lifted" or obtained in war from other Bechuana tribes. Some years before this, Mahura, assisted by another tribe, had attacked Sobiqua, king of the Bawangketse, a tribe inhabiting the borders of the great Kalahari desert, whom they routed, and succeeded in driving off the majority of their vast herds.

At 3 P.M. we inspanned, and held on till midnight with fine moonlight, crossing a desert and sandy country. In the vicinity of Chooi we passed an extensive range of old pitfalls, formed by the natives for entrapping game. They were dug in the form of a crescent, and occupied an extent of nearly a quarter of a mile. On the march I observed some enormous trunks of trees that had been destroyed by fire in by-gone years. On the following day we reached Loharon, an uninteresting and desolate spot, where we encamped for the day beside a pool of rain water. Here

I observed a few hartebeests, sassaybies, and zebras. On the 20th, having breakfasted, we inspanned, and continued our march till sunset. We passed through a very level country, covered with detached bushes. The dullness of the scene, however, was enlivened by a wondrous flight of locusts, the largest I had ever beheld. The prospect was obscured by them as far as we could see, resembling the smoke arising from a thousand giant bonfires; while those above our heads darkened our path with a double flight—the one next the ground flying north, while the upper clouds of them held a southerly course. The dogs, as usual, made a hearty meal on them.

We continued our march by moonlight, halting at midnight in a vast open plain beside a small pool of rain water. After breakfast I rode forth in quest of springboks, of which I bagged a couple. I fell in with blue and black wildebeests, zebras, ostriches, and blesboks. The plains here were bare and open, resembling the country frequented by the blesbok to the southward of the Vaal, with which country I subsequently ascertained it to be connected, in a due southerly course, by an endless succession of similar bar' plains, throughout the entire extent of which the blesbok and black wildebeest are abundant. While galloping after a herd of zebras, "The Immense Brute" put his foot into a hole, and came down with great violence on his head, pitching me over his bows. I saved my rifle at the risk of sacrificing my collar-bone, and would have escaped without further injury than the loss of a portion of the bark of my cheek, had not my horse described a somersault, coming down with the broad of his back on the calf of my right leg, and bruising it so severely as to incapacitate me from walking for several days. About mid-day we resumed our march, and in the evening we reached Great Chooi, a very large salt-pan at present full of water. Here I found, for the first time, the bones and skull of a rhinoceros long killed. My interpreter informed me that the rhinoceros had long left that country to his surprise, however, we discovered fresh spoor by the fountain. Continuing our march, on the 22nd we entered on a new description of country; boundless open plains being succeeded by endless forests of dwarfish trees and bushes, the ground slightly undulating, and covered with a variety of rich grasses and aromatic herbs.

The 2nd of June was the coldest day I had experienced in Africa, a cutting cold wind blowing oft' the Southern Ocean. On the morning of the 2nd I was waited upon Dr. Mosielely, attended by a number of his nobility and others of the tribe, who flocked around my wagons importunately requesting snuff. The appearance of the chief was mild, but not dignified. One of his generals, with whom he seemed to be on very intimate terms, was a jolly-looking old warrior with a wall eye, and a face strongly marked with the small-pox. This man's name was "Siemi." He had killed about twenty men in battle with his own hand, and bore a mark of honor for every man. This mark was a line tattooed on his ribs. Mosielely presented me with a bag of sour milk, and requested that I would tarry with him for a few days for the purpose of trading. I informed him that I was now anxious to push on to the country of the elephants, but would trade with him on my return. This intimation seemed very much to disappoint the king, who was anxious to exchange karosses for guns and ammunition. But I had resolved to part with my muskets solely for ivory, which article Mosielely on this particular occasion did not possess.

Dr. Livingstone informed me that large game was abundant on all sides to the northward of Bakatla. He stated that herds of elephants occasionally visited the territories of the adjoining chiefs, sometimes frequenting a district for half a summer, but that at present he was not aware of any elephants in the forests adjacent to Bakatla, He represented the distant and unexplored forests beyond Bamangwato, the territory of Sicomy, as being allowed by the natives to be the country where elephants were at all times abundant. There was also a prospect of obtaining there ivory in barter for my muskets. I accordingly resolved, in the first instance, to direct my attention mainly to elephants, and not to tarry in any district, however favorable, for the purpose of hunting other varieties of game. Dr. Livingstone stated that I should experience considerable difficulty in reaching Bamangwato, since there was no path nor track of any description to guide me thither. My only chance of getting there seemed to depend on being able to obtain Bechuana guides from Caachy, a subordinate chief of a branch of the "Baquaina" tribe, then resident at a place called "Booby," situated about eighty miles to the northwest of Bakatla. Without these guides it would be almost impossible to proceed, as the waters were few and very far between. The probability, however, was, that these guides would be refused, since it is the invariable policy of African chiefs to prevent all travelers from penetrating beyond themselves.

Baraangwato is distant upward of two hundred miles to the northward of Bakatla, from which it is separated by rugged and apparently impassable mountain ranges, extensive sandy deserts, which are destitute of water, and vast and trackless forests. Isaac, my interpreter, already began to lose heart, and raised a thousand objections to my proceeding to so distant a country. He recommended my rather hunting in the territory of "Sichely," the paramount chief of the Baquaines, situated about fifty miles to the north of Bakatla, where he assured me we should find elephants. Perceiving that his remonstrances did not avail, and that I was inexorable, he proposed resigning his commission, and was with difficulty prevailed on by Dr. Livingstone to agree to accompany me further.

On the 3rd I took leave of my kind friend Dr. Livingstone, and started for Bamangwato. I was accompanied by a large party of the Bakatla men and two Baquaines. They followed me in the hope of obtaining flesh, a report having spread through the tribe that I was a successful hunter. The Bechuanas are extremely fond of flesh, which they consider the only food befitting men. Corn and milk they reckon the food of women. Having no flesh at home, and being seldom able to kill large game for themselves, they entertain great respect for those who kill plenty of venison for them, and they will travel to very great distances for the purpose of obtaining it. We proceeded in a westerly course, and held up the lovely valley of Bakatla, through open glades and patches of ancient forests.

Ongoing up to them, I was astonished to behold their size and powerful appearance. Their horns reminded me of the rugged trunk of an oak-tree. Each horn was upward of a foot in breadth at the base, and together they effectually protected the skull with a massive and impenetrable shield. The horns, descending, and spreading out horizontally, completely overshadowed the animal's eyes, imparting to him a look the most ferocious and sinister that can be imagined. On my way to the wagons I shot a stag sassayby, and while I was engaged in removing his head a troop of about thirty doe pallahs cantered past me, followed by one princely old buck. Snatching up my rifle, I made a fine shot, and rolled him over in the grass.

Early in the afternoon I dispatched men with a packhorse to bring the finer of the two buffalo-heads. It was so ponderous that two powerful men could with difficulty raise it from the ground. The Bechuanas who had accompanied me, on hearing of my success, snatched up their shields and assagais, and hastened to secure the flesh, nor did I see any more of them, with the exception of the two Baquaines, who remained with me, being engaged in a plot with my interpreter to prevent my penetrating to Bamangwato. Isaac did not soon forget his adventure with the buffaloes; and at night, over the fire, he informed my men that I was mad, and that any man who followed me was going headlong to his own destruction. At an early hour on the 10th I continued my march through a glorious country of hill and dale, throughout which water was abundant.

Beautifully wooded hills and mountains stretched away on every side; some of the mountains were particularly grand and majestic, their summits being surrounded by steep precipices and abrupt parapets of rock, the abodes of whole colonies of black-faced baboons, which, astonished to behold such novel intruders upon their domains, leisurely descended the craggy mountain sides for a nearer inspection of our caravan. Seating themselves together upon a broad ledge, they seemed to hold a council as to the propriety of permitting us to proceed further through their territories. Having advanced about nine miles, I drew up my wagons on the bank of a rivulet, where the spoor of large game was extremely abundant. In the bed of the stream I discovered the scaly side of a manic, which had been newly eaten by some bird of prey. This extraordinary animal, which in its habits partakes of the nature of the hedgehog, is about three feet in length, and is covered all over with an impenetrable coat of mail, consisting of large rough scales about the size and shape of the husk of an artichoke ; these overlap one another in an extraordinary and very beautiful manner. Its tail is broad, and likewise' covered with scales; on being disturbed it rolls itself into a ball. The manis is met with throughout the interior of South Africa, but it is rare and very seldom seen.

It was on the 4th of June that I beheld for the first time the rhinoceros. Having taken some coffee, I rode out unattended, with my rifle, and before proceeding far I fell in with a huge white rhinoceros with a large calf, standing in a thorny grove. Getting my wind, she set off at top speed through thick thorny bushes, the calf, as is invariably the case, taking the lead, and the mother guiding its course by placing her horn, generally about three feet in length, against its ribs. My horse shied very much at first, alarmed at the strange appearance of "Chukuroo," but by a sharp application of spur and jambok I prevailed upon him to follow, and presently, the ground improving, I got alongside, and, firing at the gallop, sent a bullet through her shoulder. She continued her pace with blood streaming from the wound, and very soon reached an impracticable thorny jungle, where I could not follow, and instantly lost her. In half an hour I fell in with a second rhinoceros, being an old bull of the white variety. Dismounting, I crept within twenty yards, bid saluted him with both barrels in the shoulder, upon which he made off, uttering a loud blowing noise, and upsetting everything that obstructed his progress.

Shortly after this I found myself on the banks of the stream beside which my wagons were outspanned. Following along its margin, I presently beheld a bull of the borele, or black rhinoceros, standing within a hundred yards of me. Dismounting from my horse, I secured him to a tree, and then stalked within twenty yards of the huge beast, under cover of a large, strong bush. Borele, hearing me advance, came on to see what it was, and suddenly protruded his horny nose within twenty yards of me. Knowing well that a front shot would not prove deadly, I sprang to my feet and ran behind the bush. Upon this the villain charged, blowing loudly, and chased me round the bush. Had his activity been equal to his ugliness, my wanderings would have terminated here, but by my superior agility I had the advantage in the turn. After standing a short time eyeing me through the bush, he got a whiff of my wind, which at once alarmed him. Uttering a blowing noise, and erecting his insignificant yet saucy looking tail, he wheeled about, leaving me master of the field, when I sent a bullet through his ribs to teach him manners

Finding that rhinoceroses were abundant in the vicinity, I resolved to halt a day for the purpose of hunting, and after an early breakfast on the 6th I rode southeast with the two Baquiaines. They led me along the bases of the mountains, through woody dells and open glades, and we eventually reached a grand forest gray with age. Here we found abundance of spoor of a variety of game, and started several herds of the more common varieties. At length I observed an old bull eland standing under a tree. He was the first that I had seen, and was a noble specimen, standing about six feet high at the shoulder. Observing us, he made off at a gallop, springing over the trunks of decayed trees which lay across his path; but very soon he reduced his pace to a trot. Spurring my horse, another moment saw me riding hard behind him. Twice in the thickets I lost sight of him, and he very nearly escaped me; but at length, the ground improving, I came up with him, and rode within a few yards behind him. Long streaks of foam now streamed from his mouth, and a profuse perspiration had changed his sleet gray coat to an ashy blue. Tears trickled from his large dark eye, and it was plain that the eland's hours were numbered. Pitching my rifle to my shoulder, I let fly at the gallop, and mortally wounded him behind; then spurring my horse, I shot past him on his right side, and discharged my other barrel behind his shoulder, when the eland staggered for a moment and subsided in the dust. The two Baquaines soon made their appearance, and seemed delighted at my success. Having kindled a fire, they cut out steaks, which they roasted on the embers: I also cooked a steak for myself, spitting it upon a forked branch, the other end of which I sharpened with my knife and stuck into the ground.

The chase had led me close in along the northern base of a lofty detached mountain, the highest in all that country. This mountain is called by the Bechuanas the Mountain of the Eagles. The eland which I had shot in the morning lay somewhere to the southward of this mountain, but far in the level forest. Having rounded the mountain, I began to recognize the ground, and presently I had the satisfaction to behold a few vultures soaring over the forest in advance, and, on proceeding a short distance further, large groups of these birds were seated on the gray and weather-beaten branches of the loftiest old trees of the forest. This was a certain sign that the eland was not far distant; and on raising my voice and loudly calling on the name of Carollus, I was instantly answered by that individual, who, heedless of his master's fate, was actively employed in cooking for himself a choice steak from the dainty rump of the eland. That night I slept beneath the blue and starry canopy of heaven. My sleep was light and sweet, and no rude dreams or hankering cares disturbed the equanimity of my repose.

CHAPTER XII

At an early hour on the 7th he arose, and, having loaded the pack-horse with a burden of flesh and fat, I dispatched one of the Baquaines with him to camp. Carollus and I then rode for the rhinoceros to secure the horn. On nearing the carcass, a noble bull buffalo stood within thirty yards of me, but I had omitted to put on my caps. Lions had consumed a large part of the rhinoceros, and had sneaked off on hearing us approach, leaving, as is usual, matted locks from their shaggy gray manes sticking on the broken points of the projecting ribs. My dogs, on scenting them, ran baking angrily in the direction which the lions had hell, springing up into the air with their hair bristling alas their backs. With considerable difficulty we separate the horn of the muchocho from the skin by means of a long, sharp knife. It was nearly three feet in length, and measured almost a foot in diameter at the bae. This being accomplished, we returned to camp. Here I found that Isaac had not been idle in forwarding his own views. I at once saw that my followers had something unusual on their minds; blackness and dismay were plainly written on every countenance. I had scarcely seated myself beside the fire, when Isaac approached me with a slow, funereal step, and horror depicted in his face, and asked me if I had heard the news. I replied, What news? He went on to state that on the preceding evening two men of the Bamangwato tribe had passed my wagons on their way to Bakatla, to warn that tribe of the on-coming of the cruel and warlike Matabili (whose powerful chief, Moselekatse, has been so ably described in the pages of my fellow-sportsman, Captain Harris). These they represented as having a few days previously attacked and plundered various Bechuana tribes to the northward, and that they were now advancing by rapid marches to devastate the country and murder the inhabitants of these parts.

This I at once knew to be a fabrication to prevent my penetrating further, and I laughed at Isaac and told him he had dreamed it; to which he replied, "Yes, you will not listen to my advice when you are warned of danger, but both you and your men will one day acknowledge the truth of my forebodings." I had considerable difficulty in calming the minds of my followers, and prevailing on them to proceed further with me.

On the 8th we performed a short march before breakfast, halting beside a stream of delicious water. In the afternoon we resumed our march, and halted at sundown beside the broad and sandy bed of a periodical river, through which ran a crystal stream.

On the 9th we continued our march through a lovely and romantic country, steering for Sesetabie, an extremely bold and picturesque pass, in the lofty mountains in which the "Kouloubeng" or "river of wild boars," a tributary to the Ngotwani, takes its rise. As the wagons proceeded, I walked in advance with my rifle, and presently brought down a sassayby. While following a herd of pallahs, the wagons got ahead of me; and on overtaking them, I found them drawn up beside a sweet little rocky river, at a short distance from the mountain pass, which from its appearance we expected would prove a barrier to our further progress.

I ascended a lofty mountain range to the westward of the pass. Here I fell in with large colonies of baboons and a few klipspringers. I also saw for the first time green parrots and gray squirrels. A number of interesting birds, possessing melodious voices, and plumage more or less gaud, adorned the groves and forests since I had crossed the range, of the Kurrichane Mountains;

but, throughout my career in the forests of the interior, my attention was necessarily so taken up with the pursuit of larger, and to be more interesting objects of the chase, that I could rarely bestow upon the feathered creation more than a short and passing glance of admiration. Having ascended to the summit of the highest mountain of the chain, I obtained a glorious view of the surrounding country. It was truly a fair and boundless prospect; beautifully wooded plains and mountains stretched away on every side to an amazing distance, until the vision was lost among the faint blue outlines of the distant mountain ranges. Throughout all this country, and vast tracts beyond, I had the satisfaction to reflect that a never-ending succession of herds of every species of noble game which the hunter need desire pastured there in undisturbed security; and as I gazed, I felt that it was all my own, and that I at length possessed the undisputed sway over a forest, in comparison with which the tame and herded narrow bounds of the wealthiest European sportsman sink into utter insignificance.

The succeeding day we entered the gorge, and wound along the margin of the stream, which danced and sparkled down its abrupt and rocky channel, forming a pleasing succession of babbling streams and foaming waterfalls. As we advanced further up the gorge the path became extremely contracted, there being barely sufficient room to admit of the wagons passing between the steep and rocky brink of the stream, and the rugged base of the lofty, inaccessible mountain which towered on our left. On the opposite side, the mountain forming the eastern bulwark of the pass rose precipitately from the water's edge, presenting an impassable barrier. It was a wild and lonely glen, hitherto untrodden save by the wild denizens of the forests, which from time immemorial had roamed these solitudes. Large stones and masses of granite rock obstructed our progress, and several hours were occupied in rolling these to one side before we could venture to bring on the wagons.

The next morning was cold and windy, and I lay in my wagon longer than usual. My Hottentots had thought proper to leave their charge, and go in quest of honey under the guidance of a garrulous honey-bird. I had lain about twenty minutes in my wagon after they had all started, and was occupied in reading a book, when suddenly I heard the oxen come trotting along in front of the wagons, as if sharply driven. On raising my head from my pillow, I perceived a lioness following within twenty yards of them, and next moment her mate, a venerable-looking lion, with a shaggy mane which swept the ground, appeared in the yellow grass in front of the oxen, waiting for her to put them to flight. The plot had evidently been pre-concerted between them, this being the usual manner in which the lion attacks the buffaloes. Fortunately, the oxen would not run for them, and the lions seemed surprised at the confidence of their game. On springing to my feet and shouting to them, they joined one another, and stood together beneath a shady tree within a hundred and twenty yards of the wagons.

From the cool state I was in when I fired, and the steady aim which the forked branch had afforded me, I felt convinced that the lion, if not dead, must be mortally wounded, but I prudently resolved not to proceed in quest of him alone. Presently some of my men, who had gone to the carcass of a buffalo I had slain the previous day, returned, bringing the dogs; and, having informed them of what had happened, I proceeded to take up the spoor of the wounded lion. On reaching the spot where the lions had stood, my does at once commenced barking^ angrily and looking; sharply around in every direction, their hair bristling on their backs. I at once discovered blood, "which increased as I proceeded from small red drops to large frothy blotches; and before advancing two hundred yards, on approaching a dense green bush, my dogs, which led the way, sprang suddenly to one side, barking with great vehemence. By this I knew that the lion was dead, and, on cautiously rounding the bush, taking care at the same time to give it a wide berth, I had the satisfaction to behold a princely lion stretched lifeless on the ground. He was in the prime of life, having fine sharp teeth; and it being now the dead of winter, he carried the most luxuriant coat of hair, the rankness of his flowing mane exceeding in beauty anything I had hitherto seen. I considered myself extremely fortunate in having secured so noble a specimen of the lion with so little danger, and I at once set men to work to unrobe him, which they were not long in accomplishing.

About mid-day we inspanned, and trekked on till sundown through a country the most wild and primitive that can be conceived. "We proceeded under the guidance of two Bechuanas, who had joined us on the preceding day, and were proceeding to Booby. The two Baquaines who had accompanied me from Bakatla had forsaken my standard after I had shot the bull eland, so liberal a supply of flesh being far too powerful a temptation to admit of their proceeding beyond it. On gaining the neck of the mountain pass, our march for a few miles wound through beautifully-wooded grass hills, after which we descended into a rugged and densely-wooded valley, intersected with deep water-courses which threatened momentarily the destruction of my axle-trees. So dense was the jungle that we were obliged repeatedly to halt the wagons, and cut out a pathway with our axes before they could advance. Emerging from this valley, we entered upon a more level country, still, however, densely covered with forest-trees and bushes in endless variety.

On the 11th we were in the yoke soon after daybreak. It was a bitter cold morning, ice a quarter of an inch in thickness covering the pools of water. We were now clear of the extensive mountain ranges through which our road had wound since leaving Bakatla, and were approaching toward the southeastern limits of the great Kalahari desert, on whose borders Booby is situated. We continued our march, steering northwest, in which direction the distant blue hills (pointed out to me as the position of Booby) shot abruptly above the unvaried sameness of the intervening forest scenery. To the west, one eternal ocean-like expanse of gray forest stretched away in a level and unbroken plain, terminated only by the far horizon. Having performed a march of three oars, we crossed a small stream, where I outspanned to breakfast.

This day was to me rather a memorable one, as the first on which I saw and slew the lofty, graceful-looking giraffe or camelopard, with which, during many years of my life, I had longed to form an acquaintance.

Although we had now been traveling many days through the country of the giraffe, and had marched through forests in which their spoor was abundant, our eyes had not yet been gifted with a sight of "Tootla" himself; it was therefore with indescribable pleasure that, on the evening of the 11th, I beheld a troop of these interesting animals.

Our breakfast being finished, I resumed my journey through an endless gray forest of cameel-dorn and other trees, the country's lightly undulating and grass abundant. A little before the sun went down my driver remarked to me, "I was just going to say, sir, that that old tree was a camelopard." On looking where he pointed, I saw that the old tree was indeed a camelopard, and, on casting my eyes a little to the right, I beheld a troop of them standing looking at us, their heads actually towering above the trees of the forest. It was imprudent to commence a chase at such a late hour, especially in a country of so level a character, where the chances were against my being able to regain my wagons that night. I, however, resolved to chance everything; and directing my men to catch and saddle Colesberg, I proceeded in haste to buckle on my shooting-belt and spurs, and in two minutes I was in the saddle. The giraffes stood looking at the wagons until I was within sixty yards of them, when, galloping round a thick bushy tree, under cover of which I had ridden, I suddenly beheld a sight the most astounding that a sportsman's eye can encounter.

On the 12th we performed two long marches through thickly-wooded plains, the spoor of camelopard being extremely abundant. On the 18th we cast the cattle at dawn of day. Breakfast being fished, We inspanned, and having proceeded about eight miles through the forest, steering for a range of rocky mountains, we reached a gorge in the same. Here we crossed a small river, and, having followed its banks about three miles, reached Booby, a residence of Bechuanas, being a branch of the tribe of the Baquaines, and governed by a subordinate chief, who was then absent on a visit. I was, however, welcomed by his nephew, named Caachy, a man of pleasing exterior and prepossessing manners, who shortly afterward became, and now is, chief of that tribe.

As the manner in which Caachy succeeded to the chieftainship was peculiar, I may here relate the circumstances attending it. Throughout all the Bechuana tribes an absurd belief prevails in witchcraft and supernatural agencies of every end. They also believe that for every transaction there is a medicine which will enable the possessor to succeed in his object. Thus they think those among themselves who work in iron do so under the power of medicine. Their rainmakers, by the power of their medicines, can propitiate the friendly clouds during the protracted droughts of summer. They have medicines to protect them from the lightning's stroke, from the deadly bite of the viper, and from the fatal spring of the lion. They further believe that there is a medicine for guns, the possession of which will cause the gun to shoot well, and likewise one for the gunpowder, which will give it strength.

This being arranged, I gave Caachy some presents, and requested him to take charge of my buffalo and other heads until my return, which he promised to do, and ordered men to bear them directly to his kraal. About mid-day we inspanned and left Booby, accompanied by nearly the whole tribe, every man carrying two or three assagais and a battle-ax. They followed us in the hope that I would shoot large game for them. The guides at first held northeast; but presently drawing off that course and steering due east, I halted, and said that was not the road to Bamangwato. They replied, they held that course on account of water. I then directed them to place an assagai on the ground with its head pointing to Bamangwato. Thereupon the savages laid down one of their assagais, and, having pretended for some minutes to be discussing among themselves the exact position of Bamangwato, the ended by pointing it due east, declaring that Bamangwato lay in that direction. I told them that I had a needle in my pocket which I had rubbed with medicine, by which I could tell if their spear pointed to Sicomy's country. Knowing that Bamangwato lay a little to the east of north, I said that by turning the needle three times round my left wrist it would point a little to the left-hand side of the country I required. On hearing this, the savages looked at one another with surprise, and pressed round me to see if my needle possessed the power I represented. Slipping my fingers into my shooting-belt, I then pulled out my pocket compass, and, passing it three times round my left wrist with the utmost gravity, I whistled shrilly; and on opening the compass, I placed it on the ground before them. Snatching one of their assagais, I placed it beside the compass a little to the east of north, and told them that it was there Bamangwato lay. They were struck with astonishment, and at once considered me as working by supernatural agency.

Having done this, I inquired of the guides if they would lead me to waters in that direction. They all shouted that that was the desert, and that no man had ever found water there. Having said this, they all turned right about, and, retreating for about two hundred yards, they squatted on the ground. Isaac and I then approached them; but they sat in silence, and looked on the ground. I asked them why they all sat thus. They answered that they would proceed no further with me. I replied that I was happy to hear it, and that I could find the way better without them. I returned to my wagons, and ordered my men to turn about and retrace their steps to the nearest water. The savages then requested me to halt and speak with them. I told them to go home to their captain, as their presence troubled me; and having proceeded a few hundred yards, I encamped beside a pool of water.

It was plain to me that Isaac, my interpreter, was in league with the Baquaines in their designs against me; but as I did not then intend to part with him, because his presence gave confidence to my people, I deemed it best to pretend that I believed him to be sincere. My flesh being exhausted, I resolved to halt for a day for the purpose of hunting before proceeding further; and having obtained a good supply, to steer through the forests by compass a little to the east of north, and to search for water with my horses in advance of the wagons. I felt poorly in health, and was much troubled in mind. My situation was by no means an enviable one. I was far in the interior of Africa, alone and friendless, surrounded by a tribe of men who would do anything to prevent my attaining my object; but fear restrained them from using violence. What I most dreaded was their stealing my oxen or horses, which they could easily accomplish, as I was encamped in a thick forest; my men also were faint-hearted, and anxious to return toward home.

That night I slept little, from vexation and anxiety. The whole tribe of the Booby men lay encamped beside us. They lay on the ground around a number of fires, with a hedge of thorny bushes placed in a semicircle to windward of each party. After breakfast I rode east to hunt, accompanied by Kleinboy leading pack-horse; about thirty of the Bechuanas followed us in the hope of flesh. Having proceeded about two miles, I perceived a large herd of blue wildebeests and zebras. I signed to the Bechuanas to lie down, and then rode slowly forward as if to pass to leeward of the herd. Having probably never before seen a horseman, they allowed me to approach within a hundred yards, when I sprang from my horse, and with my first barrel dropped a fat blue wildebeest. The Bechuanas then rushed forward, but I beckoned to them to lie down.

Here I found Caachy with all his retinue they had come out to endeavor by cunning speaking to lead me astray. Having saluted Caachy, I said that I had yesterday promised to kill some game for him, and that I had now fulfilled my word, upon which he thanked me. I then remarked that his men did not lead me as Dr. Livingstone had told me to ride; to which he replied that the road was circuitous, and that they led me so on account of water. At length he had almost persuaded me to follow his guides, but I said I would rest till tomorrow, having determined that, as I had no friend whom I might consult, I would revolve the subject in my mind that night, and determine finally in the morning. Caachy then drank coffee with me and departed. In the evening I inquired of the guides concerning the waters and the distances between them. They replied that the first water was a moderate day's journey, but after that I must ride more than two days without water they also persevered in pointing to the east as my course, I now plainly saw that their intention was to lead me far astray, and finally to bring me to Sichely, their own paramount chief. I therefore resolved to adhere to my first resolution of steering my own course by the compass, but I kept this intention secret, fearing that they might steal some of my oxen.

CHAPTER XIII

On the morning of the 16th a large party of Caachy's men were still encamped beside us, and were under the impression that they had succeeded in prevailing upon me to follow them. Having filled all my water-casks, I ordered my men to inspan, the Bechuanas cracking their jokes and fancying that I should ride east as they led; but, to their astonishment, having inspanned, I told them that they had better all return to their captains, as I would shoot no more game for them, and I then ordered my men to ride for a conspicuous tree in the distance, bearing N.N.E. The Bechuanas sat still for some time to see how I would steer, and presently they shouldered their assagais and followed in our wake. This was a bold step on my part: the country looked very unlikely for water, and the Bechuanas swore that there was none for seven days' journey in that direction. Our march lay through a boundless forest, with no hill or landmark to give me an idea where to search for water. Fortune, however, followed me here as usual if I had lived all my life in the country, I could not have taken a more direct course for the spot I wished to reach. After we had proceeded some miles, a rising ground arose in our path, from the summit of which I fancied that a view might be obtained of the country in advance. This view only served to damp my hopes, the prospect exhibiting one slightly undulating, ocean-like expanse of forest and dense thorny jungles.

We halted for a few minutes to breathe the oxen, when the Bechuanas all came up, and sat down on the ground beside us. I asked them why they had not gone home as I had told them. They replied that they followed me because they were afraid that I should lose myself and my oxen. We held on, steering by compass N.N.E. All the Bechuanas now forsook me except the four ill-favored men whom Caachy had pointed out to me as my guides. These four, contrary to my expectations, followed in our wake at some distance. I walked a hundred yards in advance of the wagons with my compass in my hand, having ordered the men to follow my footsteps. After traveling for several hours the country became more open, and presently we entered upon a wide tract that had been recently burned by the Ba-Kalahari, or wild inhabitants of the desert. Here the trees and bushes stood scorched and burned, and there was not a blade of grass to cheer the eye—blackness and ashes stretched away on every side wherever I turned my anxious glance. I felt my heart sink within me as I beheld in dim perspective my famished and thirsty oxen returning some days hence over this hopeless desert, all my endeavors to find water having failed, and all my bright hopes of elephant-hunting dashed and crowned with bitter disappointment it was, indeed, a cheerless prospect.

I felt very sad and unhappy in my mind, for I considered that the chances were against me, and I shuddered at the idea of returning to the colony, after coming so very far, without shooting or even seeing what my heart most ardently desired, viz., a wild bull elephant free in his native Jungle. I took some wine, and, coming to the fire which the men had kindled for the night beneath a magnificent old cameel-dorn tree, I affected great cheerfulness and contentment, and, laughing at the four Bechuanas, I told them that I was not a child that they should lead me astray, but that I was an old warrior and a cunning hunter, and could, find my way in strange lands. I laughed, but it was the laugh of despair, for I expected that next evening they would be laughing at me, on seeing me compelled to retrace my steps. One of the greatest difficulties that presented itself was, that, if I rode in advance to search for water, it would be almost impossible to find my way back to the wagons through that vast and trackless forest. I went to bed, but tried in vain to sleep. Care and anxiety kept me awake until a little before morning, when I fell asleep for a short time, and dreamed that I had ridden in advance and found water. Day dawned, and I awoke in sorrow. My hopes were like a flickering flame; care sat upon my brow. I cast lose my horses and oxen, and prepared some breakfast; I then directed my men to catch "The Cow" and "Colesberg," and give them some corn. I asked the guides if they could lead me to water in a northerly direction, when they replied that no man ever found water in the desert. I did not talk more with them, but ordered my men to remain quiet during the day and listen for shots, lest I should lose my way in returning; and having given them ammunition to reply, I saddled up and held N.N.E. through thick forests, accompanied by Kleinboy. The ground was heavy, being soft sand, and the grass grew at intervals in detached bunches. We rode on without a break or a change, and found no spoor of wild animals to give me hope. I saw one duiker, but these antelopes are met with in the desert, and are independent of water.

At last we reached a more open part of the forest, and, emerging from the thicket, I perceived a troop of six or eight beautiful giraffes standing looking at us about two hundred yards to my right; but this was no time to give them chase, which I felt very much inclined to do. I allowed them to depart in peace, and continued my search for water. In this open glade I found two or three vleys that had once contained a little water, but they were now hard and dry. Re-entering the dense forest, we held one point more to the east, and rode on as before. For miles we continued our search, until my hopes sank to a very low ebb; and Kleinboy swore that we should never regain the wagons. At length I perceived a sassayby walking before me this antelope drinks every day; "fresh vigor with the hope returned." I once more pressed forward and cantered along, heedless of the distance which already intervened between me and my camp and the remonstrances of my attendant, who at last reined up his jaded steed, and said that he would not follow me further to my own destruction. I then pointed to the top of a distant gray tree that stretched its bare and weather beaten branches above the heads of its surrounding comrades, and said that, if we saw nothing to give us hope when we reached that tree, I would abandon the search, and hunt during that season in Sichely's mountains to the east of Booby.

Four signal-shots brought Kleinboy and the packhorse, and also Isaac with the four guides. The chase was all in thick forest, and had led me to within a few hundred yards of the wagons. The hungry guides seemed enchanted at the prospect of such a banquet. They at once kindled a fire, and slept that night beside the carcass. I returned to the wagons with my horses laden with flesh. My mind was now once more at rest. I went to my bed and slept soundly. During the night lions roared around us.

On the 19th I rose at dawn of day, and took a stroll through the forest. Here I found some old dung of elephants, and observed several full-grown trees torn up by the roots, and others that had been shivered by the gigantic strength of those animals. The guides, finding that they prevailed nothing, at length volunteered to lead me to Bamangwato by a northerly course, and promised that I should not lack for water. We inspanned, and held on till sundown, proceeding in a northeasterly course, when we halted in dense forest without water. Our march lay through an interesting country well adapted for hunting the eland and giraffe. The forest was in many places thin and open, with here and there gigantic old trees of picturesque tippcarance standing detached, some half dead, and others falling to pieces from age. The soil was soft yet firm, and admirably suited for riding. The spoor of eland and giraffe was abundant.

On the 20th we inspanned at dawn of day, and, having proceeded about five miles, reached a miserable little kraal or village of Bakalahari. Here was a vley of Water, beside which we outspanned. Starvation was written in the faces of these inhabitants of the forest. In their vicinity were a few small gardens, containing water-melons and a little corn. Occasionally they have the luck to capture some large animal in a pitfall, when for a season they live in plenty. But as they do not possess salt, the flesh soon spoils, when they are compelled once more to roam the forest in quest of fruits and roots, on which, along with locusts, they in a great measure subsist. In districts where game is abundant, they often construct their pits on a large scale, and erect hedges in the form of a crescent, extending to nearly a mile on either side of the pit. By this means the game may easily be driven into the pitfalls, which are carefully covered over with thin sticks and dry grass, and thus whole herds of zebras and wildebeests are massacred at once, which capture is followed by the most disgusting banquets, the poor starving savages gorging and surfeiting in a manner worthy only of the vulture or hyena.

At mid-day we resumed our march, halting at sunset without water. The first part of this march lay through dense forest, where we were obliged to cut a pathway with our axes. Here the spoor of eland was abundant. In the evening we passed through an open tract very thinly wooded, where I saw abundance of springbok and blue wildebeest. At midnight, the dogs giving chase to some animal, I sprang out of bed, and, following them in my shirt, found them standing over a jackal. The guides skinned him, and, having baked him in the ashes, they consumed him.

On the 22nd, ordering my men to move on toward a fountain in the center of the plain, I rode forth with Ruyter, and held east through a grove of lofty and wide-spreading mimosas, most of which were more or less damaged by the gigantic strength of a troop of elephants, which had passed there about twelve months before. Having proceeded about two miles with large herds of game on every side, I observed a crusty-looking old bull borele, or black rhinoceros, cocking his ears one hundred yards in advance. He had not observed us; and soon after he walked slowly toward us, and stood broadside to, eating some wait-a-bit thorns within fifty yards of me. I fired from my saddle, and sent a bullet in behind his shoulder, upon which he rushed forward about one hundred yards in tremendous consternation, blowing like a grampus, and then stood looking about him. Presently he made off. I followed, but found it hard to come up with him. When I overtook him I saw the blood running freely from his wound.

With revived spirits, I stirred my jaded steed and made for the smoke; but, alas! this only served to lead me further astray. After riding many miles in that direction, I discovered that the fire was at an amazing distance, and could not have been kindled by my men; it was the wild Bakalahari of the desert burning the old dry grass. I was now like a seaman in a hurricane—at my wit's end—I knew not how to ride nor what to do. The sun, which had just risen when I left the wagons, was about to set. There was no landmark whatever by which to steer; I might wander for days, and not discover water.

To find the wagons was comparatively a trifle. I thought little of them; it was the thought of water that harrowed my mind. Already the pangs of thirst began to seize me. I had ridden all day, under the hot sun, and had neither eaten nor drunk since early the preceding evening. I felt faint and weary, and my heart sank as horrible visions of a lingering death by maddening thirst arose before me. Dismounting from my horse, I sat down to think what I should do. I knew exactly by my compass the course we had been steering since we left Booby. I accordingly resolved to ride southwest for many miles, the course of the wagons having been northeast, and then to send Ruyter across the country a little to the north of west, while I should hold a corresponding course in an easterly direction. By this means one of us could not fail to find the spoor, and I arranged that at nightfall we should meet at some conspicuous tree. Having thus resolved, I mounted my horse, which was half dead with thirst and fatigue, and, having ridden southwest for several miles, I and Ruyter separated at a conspicuous tree, and rode in opposite directions. Before riding far I recognized the country as being the spot where I had seen the leopards in the morning. I at once followed Ruyter, and fired several signal shots, which he fortunately heard, and soon joined me. We then rode due east, and eventually, to my inexpressible gratification, we discovered the spoor of the wagons, which we reached after following it for about four miles in a northeasterly direction.

Our poor horses were completely exhausted, and could barely walk to the camp. I found my wagons drawn up beside the strong fountain of Lepeby, which, issuing from beneath a stratum of white tufous rock, formed an extensive deep pool of pure water, adorned on one side with lofty green reeds. This fountain was situated at the northern extremity of a level bare vley, surrounded by dense covers of the wait-a-bit thorns. Such a peculiar sameness characterized the country, that a person wandering only a few hundred yards from the fountain would have considerable difficulty in regaining it. It was night when I reached the wagons, and two or three cups of coffee soon restored me to my wonted vigor

On the following morning, from earliest dawn until we trekked, which we did about 10 A.M., large herds of game kept pouring in to drink from every side, completely covering the open space, and imparting to it the appearance of a cattle-fair; blue wildebeests, zebras, sassaybies, pallahs, springboks, &c., capered fearlessly up to the water, troop after troop, within two hundred yards of us. In former years a tribe of Bechuanas had frequented this fountain, and I beheld the skeletons of many rhinoceroses and of one elephant bleaching in the sun; but the powerful and cruel Matabili had attacked the tribe, and driven them to seek a home elsewhere. I shot a pallah and a wildebeest, which we secured behind the wagons. About 10 A.M. we inspanned, and within a mile of Lepeby we passed through another similar open vley, containing a strong fountain of delicious water. We continued our march till sundown through an undulating open country, thinly covered with detached trees and thorny bushes, and encamped in a sandy desert without water.

CHAPTER XIV

On the 25th, at dawn of day, we inspanned, and trekked about five hours in a northeasterly course, through a boundless open country sparingly adorned with dwarfish old trees. In the distance the long-sought mountains of Bamangwato at length loomed blue before me. We halted beside a glorious fountain, which at once made me forget all the cares and difficulties I had encountered in reaching it. The name of this fountain was Massouey, but I at once christened it "the Elephant's own Fountain." This Mas a very remarkable spot on the southern borders of endless elephant forests, at which I had at length arrived. The fountain was deep and strong, situated in a hollow at the eastern extremity of an extensive vley, and its margin was surrounded by a level stratum of solid old red sandstone. Here and there lay a thick layer of soil upon the rock, and this was packed flat with the fresh spoor of elephants. Around the water's edge the very rock was worn down by the gigantic feet which for ages had trodden there.

The soil of the surrounding country was white and yellow sand, but grass, trees, and bushes were abundant. From the borders of the fountain a hundred well trodden elephant foot-paths led away in every direction, like the radii of a circle. The breadth of these paths was about three feet; those leading to the northward and east were the most frequented, the country in those directions being well wooded. We drew up the wagons on a hillock on the eastern side of the water. This position commanded a good view of any game that might approach to drink. I had just cooked my breakfast, and commenced to feed, when I heard my men exclaim, "Almagtig keek de ghroote clomp cameel;" and, raising my eyes from my sassayby stew, I beheld a truly beautiful and very unusual scene. From the margin of the fountain there extended an open level vley, without a tree or bush, that stretched away about a mile to the northward, where it was bounded by extensive groves of wide-spreading mimosas. Up the middle of this vley stalked a troop of ten colossal giraffes, flanked by two large herds of blue wildebeests and zebras, with an advanced guard of pallahs. Here he became obstreperous; so, loading one barrel, and pointing my rifle toward the clouds, I shot him in the throat, when, rearing high, he fell backward and expired. This was a magnificent specimen of the giraffe, measuring upward of eighteen feet in height. I stood for nearly half an hour engrossed in the contemplation of his extreme beauty and gigantic proportions; and, if there had been no elephants, I could have exclaimed, like Duke Alexander of Gordon when he killed the famous old stag with seventeen tine, "Now I can die happy." But I longed for an encounter with the noble elephants, and I thought little more of the giraffe than if I had killed a gemsbok or an eland.

In the afternoon I removed my wagons to a correct distance from the fountain, and drew them up among some bushes about four hundred yards to leeward of the water. In the evening I was employed in manufacturing hardened bullets for the elephants, using a composition of one of pewter to four of lead; and I had just completed my work, when we heard a troop of elephants splashing and trumpeting in the water. This was to me a joyful sound; I slept little that night.

On the 26th I arose at earliest dawn, and, having fed four of my horses, proceeded with Isaac to the fountain to examine the spoor of the elephants which had drunk there during the night. A number of the paths contained fresh spoor of elephants of all sizes, which had gone from the fountain in different directions. We reckoned that at least thirty of these gigantic quadrupeds had visited the water during the night.

We hastily returned to camp, where, having breakfasted, I saddled up, and proceeded to take up the spoor of the largest bull elephant, accompanied by after riders and three of the guides to assist in sporing. I was also accompanied by my dogs. Having selected the spoor of a mighty bull, the Bechuanas went ahead, and I followed them. It was extremely interesting and exciting work. The foot-print of this elephant was about two feet in diameter, and was beautifully visible in the soft sand. The spoor at first led us for about three miles in an easterly direction, along one of the sandy foot-paths, without a check. We then entered a very thick forest, and the elephant had gone a little out of the path to smash some trees, and to plow up the earth with his tusks. He soon, however, again took the path, and held along it for several miles.

Having reached the wagons, while drinking my coffee I reviewed the whole day's work, and felt much regret at my want of luck in my first day's elephant hunting, and I resolved that night to watch the water, and try what could be done with elephants by night shooting. I accordingly ordered the usual watching hole to be constructed, and, having placed my bedding in it, repaired thither shortly after sundown. I had lain about two hours in the hole, when I heard a low rumbling noise like distant thunder, caused (as the Bechuanas affirmed) by the bowels of the elephants which were approaching the fountain. I lay or my back, with my mouth open, attentively listening, and could hear them plowing up the earth with their tusks. Presently they walked up to the water, and commenced drinking within fifty yards of me. They approached with so quiet a step that I fancied it was the footsteps of jackals which I heard, and I was not aware of their presence until I heard the water, which they had drawn up in their trucks and were pouring into their mouths, dropping into the fountain. I then peeped from my sconce with a beating heart, and beheld two enormous bull elephants, which looked like two great castles, standing before me. I could not see very distinctly, for there was only starlight. Having lain on my breast sometime taking my aim, I let fly at one of the elephants, using the Dutch rifle carrying six to the pound. The ball told loudly on his shoulder, and, uttering a loud cry, he stumbled through the fountain, when both made off in different directions.

All night large herds of zebras and blue wildebeests capered around me, coming sometimes within a few yards. Several parties of rhinoceroses also made their appearance. I felt a little apprehensive that lions might visit the fountain, and every time that hyenas or jackals lapped the water I looked forth, but no lions appeared. At length I fell into a sound sleep, nor did I again raise my head until the bright star of morn had shot far above the eastern horizon.

The elephant entertains an extraordinary horror of man, and a child can put a hundred of them to flight by passing at a quarter of a mile to windward; and when thus disturbed, they go a long way before they halt. It is surprising how soon these sagacious animals are aware of the presence of a hunter in their domains. When one troop has been attacked, all the other elephants frequenting the district are aware of the fact within two or three days, when they all forsake it, and migrate to distant parts, leaving the hunter no alternative but to inspan his wagons, and remove to fresh ground. This constitutes one of the greatest difficulties which a skillful elephant-hunter encounters. Even in the most remote parts, which may be reckoned the head-quarters of the elephant, it is only occasionally, and with inconceivable toil and hardship, that the eye of the hunter is cheered by the sight of one. Owing to habits peculiar to himself, the elephant is more inaccessible, and much more rarely seen, than any other game quadruped, excepting certain rare antelopes. They choose for their resort the most lonely and secluded depths of the forest, generally at a very great distance from the rivers and fountains at which they drink. In dry and warm weather they visit these waters nightly, but in cool and cloudy weather they Irink only once every third or fourth day. About sundown the elephant leaves his distant mid-day haunt, and commences his march toward the fountain, which is probably from twelve to twenty miles distant. This he generally reaches between the hours of nine and midnight, when, having slaked his thirst and cooled his body by spouting large volumes of water over his back with his trunk, ho resumes the path to his forest solitudes. I have repeatedly ridden through, forests where the trees thus broken lay so thick across one another that it was almost impossible to ride through the district, and it is in situations such as these that attacking the elephant is attended with most danger. During the night they will feed in open plains and thinly-wooded districts, but as day dawns they retire to the densest covers within reach, which nine times in ten are composed of the impracticable wait-a-bit thorns, and here they remain drawn up in a compact herd during the heat of the day. In remote districts, however, and in cool weather, I have known herds to continue pasturing throughout the whole day.

The appearance of the wild elephant is insensibly majestic and imposing. His gigantic height and colossal bulk, so greatly surpassing all other quadrupeds. combined with his sagacious disposition and peculiar habits, impart to him an interest in the eyes of the hunter which no other animal can call forth. The pace of the elephant, when undisturbed, is a bold, free, sweeping step; and from the peculiar spongy formation of his foot, his tread is extremely light and inaudible, and all his movements are attended with a peculiar gentleness and grace. This, however, only applies to the elephant when roaming undisturbed in his jungle; for, when roused by the hunter, he proves the most dangerous enemy, and far more difficult to conquer than any other beast of the chase.

On the 27th, as day dawned, I left my shooting, hole, and proceeded to inspect the spoor of my wounded, elephant. After following it for some distance I came to an abrupt hillock, and fancying that from the summit a good view might be obtained of the surrounding country, I left my followers to seek the spoor while I ascended. I did not raise my eyes from the ground until I had reached the highest pinnacle of rock. I then looked east, and, to my inexpressible gratification, beheld a troop of nine or ten elephants quietly browsing within a quarter of a mile of me. I allowed myself only one glance at them, and then rushed down to warn my followers to be silent. A council of war was hastily held, the result of which was my ordering Isaac to ride hard to camp, with instructions to return as quickly as possible, accompanied by Kleinboy, and to bring me my dogs, the large Dutch rifle, and a fresh horse. I once more ascended the hillock to feast my eyes upon the enchanting sight before me, and, drawing out my spy-glass, narrowly watched the motions of the elephants. The herd consisted entirely of females, several of which were followed by small calves.

Presently, on reconnoitering the surrounding country, I discovered a second herd, consisting of five bull elephants, which were quietly feeding about a mile to the northward. The cows were feeding toward a rocky ridge that stretched away from the base of the hillock on which I stood. Burning with impatience to commence the attack, I resolved to try the stalking system with these, and to hunt the troop of bulls with dogs and horses. Having thus decided, I directed the guides to watch the elephants from the summit of the hillock, and with a beating heart I approached them. The ground and wind favoring me, I soon gained the rocky ridge toward which they were feeding. They were now within one hundred yards, and I resolved to enjoy the pleasure of watching their movements for a little before I fired. They continued to feed slowly toward me, breaking the branches from the trees with their trunks, and eating the leaves and tender shoots. I soon selected the finest in the herd, and kept my eye on her in particular. At length two of the troop had walked slowly past at about sixty yards, and the one which I had selected was feeding with two others, on a thorny tree before me.

My hand was now as steady as the rock on which it rested; so, taking a deliberate aim, I let fly at her head a little behind the eye. She get it hard and sharp, just where I aimed, but it did not seem to affect her much. Uttering a loud cry, she wheeled about, when I gave her the second ball close behind the shoulder. All the elephants uttered a strange rumbling noise, and made off in a line to the northward at a brisk am bring pace, their huge, fan-like ears flapping in the ratio of their speed. I did not wait to load, but ran back to the hillock to obtain a view. On gaining its summit, the guides pointed out the elephants; they were standing in a grove of shady trees, but the wounded one was some distance behind with another elephant, doubtless its particular friend, who was endeavoring to assist it. These elephants had probably never before heard the report of a gun, and, having neither seen nor smelt me, they were unaware of the presence of man, and did not seem inclined to go any further. Presently my men hove in sight, bringing the dogs; and when these came up, I waited some time before commencing the attack, that the dogs and horses might recover their wind. We then rode slowly toward the elephants, and had advanced within two hundred yards of them when, the ground being open, they observed us, and made off in an easterly direction; but the wounded one immediately dropped astern, and the next moment was surrounded by the dogs, which, barking angrily, seemed to engross her attention.

The friend now seemed resolved to do some mischief, and charged me furiously, pursuing me to a distance of several hundred yards. I therefore deemed it proper to give her a gentle hint to act less officiously, and, accordingly, having loaded, I approached within thirty yards, and gave it her sharp, right and left, behind the shoulder, upon which she at once made off with drooping trunk, evidently with a mortal wound. I never recur to this my first day's elephant shooting without regretting my folly in contenting myself with securing only one elephant. The first was now dying, and could not leave the ground, and the second was also mortally wounded, and I had only to follow and finish her; but I foolishly allowed her to escape, while I amused myself with the first, which kept walking backward, and standing by every tree she passed. Two more shots finished her on receiving them, she tossed her trunk up and down two or three times, and, falling on her broadside against a thorny tree, which yielded like grass before her enormous weight, she uttered a deep hoarse cry and expired. This was a very handsome old cow elephant, and was decidedly the best in the troop. She was in excellent condition, and carried a pair of long and perfect tusks. I was in high spirits at my success, and felt so perfectly satisfied with having killed one, that, although it was still early in the day, and my horses were fresh, I allowed the troop of five bulls to remain unmolested, foolishly trusting to fall in with them next day. How little did I then know of the habits of elephants, or the rules to be adopted in hunting them, or deem it probable I should never see them more!

Having knee-haltered our horses, we set to work with our knives and assagais to prepare the skull for the hatchet, in order to cut out the tusks, nearly half the length of which, I may mention, is imbedded in bone sockets in the fore part of the skull. To cut out the tusks of a cow elephant requires barely one fifth of the labor requisite to cut out those of a bull; and when the sun went down, we had managed by our combined efforts to cut out one of the tusks of my first elephant, with which we triumphantly returned to camp, having left the guides in charge of the carcass, where they volunteered to take up their quarters for the night. On reaching my wagons I found Johannus and Carollus in a happy state of indifference to all passing events they were both very drunk, having broken into my wine-cask and spirit-case.

We were now within two days' march of the kraal of the great chief Sicoray, king of the extensive territory of Bamangwato. This chief was reported to be in the possession of large quantities of ivory; and as I had brought a number of muskets and other articles for barter, I was anxious to push on and first get over my trading before resuming elephant hunting, more especially since it was not improbable that, having once led the way, other adventurers might follow in my track, and perhaps spoil my market. Taking this into consideration, I deemed it proper, on the morning of the 30th, to march upon the kraal of Sicomy; and, accordingly, about 10 A.M. we inspanned, and held for the Bamangwato mountains, whose summits we could see peering above the intervening forest in an easterly direction. On our march we passed near to the carcass of the elephant which I had slain three days before. The number of vultures which were here congregated was truly wonderful. My guides had baked a part of the trunk and two of the feet of the elephant, and these they now brought to the wagons.

Here we were joined by three of Sicomy's men, who informed us that they were in daily apprehension of an attack from the Matabili, who they heard were marching against them. In consequence of this, Sicomy and all his tribe had forsaken their kraals, and were now living in wild caves and other secluded retreats in the sides and on the summits of these rocky mountains. They led us round the base of a bold projecting rock, and then up a wild and well-wooded rocky ravine, bearing no traces of men. On raising our eyes, however, we perceived the summits of the rocks covered with women and children, and very soon detached parties of Sicomy's warriors came pouring in from different directions, to gaze upon the white man, I being the first that many of them had seen. These men were all armed and ready for action, each bearing an oval shield of ox, buffalo, or camelopard's hide, a battle-ax, and three or four assagais. They wore karosses of jackal's and leopard's skins, which depended gracefully from their shoulders; and many of them sported a round tuft of black ostrich feathers on their heads, while others had adorned their woolly hair with one or two wavy plumes of white ones. Both men and women wore abundance of the usual ornaments of beads and brass and copper wire.

We were presently met by a messenger from Sicomy, saying that the king was happy we had arrived, and that he would shortly come to see me. We proceeded up the bold and narrow ravine of Lesausau as far as it was practicable, the water being situated at its upper extremity. Soon after we had encamped Sicomy drew nigh, accompanied by a large of his principal men and warriors. He appeared to me to be about thirty years of age, and was of middle stature. His distinguishing feature is a wall-eye, which imparts to his countenance a roguish look that does not belie the cunning and deceitful character of the man. As he came up to the wagons I met and shook hands with him, and invited him to partake of coffee with me. I could see that he was enchanted at my arrival. He talked at a very rapid pace, and assumed an abrupt and rather dictatorial manner, occasionally turning round and cracking jokes with his counselors and nobility. He was very anxious to ascertain from Isaac the contents of the wagons, and said that he would buy everything I had brought, and that he would give me a large bull elephant's tusk for each of my muskets.

At an early hour on the following morning the king made his appearance, attended by a number of his warriors, all carrying their battle gear. I was still in bed, and, seeing the king peeping into my wagon, I pretended to be asleep. Presently I observed a savage coming up the glen bearing on his shoulders a bull 'elephant's tooth, which he laid under the wagon. Coffee was now announced, so I arose, and the king breakfasted with me. I had resolved to say as little as possible about the trading, and to appear Very indifferent, a system indispensable in trading with the natives, which at all times progresses slowly, but much more so if the trader allows them to imagine that he is very anxious to obtain possession of their goods.

While Sicomy was taking his coffee, he told me that he had dispatched men to bring elephants' teeth, which he said were at a distance, and that ho would purchase everything as quickly as possible, that I might be enabled to leave the country before the Matabili should come. This rumor about the Matabili I at the time suspected to be a fabrication, but I subsequently ascertained that it was a fact.

In the forenoon I occupied myself in writing my journal in my wagon, and I could see that the king was annoyed at ray indifference about the trading. At length he asked me to come out of the wagon, saying that he had got a present for me, and he brought forward the elephant's tusk which lay beneath the wagon. Having thanked him, I expressed myself satisfied with his present, and, in return, immediately presented him with what he reckoned an equivalent in beads. He asked me the price of my muskets, and I answered four large bull's teeth for each. He then retired to an adjacent grove of shady trees, where he sat consulting with his men for hours. Two men at length appeared, coming from opposite directions, each bearing a bull's tooth. When these arrived, Sicomy ordered them to be placed before me, and, calling Isaac, he inflicted on me a long harangue, talking all manner of nonsense, and endeavoring to obtain a musket for these two teeth. At length a third tusk was brought, but it was a small one. It was now late in the afternoon, so I told the king that I was going to take a walk in the mountains to obtain a view of his country. He said that he was going to buy one of the muskets immediately, and requested that I would not leave the wagons. After sitting talking with his men till it was near sunset, he once more offered me two tusks for a gun. I replied that I had already spoken. He then said he was going home, and that he did not know if he would come again to trade with me. If the king had indeed resolved not to trade with me, no request on my part would have altered the case. So I replied that I had never asked him to purchase any thing, and was perfectly indifferent whether he did or not; that there were other thief who were anxious to purchase my goods, and that my reason for visiting his territory was to enjoy the sport of elephant hunting. Having thus spoken, I wished him good evening, and, shouldering my rifle, stalked up the rocky ravine and shot two baboons.

Although I voted the trading an intense bore, it was nevertheless well worth a little time and inconvenience, on account of the enormous profit I should realize. The price I had paid for the muskets was 16 for each case containing twenty muskets, and the value of the ivory I required for each musket was upward of £30, being about 3000 percent., which I am informed is reckoned among mercantile men to be a very fair profit. Sicomy was in those days in the possession of very large quantities of splendid ivory, and still considerable quantities pass annually through his hands. Since I first visited Bamangwato, and taught the natives the use of firearms, they have learned to kill the elephant themselves; but previous to my arrival they were utterly incapable of subduing a full-grown elephant, even by the united exertions of the whole tribe. All the ivory which Sicomy then possessed, and the majority of that which still passes through his hands, is obtained from elephants slain with assagais by an active and daring race of Bushmen inhabiting very remote regions to the northward and northwest of Bamangwato.

The manner in which Sicomy obtained this ivory was by sending a party of his warriors to the Bushman, who first obtained the tusks in barter for a few beads, and then compelled some of the poor Bakalahari, or wild natives of the desert, over whom Sicomy conceives that he has a perfect right to tyrannize, to bear them on their shoulders across extensive deserts of burning sand to his headquarters at Bamangwato. So great was the fatigue endured by the poor Bakalahari on these occasions, that many of them died of exhaustion before reaching Bamangwato. At an early hour on the 4th, Sicomy not appearing, I proceeded to visit him at his mountain residence, accompanied by Isaac and a party of his own men. We wound along the base of the mountains for the distance of half a mile, and then commenced ascending the almost perpendicular and rugged mountain side, consisting of immense masses of rock heaped together in dire confusion. Having gained the summit, which was of a tabular character, we advanced a short distance through a succession of heaps of disjointed masses of rock, and presently we reached the chief's temporary retreat, which consisted of a small circular hut, composed of a framework of boughs of trees, interlined with twigs and covered with grass. A number of similar huts were erected around the royal dwelling, on areas which his men had cleared among the rocks. This, however, was the abode of only a very small part of his tribe, which was extensively scattered over different parts of the mountain range, and occupied sundry distant cattle outposts.

I also effected several exchanges of beads and ammunition for the tusks of cow elephants. I had resolved to purchase fine specimens of the native costume and arms, &c.; but ivory being the most important article, it was best to defer all minor transactions until our trade in it was concluded. The king seemed highly delighted with his purchases, and insisted on discharging each of the muskets as he bought it. It was amusing to see the manner in which he performed this operation. Throwing back his kaross, and applying the stock to his naked shoulder, he shut his good eye, and kept the wall-eye open, to the intense amusement of the Hottentots, who were his instructors on the occasion. Each report caused the utmost excitement and merriment among the warriors, who pressed forward, and requested that they also might be permitted to try their skill with these novel implements of war.

The king had in his possession a most wonderful knob-kerry, which I was determined to obtain. It was made of the horn of the kobaoba, a very rare species of the rhinoceros, and its chief interest consisted in its extraordinary length, which greatly exceeded anything I had ever seen of the kind before, or have since met with. Handing Sicomy my snuff-box, I pointed to the kerry, and asked him where the kobaoba had been killed. He replied that that kerry had been sent him by a chief who resided at an amazing distance on the borders of the Lake of Boats. I then asked him to present it to me, that I might have something to keep in remembrance of him; but he replied that it belonged to his wife, and he could not part with it. Presently, however, while sipping his coffee, he said that if I chose I might purchase it. I asked him what he required for it, and he answered, the cup which he then held full of gunpowder.

At an early hour on the morning of the 5th, I commenced to trade with Sicomy's men for karosses and Bechuana arms, of each of which I obtained some very fine specimens. With these, as with the ivory, there was considerable discussion before the prices could be agreed on in the first instance, after which exchanges were effected rapidly. I had, however, to pay them long prices for their "chakas" or battle-axes, on which all the Bechuana tribes place a very great value.

I had intended to penetrate beyond Bamangwato, with a wish to explore the country, and for the purpose of hunting elephants; but, owing to gross misrepresentations made to me by Isaac relative to Sicomy's wishes on the subject, and partly owing to the threatened attack from the Matabili, I resolved for the present not to extend my peregrinations beyond Bamangwato, but to occupy my time for the remainder of that season in hunting throughout the fine country between Bamangwato and Sichely's mountains. As Isaac's character, however, gradually unfolded itself to me, and as I became more intimate and conversant with the natives, I discovered that he had interpreted Sicomy's wishes to me in utterly false colors; and I afterward ascertained from the natives, whose language I very soon began to understand, that Sicomy and his people were not only willing, but anxious that I should remain and hunt elephants in their territory. In consequence of this, as the reader will shortly learn, being informed by Sicomy's men that the invasion by the Matabili was no longer apprehended, I returned to Bamangwato, and penetrated into the extensive forest to the northward and eastward of that mountain range where for several months I continued hunting elephants, accompanied by large parties of Sicomy's.

CHAPTER XV

About 11 o'clock A.M. on the 5th of July, everything being ready, I took leave of Sicomy and retraced my steps for Corriebely. It caused me much pain and anxiety to observe that my cattle were extremely hollow-looking and spiritless from want of water, not one of them having obtained a sufficiency of that essential of life since they had last drunk at Corriebely, and several appearing so distressed that I entertained considerable fears of their being able to reach that fountain. I was accompanied by a small party of Sicomy's men, who followed me in the hope of obtaining flesh. Having proceeded about a mile, I missed my greyhound "Flam," which had been doubtless stolen by Sicomy's orders, he being notorious for his predilection for that variety of dog. I therefore at once dispatched a messenger to the king, to say that I required him to find my dog; and shortly after this men overtook me, bearing a kaross which they said the king had sent to purchase one of my dogs. I replied that they had already taken the dog, but that I would not have the kaross They then departed, and I continued my march. After trekking about six miles we reached a deep gravel, hole beside a mass of red granite rock, at the bottom of which there was about a bucketful of spring water; and here was the fresh spoor of a huge bull elephant, which had scooped out large portions of the gravel with his trunk on the preceding evening, but on turning about he had entirely undone what he had accomplished by trampling it down- again into the well with his huge feet.

On inspecting the spot I fancied that by digging we might obtain a little water for the unfortunate cattle, which at this moment was an object of the utmost importance, the fountain of Corriebely being still very distant. I accordingly set to work hard with all my followers, assisted by the Bechuanas; and having removed an immense quantity of the gravel, I had the satisfaction to discover a small spring of excellent water, which issued from beneath the granite rock, and ran as fast as we could catch it in our pails. I then placed my large flesh-pot near the pit, and ordering the men to bring up the cattle in small detachments, we bailed out the water as fast as they could drink it, the buckets being handed along by a line of men extending up the gravel bank to the cattle, and thus, in a short time, every one of them obtained a sufficiency. This opportune supply of water was to me invaluable, my poor dogs having also been much distressed, and requiring water no less than the cattle.

In the afternoon we inspanned, and marched to the scene of the fall of my first elephant, where we halted for the night. On reaching Massouey I commenced examining the elephants' foot-paths on the side on which were my strongest hopes. I had almost made the circuit of the fountain, and hope had died within me, when, lo! broad and long, and fresh as fresh could be, the enormous spoor of two mighty bull elephants which had drunk there during the night. This was glorious! I had great faith in the sporing powers of the Bamangwato men, and I felt certain that at length the day had arrived on which I was to kill my first bull elephant. The Bechuanas at once took up the spoor, and went ahead in a masterly manner, and with buoyant spirits I followed in their steps. The spoor led about due west, a direction in which I had not yet been. Having followed it for many miles through this desert country, we reached a district where the bushes, to whose berries Knop-kop was so partial, grew in great abundance; and here the elephants had commenced to feed upon their roots, plowing up the sand extensively with their tusks.

On the morning of the 8th I walked to the fountain and examined all the elephants' foot-paths, but there was no fresh spoor. Having breakfasted, I rode for a conical hill, distant from the wagons about five miles in a northerly direction, from whose summit I fancied that elephants might be seen. It was a charming cool day, with a fine bracing wind, the sky beautifully overcast with clouds. I rode along, holding the elephants' foot-paths. The marks of their strength were visible in every grove, and all the large trees in the vicinity of the muddy vleys, which at this season were dry, were plastered with sun baked mud to a height of twelve feet from the ground. On reaching the base of the conical hill I secure my horse to a tree, and ascended to its summit, from which I carefully examined the distant forest landscape with my spy-glass, but sought in vain for elephants.

In the evening I took my heavy single-barreled rifle and sauntered toward the fountain A. large herd of blue wildebeests were slowly advancing up the vley to drink. I accordingly took up a position behind a low bush near which they must pass, and lay flat on the ground, waiting their approach. Presently I raised my head to see how they were coming on, when I perceived a pair of the rare and beautiful roan antelope or bastard gemsbok warily approaching the fountain. These came up, and were passing within a hundred and twenty yards of me, when selecting the buck, I let fly, and missed. The whole herd of wildebeests now wheeled to the right-about, and thundered down the vley, enveloped in a cloud of dust; but the two roan antelopes, which had probably never before heard the report of a gun, stood looking about them, while I hastily loaded, lying flat on my side. This being accomplished, I again let fly, and the old buck dropped to the shot; the ball had entered his shoulder, and he lay kicking and roaring until I had almost reloaded, when he regained his feet and made off after his comrade. At this moment "Aigyll" and "Bonteberg," two right good dogs, came up, having heard the shots, and, perceiving the bastard gemboks, they gave chase. To my surprise, the wounded buck, instead of turning to bay, now set off at a rapid pace.

On reaching camp I inquired of the men if they had seen the buck, and they answered Yes, but that he was not wounded. This I fancied must be the case, and that the dogs had followed the fresh buck; and as two of them made their appearance, I thought that the affair was at an end. In the meantime, however, Kleinboy had seen the chase, and, hastily bridling a horse, had followed. He now rode breathless to the wagons, and reported that the buck was at bay beyond a low ridge within half a mile of camp, and that he was killing the dogs right and left. Seizing my rifle, I mounted a horse and followed after Kleinboy in the dark. Presently I heard the music of my pack, and on coming up I found the bastard gemsbok lying beside a bush, with the dogs barking round him. Three dogs that had followed me from camp, on seeing the buck lying, rushed in upon him, when he struck furiously right and left, and killed one dead on the spot, severely wounding the other behind the shoulder; these were Vitfoot and Argyll, two of my best dogs. Again he struck right and left, and knocked over Wolf and Flam with amazing violence, severely injuring their stomachs. He had killed Bles, my stoutest and fiercest dog, before I came up, the horn having entered his heart. It was a long time before I could fire, for the night was dark, and the buck lay on the ground, with the surviving dogs fill pressing close around him.

After remaining in the neighborhood of the fountain for several days, and finding that it was entirely deserted by the elephants, I determined to retrace my steps and seek for them beyond Bamangwato, and on the 18th we again came to the camp of Sicomy upon the Rocky Mountains. I found the king in a kraal which I had not hitherto visited. He was seated beneath a low shady tree, with a few friends and some of his wives. A number of splendid koodoos' skulls and horns lay rotting about the kraal, among which were several pairs exceeding any I had yet beheld. Casting my eyes to the southeast, I obtained a very distant view of the country in that direction. From the base of the mountain on which I stood stretched a dead-level park through a bold opening in the mountains. This park was regularly ornamented with groves and forest-trees, and extended without the slightest break or change as far as I could see. The scene exactly resembled the ocean when viewed from the summit of some bold mountain standing near its shore. Having partaken of the king's beer, I descended to my wagons, when we continued our march along the aforesaid valley.

We held a northerly course, and on the second day we reached Letlochee, a strong perpetual fountain, situated in an abrupt and rocky ravine. This ravine lay in a range of low rocky hills, which were bounded on the north and west by a wide and gently-sloping basin or hollow, diversified with extensive groves and open glades. This hollow extended to a breadth of from six to eight miles, and was much frequented by elands and giraffes, and beyond it stretched the boundless extent of the sandy Kalahari desert. Here I daily enjoyed excellent sport with these two varieties of game; but, though elephants occasionally visited the water, and we followed on their tracks to an amazing distance, we always failed to obtain a view of them.

On the forenoon of the 23rd a native came and informed me that he had discovered a white rhinoceros lying asleep in thick cover to the south. I accordingly accompanied him to the spot, and commenced stalking in upon the vast muchocho. He was lying asleep beneath a shady tree, and his appearance reminded me of an enormous hog, which in shape he slightly resembles. He kept constantly flapping his ears, which they invariably do when sleeping. Before I could reach the proper distance to fire, several "rhinoceros birds," by which he was attended, warned him of his impending danger by sticking their bills into his ear, and uttering their harsh, grating cry. Thus aroused, he suddenly sprang to his feet and crashed away through the jungle at a rapid trot, and I saw no more of him.

In the evening one of the parties sent out to seek for the spoor of elephants returned to camp, stating that a small tribe of Baivalahari, who resided in a range of mountains to the east, reported these beasts to frequent the forests in the vicinity of their abode, and Mutchuisuo, Sicomy's uncle, who attended me while hunting his country, accordingly requested me to hold myself in readiness to accompany him in quest of the elephants at an early hour next day. It was customary with me to console myself, when hope had almost died under a long-continued run of bad luck, by saying to myself that "Patience will have her perfect work;" thus making up my mind that a man who is a good stalker and a fair rifle-shot must eventually obtain by perseverance whatever game he seeks to kill. But in the present instance things looked so bad that I had begun to think it not improbable that I might be compelled to leave the Bamangwato country without again even seeing what my heart so ardently desired, viz., an old bull elephant free in his native forests, and day and night I mourned my folly in losing the opportunity which I had neglected on the 27th day of June.

But Patience will have her perfect work, and the day had at last arrived which was to repay my steady perseverance with complete success. At an early hour on the 24th, upon the strength of the report brought to us on the preceding evening, I took the field with Isaac and

Kleinboy as after-riders, accompanied by Mutchuisho and a hundred and fifty of his tribe. We held a northeasterly course, and, having proceeded about five miles through the forest, reached a fountain, where I observed the spoor of a herd of cow elephants, two days old. Here we made a short halt, and snuff was briskly circulated, while the leading men debated on the course we were to follow, and it was agreed that we should hold for the Bakalahari kraal. Having continued our course for several miles, we rounded the northern extremity of a range of rocky mountains which rose abruptly in the forest and stretched away to the south of east in a long-continued chain. Here we were met by men whom Mutchuisho had dispatched before daybreak, who said that, the Bakalahari women had that morning seen elephants. This was joyous news. My hopes were high, and I at once felt certain that the hour of triumph was at hand. But disappointment was still in store for me. We all sat down on the grass, while men were dispatched to bring the Bakalahari, and when these came we ascertained that it was only spoor and not elephants they had seen. We held on for an inspection of it; and here I was further to be disappointed, the spoor proving to be two days old.

The country now before me was a vast level forest, extending to the north and east for about twenty miles without a break. At that distance, however, the landscape was shut in by blue mountain ranges of considerable height, and two bold conical mountains standing close together rose conspicuous above the rest. These mountains the Bamangwato men informed me were their ancient habitation, and that of their forefathers, but the cruel Matabili had driven them from thence to the rocky mountains which they now occupy. We continued our course in an easterly direction, and twice crossed the gravelly bed of a periodical river, in which were several small springs of excellent water. These springs had been exposed by elephants, which had cleared away the gravel with their trunks. Around these springs the spoor of rhinoceros was abundant. After proceeding several miles through a dry and barren tract, where wait-a-bit thorns prevailed, we entered upon more interesting ground. The forest was adorned with very picturesque old trees of various sorts and sizes, which stood singly and in shady groups, while the main body of the forest consisted of a variety of trees of other sorts, averaging the height of a giraffe.

All this was extremely interesting and gratifying; but I had been so often disappointed, and it was now so very near sunset, that I entertained but faint hopes of finding them that evening. Mutchuisho was very anxious that I should see the elephants; he had divested himself of his kaross, and, carrying one of the muskets which Sicomy had bought from me, he led the spooring party, consisting of about fifteen cunning old hands The great body of the men he had ordered to sit down and remain quiet until the attack commenced Having followed the spoor for a short distance, old Mutchuisho became extremely excited, and told me that you were close to the elephants. A few minutes after several of the spoorers affirmed that they had heard the elephants break a tree in advance; they differed, however, about the direction, some saying it was in front, and others that it was away to our left. Two or three men quickly ascended the tallest trees that stood near us, but they could not see the elephants. Mutchuisho then extended men to the right and left, while we continued on the spoor.

In a few minutes one of those who had gone off to our left came running breathless to say that he had seen the mighty game. I halted for a minute and instructed Isaac, who carried the big Dutch rifle, to act independently of me, while Kleinboy was to assist me in the chase; but, as usual, when the row began, my followers thought only of number one. I bared my arms to the shoulder, and, having imbibed a draught of aqua pure from the calabash of one of the spoorers, I grasped my trusty two-grooved rifle, and told my guide to go ahead. We proceeded silently as might be for a few hundred yards, following the guide, when he suddenly pointed, exclaiming, "Klow I" and before us stood a herd of mighty bull elephants, packed together beneath a shady grove about a hundred and fifty yards in advance. I rode slowly toward them, and, as soon as they observed me, they made a loud rumbling noise, and, tossing their trunks, wheeled right about and made off in one direction, crashing through the forest and leaving a cloud of dust behind them. I was accompanied by a detachment of my dogs, who assisted me in the pursuit.

When he pulled up in his charge, I likewise halted; and as he slowly turned to retreat, I let fly at his shoulder, "Sunday" capering and prancing, and giving me much trouble. On receiving the ball the elephant shrugged his shoulder, and made off at a free majestic walk. This shot brought several of the dogs to my assistance which had been following the other elephants, and on their coming up and barking another headlong charge was the result, accompanied by the never-failing trumpet as before. In his charge he passed close to me, when I saluted him with a second bullet in the shoulder, of which he did not take the slightest notice, I now determined not to fire again until I could make a steady shut; but, although the elephant turned repeatedly, "Sunday" invariably disappointed me, capering so that it was impossible to lire. At length, exasperated, I became reckless of the danger, and, springing from the saddle, approached the elephant under cover of a tree, and gave him a bullet in the side of the head, when, trumpeting so shrilly that the forest trembled, he charged among the dogs, from whom he seemed to fancy that the blow had come; after which he took up a position in a grove of thorns, with his head toward me. I walked up very near, and, as he was in the act of charging (being in those days under wrong impressions as to the impracticability of bringing down an elephant with a shot in the forehead), stood coolly in his path until he was within fifteen paces of me, and let drive at the hollow of his forehead, in the vain expectation that by so doing I should end his career. The shot only served to increase his fury—an effect which, I had remarked, shots in the head invariably produced; and, continuing his charge with incredible quickness and impetuosity, he all but terminated my elephant-hunting forever.

The sun had now sunk behind the tops of the trees it would very soon be dark, and the elephant did not seem much distressed, notwithstanding all he had received. I recollected that my time was short, and therefore at once resolved to fire no more from the saddle, but to go close up to him and fire on foot. Riding up to him, I dismounted and, approaching very near, I gave it him right and left in the side of the head, upon which he made a long and determined charge after me; but I was now very reckless of his charges, for I saw that he could not overtake me, and in a twinkling I was loaded, and, again approaching, fired sharp right and left behind his shoulder. Again he charged with a terrific trumpet, which sent "Sunday" flying through the forest. This was his last charge. The wounds which he had received began to tell on his constitution, and he now stood at bay beside a thorny tree, with the dogs barking around him. These, refreshed by the evening breeze, and perceiving that it was nearly over with the elephant, had once more come to my assistance. Having loaded, I drew near and fired right and left at his forehead. On receiving these shots, instead of charging, he tossed his trunk up and down, and by various sounds and motions, most gratifying to the hungry natives, evinced that his demise was near. Again I loaded, and fired my last shot behind his shoulder on receiving it, he turned round the bushy tree beside which he stood, and I ran round to give him the other barrel, but the mighty old monarch of the forest needed no more; before I could clear the bushy tree he fell heavily on his side, and his spirit had fled. My feelings at this moment can only be understood by a few brother Nimrods who have had the good fortune to enjoy a similar encounter. I never felt so gratified on any former occasion as I did then.

By this time all the natives had come up; they were in the highest spirits, and flocked around the elephant, laughing and talking at a rapid pace. I climbed on to him, and sat enthroned upon his side, which was as high as my eyes when standing on the ground. In a few minutes night set in, when the natives, having illuminated the jungle with a score of fires, and formed a semicircle of bushes to windward, lay down to rest without partaking of a morsel of food. Mutchuisho would not allow a man to put an assagai into the elephant until the morrow, and placed two relays of sentries keep watch on either side of him. My dinner consisted of a piece of flesh from the temple of the elephant, which I broiled on the hot embers. In the conflict I had lost my shirt, which was reduced to streamers by the wait-a-bit thorns, and all the clothing that remained was a pair of buckle skin knee-breeches.

The night was very cold, it being now the dead of the African winter. Having collected dry grass, I spread it beside my fire, and lay down for the night with no other covering than an old sheep-skin which I had used for a saddle-cloth. Shortly after T had dropped asleep. Mutchuisho, commiserating my bare condition, spread an old jackal kaross over me. This kaross, as all Beehuana garments are, was thickly tenanted by small transparent insects, usually denominated lice. These virulent creatures, probably finding my skin more tender than that of the owner of the kaross, seemed resolved to enjoy a banquet while they could; and presently I awolce with my whole body so poisoned and inflamed that I felt as if attacked with a severe fever. All further rest that night was at an end. I returned the kaross to Mutchuisho, with grateful acknowledgments for his polite intentions; and piling dry wood on the fire, which emitted a light as bright as day, I aroused the slumbering Kleinboy to assist me in turning my buckskins outside in, when an animating "chasse" commenced, which terminated in the capture of about fourscore of my white-currant colored visitors. I then lit another fire opposite to the first, and spent the remainder of the night squatted between the two, thus imbibing caloric before and behind.

The manner in which the elephant is cut up is as follows: The rough outer skin is first removed, in large sheets, from the side which lies uppermost. Several coats of an under skin are then met with. This skin is of a tough and pliant nature, and is used by the natives for making water-bags, in which they convey supplies of water from, the nearest vley or fountain (which is often ten miles distant) to the elephant. They remove this inner skin with caution, taking care not to cut it with the assagai and it is formed into water bags by gathering the corners and edges, and transfixing the whole on a pointed wand. The flesh is then removed in enormous sheets from the ribs, when the hatchets come into play, with which they chop through, and remove individually, each colossal rib. The bowels are thus laid bare; and in the removal of these the leading men take a lively interest and active part, for it is throughout and around the bowels that the fat of the elephant is mainly found.

There are few things which a Bechuana prizes so highly as fat of any description; they will go an amazing distance for a small portion. of it. They use it principally in cooking their sun-dried biltongue, and they also eat it with their corn. The fat of the elephant lies in extensive layers and sheets in his inside, and the quantity which is obtained from a full-grown bull, in high condition, is very great. Before it can be obtained, the greater part of the bowels must be removed. To accomplish this, several men eventually enter the immense cavity of his inside, where they continue mining away with their assagais, and handing the fat to their comrades outside until all is bare. While this is transpiring with the sides and bowels, other parties are equally active in removing the skin and flesh from the remaining parts of the carcass. The natives have a horrid practice on these occasions of besmearing their bodies, from the crown of the head to the sole of the foot, with the black and clotted gore; and in this anointing they assist one another, each man taking up the fill in both his hands, and spreading it over the back and shoulders of his friend. Throughout the entire proceeding an incessant and deafening clamor of many voices and confused sounds is maintained, and violent jostling and wrestling are practiced by every man, elbowing the breasts and countenances of his fellows, all slippery with gore, as he endeavors to force his way to the venison through the dense intervening ranks, while the sharp and ready assagai gleams in every hand. The angry voices and gory appearances of these naked savages, combined with their excited and frantic gestures and glistening arms, presented an effect so wild and striking, that when I first beheld the scene I contemplated it in the momentary expectation of beholding one half of the gathering turn their weapons against the other.

The trunk and feet are considered a delicacy, and a detachment are employed on these. The four feet are amputated at the fetlock joint, and the trunk, which at the base is about two feet in thickness, is cut into convenient lengths. Trunk and feet are then baked, preparatory to their removal to head-quarters. The manner in which this is done is as follows: A party, provided with sharp-pointed sticks, dig a hole in the ground for each foot and a portion of the trunk. These holes are about two feet deep, and a yard in width; the excavated earth is embanked around the margin of the hole. This work being completed, they next collect an immense quantity of dry branches and trunks of trees, of which there is always a profusion scattered around, having been broken by the elephants in former years. These they pile above the holes to the height of eight or nine feet, and then set fire to the heap. When these strong fires have burned down, and the whole of the wood is reduced to ashes, the holes and the surrounding earth are heated in a high degree. Ten or twelve men then stand round the pit, and rake out the ashes with a pole about sixteen feet in length, having a hook at the end. They relieve one another in quick succession, each man running in and raking the ashes for a few seconds, and then pitching the pole to his comrade and retreating, since the heat is so intense that it is scarcely to be endured. When all the ashes are thus raked out beyond the surrounding bank of earth, each elephant's foot and portion of the trunk is lifted by two athletic men, standing side by side, who place it on their shoulders, and, approaching the pit together, they heave it into it.

The feet, thus cooked, are excellent, as is also the trunk, which very much resembles buffalo's tongue. The reason why such large fires are requisite is owing to the mass of the flesh that must be baked. In raking the sand on the foot, the natives are careful not to rake the red-hot embers in with it, which would burn and destroy the meat; whereas the sand or earth protects it, imparting an even and steady heat. When the natives have cut up the elephant, and removed the large masses of flesh, &c., to their respective temporary kraals around, they sit down for a little to rest and draw their breath, and for a short time smoking and snuffing are indulged in.

The Bechuana pipe is of a very primitive description, differing from any I had ever seen. When they wish to smoke they moisten a spot of earth, not being particular whence they obtain the water. Into this earth they insert a green twig, bent into a semicircle, whose bend is below the said earth, and both ends protruding. They then knead the moist earth down with their knuckles on the twig, which they work backward and forward until a hole is established, when the twig is withdrawn, and one end of the aperture is enlarged with the fingers, so as to form a bowl to contain the tobacco. The pipe is thus finished and ready for immediate use, when tobacco and fire are introduced, and the smoker drops on his knees, and, resting on the palms of his hands, he brings his lips in contact with the mud at the small end of the hole, and thus inhales the grateful fumes. Large volumes of smoke are emitted through the nostrils, while a copious flow of tears from the eyes of the smoker evinces the pleasure he enjoys. One of these pipes will serve a large party, who replenish the bowl and relieve one another in succession.

The natives, having drawn their breath, once more devote their attention to the flesh, which they next reduce to biltongue, cutting every morsel into thin strips from six to twenty feet in length. These strips are of the breadth and thickness of a man's two fingers. When all is reduced to biltongue, they sally forth with their tomahawks, and cut down a number of poles of two sorts, for uprights and cross-poles. The uprights are eight feet long, and forked at one end. They place them upright in the ground around their respective trees, laying the cross-poles resting on the forks, and these are adorned with endless garlands of the raw meat, which is permitted to hang in the sun for two or three days, when it will have lost much of its weight, and be stiff and easy to be carried. They then remove the biltongue from the poles, and, folding it together, they form it into bundles, which are strongly lashed and secured with long strips of the tough inner bark of thorny mimosas. Their work in the forest is now completed, and, each man placing one bundle on his head, and slinging several others across his shoulders, returns to his wife and family at head-quarters.

The appearance which the flesh of a single elephant exhibits when reduced to strips and suspended from the poles is truly, surprising, the forest far around displaying a succession of ruby festoons, and reminding one of a vineyard laden with its clustering fruits. When the skull of my elephant was ready for the ax, Mutchuisho caused a party to hew out for me the tusks—a work of great labor, and needing considerable skill. In the present instance the work was clumsily executed, the native hacking and injuring the ivory in removing the bone with their little tomahawks. In consequence of this, I invariably afterward performed the task myself, using superior American hatchets, which I had provided expressly for the purpose. When the tusks had been extracted, I saddled up and started for the camp, accompanied by my after-riders and a party of the natives bearing the ivory, with a supply of baked foot and trunk and a portion of the flesh. The natives had appropriated all the rest, and when I left them they were quarreling over the remnant of the skull, whose marrowy bones were in high demand. They fought for every chip as it flew from the ax, and chewed it raw. On our way to camp we passed through the kraal of the Bakalahari, situated in the mountain range. In the valleys they had formed considerable gardens, in which corn and water-melons were extensively grown. I was right glad to reach my comfortable camp, and get a bowl of coffee.

On the evening of the 26th men kept pouring into camp heavily laden with the flesh of the elephant, a large part of which was for Sicomy they halted with me for the night, and resumed their march in the morning.

CHAPTER XVI

On the 27th of July I resolved to move my wagons further to the east, and informed the wagon-drivers of my intentions: they, however, raised many objections, and all but gave me a direct refusal. As I was not aware of the position of the waters, and knowing well that Isaac would not assist me in discovering them, I deemed it prudent first to make an excursion to the east on horseback. I accordingly stowed some ammunition and a washing-rod in my old game-bag (to the inside of which, by-the-by, adhered a goodly coating of the scales of grilse and salmon, along with sundry speckled and blood-stained feathers of the grouse and partridge), and having made bread and ground coffee sufficient for three days' consumption, I ordered two of my men to be ready to accompany me next morning. My interpreter's countenance never lacked a scowl; and, instead of forwarding my interests, he actively employed his energies in sowing dissension between me and the natives, and disseminating mutiny among my Hottentots. I discovered that all along he had deceived me, and carefully concealed the direction where elephants most abounded, and I began to think that, in justice to myself, it was high time that he should be ignominiously dismissed the service.

On the 28th, as I was breakfasting, natives arrived and reported fresh spoor within a mile of camp. I therefore resolved to defer for the present the trip to the eastward on which I had determined; but it so happened that the spoor which was reported led me in that direction, and was the means of introducing me to a succession of fine hunting districts, throughout which elephant and rhinoceros were abundant. Everything being ready, I proceeded to take up the spoor, accompanied by after-riders and about a hundred of the Bamangwato men, fresh parties having joined me it was the spoor of a small troop of cow elephants. Mutchuisho and the spooring party took it up in a masterly manner, and went along at a rapid pace all day, with scarcely a check, until we found the elephants. The spoor led us first through a gorge in the mountains, which I mentioned as having rounded on the 24th; after which we followed it in an easterly course, skirting the base of the mountain chain. The country increased in beauty as we advanced; and, having followed the spoor some hours, it led us into a new variety of country, and, as I fancied, into a new climate. Here large trees were abundant, and the grass and leaves were much greener than in the country we had left behind. We crossed the gravelly beds of two periodical rivers. In one of these I observed the recent spoor of a heard of bull elephants deeply imprinted in the sand. This day the wind, which had for weeks been cold and blighting, blowing off the icebergs of the Southern Ocean, shifted to northeast, and breathed warm and balmy upon us.

As we advanced the work of elephants became more and more apparent on the trees and in the earth, and late in the afternoon we reached ground where a large herd of cows had fed that morning. Here we had a short check, when Mutchuisho rated the trackers for their negligence; and, having dispatched parties to try back upon the spoor, and extended others to make casts on our right and left, he leisurely ensconced himself beneath a shady tree, and proceeded, along with several of his cronies, to enjoy the luxury of taking snuff which important ceremony having been duly performed, they began with the utmost gravity to smooth a portion of the ground before them, preparatory to casting the mystic dice which most of the Bechuanas carry strung around their necks. These dice, which are of sundry indescribable shapes, are formed of ivory, and the Bechuanas invariably appeal to them before entering upon any project of importance, to ascertain the probability of its ultimate success. Having unstrung the dice, which are four in number, they rattle them between their hands, and drop them on the ground, when the long-headed old men carefully study the directions of the points, and decide the merits of the case accordingly.

Once more all was quiet; my dogs were jaded with the sun, and would not fight. Fancying that the elephants had gone ahead, and fearing to lose them, I again pushed on, holding the foot-path as before, when crash came a second charge of elephants at our very elbows, accompanied by a trumpeting which caused our ears to tingle. They charged upon us from opposite directions, and we were actually in the very middle of them. They were extremely tierce, and, but for the dogs, not a man of us had escaped to tell the tale. Fortunately, the dogs, which they seemed to think designed the capture of their calves, engrossed their whole attention; whereas, by reason of the color of the horses on which we rode, they took us for gregarious creatures like themselves, and actually grazing our animals' haunches with their legs, they left us scatheless and pursued the dogs. Spurs and jamboks were energetically plied; there was no time to select a path. Placing my head below my horse's neck and trusting to Providence, I charged through the thickest of the thorns, and presently found myself out of the way of the elephants. After a few such lessons he will have learned to bring his breast in contact with the side of his horse's neck, his head being well under it, whereby his prominent feature will be secured, and, agitating his persuaders, he will dive through the most impracticable "wait-a-bits" with apparently the facility with which an Eton boy takes a header into the Thames at the Lion's Leap.

With very great difficulty, we got clear of the cover and gained the level forest on the lower side. By the time the natives had lined the side of the mountain above the cover, and were shouting and yelling in the hope of driving out the elephants; but not a man would venture in. Presently some of them came round to me, and I proposed to go in on foot, but they would not hear of it, saying that the elephants were extremely fierce and would kill mc to a certainty. I then proposed that all the natives should enter the jungle in a line, and try to drive them out; but they said that no power could force the elephants from their stronghold until night set in.

The elephants now shifted their ground a little, forcing their way through the jungle to the higher side of the basin. Leaving the horses in charge of a native, I went round to the line of men above. Here I commanded a fine view of the exasperated elephants, being high above them, and distant about two hundred and fifty yards, and I observed that they displayed considerable cunning in their movements. Placing my rifle on a forked branch, and giving it the proper elevation, I let drive at the nearest cow, and wounded her severely. The shot reverberated through the dale, and the dogs once more ran into the midst of them, when a general charge and trumpeting ensued, which was truly terrific. They rushed after the dogs, following them up to a great distance, crashing through and upsetting the high, bushy wait-a-bits and other trees like grass. They then turned and formed in two separate detachments, standing thick together; but two wicked old cows that had calves stood far out from the others, with their heads turned to us, ready to charge whatever might approach. I then stalked in within twenty yards, and fired at the side of the head of the elephant that stood next to me; and before the smoke had cleared, my back was to them, and I was running for the outside of the cover at my utmost speed. The elephants held their ground; so, having loaded, I again drew near, and fired sharp right and left into another, and, turning my back, ran for it once more. Re-entering the cover a third time, I was listening which way they had gone, when, casting my eyes to the left, a noble elephant lay dead before me. The ball had penetrated to her brain, and she had dropped dead upon the spot.

A little after this an old cow came charging after the dogs, and took up a position in the jungle close beside us. We heard her preparing for a second charge, when the natives beat a precipitate retreat; but I very rashly waited to receive her, and just as she cleared the cover I let fly at her forehead. Regardless of my shot, she came down upon me at a tremendous pace, shrilly trumpeting. It was rather a near thing, for I was burdened with my rifle and rhinoceros-horn loading-rod, and my shooting-belt containing about forty rounds of ammunition. I escaped her by my speed, and the instant she halted I faced about, and gave her the other barrel behind the .shoulder.

Night now set in, and I saw no more of the elephants. A number of them were wounded and must have died; I, however, felt satisfied with the one I had secured. The natives made me more cautious than I should otherwise have been, and, had we found them at an earlier hour, I should probably have killed one half the troop. Weary and hungry, we formed our kraals and kindled fires; after which, having partaken of the elephant, I lay down to sleep beside my fire.

On the 29th I sent Carollus to the wagons with instructions to bring all the horses and the Bushman, with bread, coffee, and ammunition. In the forenoon I ascended the neighboring mountain range to obtain a view of the surrounding country. On clearing the first ridge I looked down upon a bold and romantic gorge, which here intersected the mountain chain, connecting the forests on either side. Far below me, through the bottom of the ravine, twined the gravelly bed of a periodical river, which in the rainy season flows in an easterly direction. Though in all other parts this gravelly channel was now dry, yet just at this spot, deep in the bosom of the mountains, its bed was covered with delicious spring water to a depth of several inches; and here the elephants had excavated sundry holes, about two feet deep, for the purpose of drinking. I descended to the water by an elephant path, and stood long contemplating the interesting spot. The bed of the river was deeply imprinted with the spoor of elephants, buffaloes, and rhinoceros, of various dates.

In the evening Carollus arrived, bringing the horses and ammunition, and accompanied by a numerous body of the natives. At an early hour on the 30th I started with Mutchuisho and a numerous retinue to search for elephants in an easterly direction, and we crossed the gravelly bed of the River Mahalapia, about a mile below the gorge I had visited on the preceding day. In after years I renewed my acquaintance with the Mahalapia, on the banks of the fair Limpopo, into which it empties itself several days' journey to the east.

This was one of the loveliest spots I had seen in Southern Africa a bold bend of the river was adorned with groves of remarkably lofty and picturesque acacias. Three trees in particular, of the same description, graced the spot, which in size and beauty surpassed any I had hitherto met with, carrying their thickness to an immense height from the ground, when they divided into goodly branches, which stretched away in beauty to the skies.

Here, in the bed of the river, we took up the spoor of a huge bull elephant, and, having followed it a short distance through the verdant forest, we started the old fellow, but no man saw him. The great body of the relatives never would be quiet, and ever pressed upon the spooring party, notwithstanding my remonstrances. One native heard him, but said he thought it was a rhinoceros. In half a minute, however, we discovered our mistake, and there ensued a general rush upon the spoor, at a pace which must shortly have overtaken him, for he had not started in great alarm. Whistling to my dogs, they took up the scent and went ahead; but as I galloped after them, expecting every instant to behold the elephant, whose spoor I now saw beneath my horse's feet, an unlucky troop of camelopards dashed across our path, and away went all the dogs, leaving me in the lurch just as I was upon the elephant. The trackers, however, soon came up, and we again held briskly on, but had not proceeded far when we entered upon ground so covered with fresh footmarks that the trackers in their haste overran the spoor we followed, and a long check was the result. Here, to add to my annoyance, another large herd of camelopards came cantering up the wind, and dashed away before us, to spread further alarm. Old Mutchuisho now came up in a state of intense excitement, his watery eyes fixed upon the ground, and his tongue going like perpetual motion.

We renamed the spoor at a rapid pace, with a widely-extended front, and presently on my left I heard the joyous signal of the presence, "Kiow;" and, cantering in that direction, I came full in sight of an enormous bull elephant, marching along at a free majestic pace, and in another minute I was riding by his side. The horse which I bestrode on this occasion was "The Cow," one of my best and stotidiest shooting-horses; and the forest being tolerably suited for the sport, I was not long in finishing the elephant. I fired thirteen bullets at his head and shoulder; on receiving the last two shots sharp right and left behind the .shoulder, he made a rapid charge, and disappeared among the trees. Cautiously following, I discovered him lying in an upright position, with his two fore legs stretched out before him. Fancying he was still alive, I fired both barrels at his car; but, though the balls rang loudly on his venerable head, the noble elephant heeded not their force; his ancient spirit had departed.

This was a very large old elephant; but his tusks were much destroyed, being worn down, and having been broken (probably in rocky ground) in former years. Mutchuisho appeared in the highest glee, and dispatched messengers through the gorge in the mountains, the name of which is Sabie, to advise Sicomy of the death of the elephant. The chase had led me to within rifle range of the three veteran acacias T admired in the morning. I made my bower and a couch of grass beneath a shady wait-a-bit thorn-tree, and encircled my fire with a hedge of the same description.

Observing the lioness, I shouted to the natives, who were pressing forward, that it was "Tao," when a headlong retreat was the immediate result, a number of the party taking refuge in the trees. I dismounted, and, advancing to within twenty yards of the lioness, waited till she turned her head, when I fired at the back of her neck, and stretched her lifeless on the ground. The bullet had passed along the spine, and, penetrating the skull, rested in her brain. On shouting to the natives for a long time none of them would venture to approach and when at length they did, their astonishment know no bounds at beholding their formidable enemy so easy, disposed of. Having resumed the spoor of the elephants, we soon ascertained that the hubbub with the lioness had started them; and after following the spoor some distance through dense jungle, and over very rocky ground, along the mountain side, the trackers declaimed themselves to be fairly beaten, and we gave it up.

At an early hour on the 3rd I again held east with a large retinue to seek for elephants We took up spoor at the fountains where I discovered bored; on the preceding day. This spoor led us in a southeasterly course, first through verdant forest, and then over an extremely rugged ridge that stretched into the forest from the mountain chain. Beyond this ridge was an extensive and almost impracticable jungle of wait-a-bit thorns, and in this jungle we now heard the rumbling sound of elephants. As we advanced, I perceived from the nature of the ground that success was very doubtful, and in a few minutes the dogs, winding the elephants, ran in upon them and gave tongue; a crashing and trumpeting ensued, and all the natives shouted out "Machoa" (signifying white man). With the utmost difficulty I pressed through the jungle, and obtained a view of one of the elephants, around which my dogs were barking angrily; but perceiving that it was a small cow, and knowing well that if I shot her the natives would not take up spoor again for at least a couple of days, I reserved my fire and the dogs being jaded by the sun, and returning to my call, we left the elephants to their own devices.

A few minutes afterward we discovered the fresh spoor of two enormous bull elephants, which had pastured toward the hills. Having followed it a short distance, we came upon some dung, the outside of which the sun had not yet dried, from which we might presume that the elephants were at that moment in the same valley with ourselves. Two young men were dispatched in haste to ascend the beetling crags of the adjacent mountain, from which they could obtain a bird's-eye view of the length and breadth of that and the surrounding valleys. The main body of the natives squatted on the ground, and I sat down to eat some bread and elephant, and take a drink of water. I had scarcely time to finish my luncheon when the two young when returned breathless with excitement to report that they had discovered the two bull elephants browsing in a grove of thorny trees on the mountain side within a quarter of a mile of us. I approached under cover of a bushy tree, on clearing which I beheld two of the finest elephants in Africa standing broadside on within fifty yards. The finer of these had one of his tusks broken short off by the lip; I therefore chose his comrade, which carried a pair of very long and perfect tusks. I had hard work with this elephant, and the sun was under before I laid him low.

On the 4th I rode for my bower on the Mahalapia, in the hope of finding my wagons waiting for me; but I had misgivings about my men, who ought to have appeared on the evening of the 2nd. On reaching my bower where the former elephant had died, I found the fires still smoking, but every man had disappeared Carollus, whom I had ordered to await me, had vanished with the rest. I now fancied that I must have missed the natives who had passed me on their way to the elephant of the previous day, and that Carollus had joined the wagons wherever they might be. I was right in my conjecture, and presently, on firing a signal shot, I received an answer from the wagons, which were drawn up in the romantic gorge of Sabie, as near as might be to the water. Drunkenness and disorder had prevailed during my absence, as I had feared ; my chests were broken open, the fine contents of both my wagons were most seriously damaged, oxen had been lost, and horses ridden off their legs in search of them.

I remember having a discussion with the commanding officer of a regiment of heavy dragoons on this subject, and he and I agreed that nothing can surpass a double-barreled smooth bore for practical utility. When a two-grooved rifle has been once or twice discharged, the bullet requires considerable power to drive it home; and to a mounted man this is extremely inconvenient I consider that no regiment in the service was more effectually armed than my own old corps, the Cape Mounted Rifles, who were furnished with short double-barreled smooth-bored pieces, carrying a ball of twelve to the pound, and having stout percussion locks. Give me a weapon of this description to war against the large game of Africa. To accelerate loading, the hunter ought have his balls stitched up in their patches, and well greased before taking the field. This was my invariable custom I found it a great convenience, and after a little practice I could load and fire in the saddle, although riding in rough ground at a swinging gallop.

On the evening of the 12th a herald from Sicomy stood up in the center of my camp, and loudly proclaimed that it was the king's orders that on the following day every man should return to headquarters; and, accordingly, next day all hands shouldered their impedimenta and forsook me. I could not rightly divine the cause of this mysterious command; but I attributed it to some plotting scheme of Isaac's, who, I understood, was living with Sicomy. I saw very plainly that Mutchuisho was against the move. In consideration of his services, I begged his acceptance of several considerable presents, and I also sent some presents to the king. On parting, Mutchuisho promised shortly to return, and he informed me that he had instructed a party of Bakalahari to assist me in my hunting during his absence.

CHAPTER XVII

I remained at Sabie, hunting elephant and rhinoceros with various success, till the morning of the 22nd of August, when I inspanned, and marched for Mangmaluky, which we reached at sundown, and I drew up my wagons in an open grassy glade on a rather elevated position, commanding a fine view of the bold outline of the surrounding mountains. On the march I shot a white rhinoceros in the act of charging down a rocky face, with all the dogs in full pursuit of him. The ball disabled him in the shoulder, when, pitching upon his head, he described the most tremendous somersault, coming down among the stones and bushes with the overwhelming violence of an avalanche.

On the 27th I cast lose my horses at earliest dawn of day, and then lay half asleep for two hours, when I arose to consume coffee and rhinoceros. Having breakfasted, I started with a party of the natives to search for elephants in a southerly direction. We held along the gravelly bed of a periodical river, in which were abundance of holes excavated by the elephants in quest of water. Here the spoor of rhinoceros was extremely plentiful, and in every hole where they had drunk the print of the horn was visible. We soon found the spoor of an old bull elephant, which led us into a dense forest, where the ground was particularly unfavorable for spooring; we, however, thridded it out for a considerable distance, when it joined the spoor of other bulls. The natives now requested me to halt, while men went off in different directions to reconnoiter.

In the meantime a tremendous conflagration was roaring and crackling close to windward of us. It was caused by the Bakalahari burning the old dry grass to enable the young to spring up with greater facility, whereby they retained the game in their dominions. The fire stretched away for many miles on either side of us, darkening the forests far to leeward with a dense and impenetrable canopy of smoke. Here we remained for about half an hour, when one of the men returned, reporting that he had discovered elephants. This I could scarcely credit, for I fancied that the extensive fire which raged so fearfully must have driven, not only elephants, but every living creature out of the district. The native, however, pointed to his eye, repeating the word "Klow," and signed to me to follow him. My guide led me about a mile through dense forest, when we reached a little well-wooded hill, to whose summit we ascended, whence a view might have been obtained of the surrounding country, had not volumes of smoke obscured the scenery far and wide, as though issuing from the funnels of a thousand steam-boats. Here, to my astonishment, my guide halted, and pointed to the thicket close beneath me, when I instantly perceived the colossal backs of a herd of bull elephants. There they stood, quietly browsing on the lee side of the hill, while the fire in its might was raging to windward within two hundred yards of them.

I directed Johannus to choose an elephant, and promised to reward him should he prove successful. Galloping furiously down the hill, I started the elephants with an unearthly yell, and instantly selected the finest bull in the herd. Placing myself alongside, I fired both barrels behind his shoulder, when he instantly turned upon me, and in his impetuous career charged head foremost into a large bushy tree, which he sent flying before him high in the air with tremendous force, coming down at the same moment violently on his knees. He then met the raging fire, when, altering his course, he wheeled to the right-about. As I galloped after him I perceived another noble elephant meeting us in an opposite direction, and presently the gallant Johannus have in sight, following his quarry at a respectful distance. Both elephants held on together; so I shouted to Johannus, " I will give your elephant a shot in the shoulder, and you must try to finish him." Spurring ray horse, I rode close alongside, and gave the fresh elephant two balls immediately behind the shoulder, when he parted from mine, Johannus following; but before many minutes had elapsed that mighty Nimrod reappeared, having fired one shot and lost his prey.

This animal was first discovered by Captain Harris, of the Bombay Engineers, in 1837. As I subsequently devoted a great deal of time in the pursuit of this antelope, I shall not here make any remarks concerning him. The one which was now before me was the first I had seen, and I shall never forget the sensations I experienced on beholding a sight so thrilling to the sportsman's eye. He stood with a small troop of pallahs right in our path, and had unfortunately detected us before we saw him. Shouting to my pack, I galloped after him; but the day was close and warm, and the dogs had lost their spirit with the sun. My horse being an indifferent one, I soon lost ground, and the beautiful sable antelope, gaining a rocky ridge, was very soon beyond my reach, and vanished forever from my view. I then rode on for the carcass of the elephant, where I took up my quarters for the night, but I sought in vain to close my eyelids the image of the sable antelope was still before me, and I slept little throughout the night.

On the 31st I held southeast in quest of elephants, with a large party of the natives. Our course lay through an open part of the forest, where I beheld a troop of springboks and two ostriches, the first I had seen for a long time. We held for Towannie, a strong fountain in the gravelly bed of a periodical river: here two herds of cow elephants had drunk on the preceding evening, but I declined to follow them ; and presently, at a muddy fountain a little in advance, we took up the spoor of an enormous bull, which had wallowed in the mud, and then plastered the sides of several of the adjacent veteran-looking trees. We followed the spoor through level forest in an easterly direction, when the leading party overran the spoor, and casts were made for its recovery. Presently I detected an excited native beckoning violently a little to my left, and, cantering up to him, he said that he had seen the elephant. He led me through the forest a few hundred yards, when, clearing a wait-a-bit, I came full in view of the tallest and largest bull elephant I had ever seen. He stood broadside to me, at upward of one hundred yards, and his attention at the moment was occupied with the dogs, which, unaware of his proximity, were rushing past him, while the old fellow gem at their unwonted appearance with surprise

Halting my horse, I fired at his shoulder, and ,neon red him with a single shot. The ball caught him upon the shoulder-blade, rendering him instantly dead lame; and before the echo of the bullet could reach my ear, I plainly saw that the elephant was mine. The dogs now came up and barked around him, but, finding himself incapacitated, the old fellow seemed determined to take it easy, and, limping slowly to a neighboring tree, he remained stationary, eyen his pursuers with a resigned and philosophic air.

I resolved to devote a short time to the contemplation of this noble elephant before I should lay him low; accordingly, having off-saddled the horses beneath a shady tree which was to be my quarters for the night and ensuing day, I quickly kindled a fire and put on the kettle, and in a very few minutes my coffee was prepared. There I sat in my forest home, coolly sipping my coffee, with one of the finest elephants in Africa awaiting my pleasure beside a neighboring tree.

It was, indeed, a striking scene; and as I gazed upon the stupendous veteran of the forest, I thought of the red deer which I loved to follow in my native land, and felt that, though the Fates had driven me to follow a more daring and arduous avocation in a distant land, it was a good exchange which I had made, for I was now a chief over boundless forests, which yielded unspeakably more noble and exciting sport.

On the 1st of September—so full of interest to the British Nimrod—we saddled our steeds and steered our course for Mangmaluky. Cantering along the base of a mountain range, I started two klipspringers, which went bounding up the mountain side with the elasticity of an India-rubber ball, selecting for their path the most prominent points of the large fragments of rock of which the mountain side was chiefly composed. I shot one of these, being the first of the species I had killed, though in subsequent years, while hunting the sable antelope, I secured a number of fine specimens. This darling little antelope frequents precipitous rocky hills and mountains, and bounds along over the broken masses of rock with the most extraordinary ease and agility it may often be seen perched, like a chamois, on the sharp pinnacle of some rock or stone, with its four feet drawn close up together. Its hoofs are different from those of other antelopes, being suited solely for rocky ground, and are so formed that the weight of the animal rests upon their tips. On looking down a precipice I have often seen two or three of this interesting antelope lying together on a large flat mass of rock, and sheltered from the power of the noonday sun by the friendly shade of some sandal-wood or other mountain tree. They are about half the size of the Scottish roebuck, whose winter coat the texture of their hair very much resembles, but it is stiffer, and of a yellower color.

On the afternoon of the 2nd, as I was sitting in my wagon writing up my journal, a koodoo charged past me, closely followed by a pack of hungry wild dogs, which maintained their position although my kennel joined them in the chase, and, holding on, the wild dogs killed the koodoo just as it reached the water where my oxen drank. On the 3rd I took the field with Johannus and a small party of Bakalahari, and held a northerly direction. After following the spoor of four bull elephants for many miles in a semicircular course, we came up with them in extremely dangerous and unfavorable ground, when I was fortunate enough to secure the finest, after a severe and dangerous conflict, during which, on three separate occasions, I narrowly escaped destruction. The horse I rode was "Colesberg," which, as usual, capered and balked me when I tried to fire from his back; when I dismounted, he seemed to take a pleasure in jerking my arm as I was taking aim; and on the elephant charging, he declined permitting me to regain the saddle.

In the afternoon I was engaged for many hours combating with a vicious elephant, which I finished with thirty-five bullets in the shoulder, in an impracticable jungle of wait-a-bit thorns. The conflict was greatly prolonged by "The Immense Brute," which capered continually, and constantly destroyed the correctness of my aim. While I was fighting with this elephant, my dogs were combating with a younger bull, which they hunted backward and forward in the same thicket with myself. This elephant took up a position beside the one which had fallen, and the dogs continued barking around him. My rifle being now extremely dirty, I experienced considerable difficulty in ramming home the balls, notwithstanding the power of my rhinoceros horn loading-rod. This being accomplished, I ran cautiously within twenty yards of this second elephant, and, resting my rifle on a branch, aimed for his heart and pressed the trigger. Alas ! it was for the last time. The barrel burst with a terrific explosion, sending the Locks and half the stock flying right and left, and very nearly sending me to "the land of the heal." I, however, received no further damage than a slight burn on my left arm, and the loss for many days of the use of my left ear, a fragment of the barrel having whizzed close past it. At first I was so stunned that I knew not if I were wounded or not, and on recovering from the shock my person underwent a strict scrutiny. Before I discovered these elephants I was faint from thirst, and quite done up with the power of the sun, owing to which I considered that I did not attack the elephant so bravely as I might otherwise have done.

The loss of my trusty two-grooved rifle, in such a remote corner of the world, was irreparable, and cut me to the heart. It was my main stay; and as I thought of the many services it had performed for me in the hour of need, I mourned over it as David mourned for Absalom, On the evening of the 7th I returned to Mangmaluky under a burning sun, which continued oppressive throughout the day. Having lost my two grooved rifle, I resolved to try what could be done with the double-barreled Moore and Purdey rifles, carrying sixteen to the pound, and I accordingly set about casting hardened bullets to suit them. For this purpose I had brought in with me a quantity of solder, but I now had the mortification to discover that all that I had possessed of this important article had mysteriously vanished by some underhand transaction between my followers and Sicomy. I was thus reduced to the extremity of melting the contents of my old military canteen to harden the bullets; and upon overhauling it, I ascertained that the tray of the snuflers, the spoons, candlesticks, tea-pots, and two drinking-cups, were admirably suited for this purpose, and I accordingly sentenced them to undergo the fiery ordeal of the ladle.

In the evening I had much pleasure to behold my old friend Mutchuisho walk into my camp, followed by a numerous party of the natives. He seemed glad to see me, and we at once arranged to make an expedition to the eastward on the following day. Accordingly, on the morning of the 9th I took the field with Johannus and Mutchuisho, and about eighty men, and proceeded in a southeasterly direction. We continued our course till the sun went down without finding fresh spoor, when we halted for the night to leeward of a fountain, where we hoped that elephants would come to drink. The heat throughout the day had been most oppressive, the dense level forest rendering it still more insupportable. On the morrow we cast loose the horses so graze long before the dawn of day. No elephants had visited the fountain; so, after an early breakfast, we saddled up, and again held on in an easterly direction through boundless forests, till I found myself in a country which I had not hitherto visited. Passing along beneath a rocky hillock, we started a detachment of hideous hyenas, which sought shelter from the sun beneath the shadow of the rocks. We passed several large herds of lovely camelopards, and I also obtained two very deadly chances of rhinoceros, both fine old bulls; but knowing well from past experience that my policy was to keep my followers hungry, I refrained from firing a single shot.

In the afternoon we reached a small vley, where five first-rate bull elephants had drunk on the preceding evening. Here my followers all sat down and rested for a quarter of an hour, a wild duck swimming fearlessly beside us. We then took up the spoor, but, as it was late in the day, I had not the slightest expectation of success, and was so done up with the power of the sun that I felt it irk soroc to sit in the saddle. The spoor led east, right away from camp, but the elephants seemed to have proceeded slowly, having extended widely from one another, and rent and uprooted an amazing number of goodly trees. Presently the spoor took a turn to our left, when I grieved to remark that we were following it down the wind; thus we eventually started the elephants, which were feeding in the forest at no great distance, but, owing to a check among the trackers, we were not aware of this until the elephants had gained a considerable start.

The nearest water to this elephant was in a vley situated several miles to the eastward; and when the natives had constructed a number of water-bags of the under skin of the elephant, a watering party was dispatched with these and a number of calabashes which they always carried along with them. This party rejoined us at the hour of midnight, and reported that while they were filling their water-bags at one side of the vley, a troop of bull elephants were drinking at the other. Accordingly, on the morrow I went in quest of these, accompanied by Mutchuisho and a small party, and on the second day came up with them and bagged an old bull, whose tusks were the stoutest I had ever seen.

On the morrow I cast loose the steeds at earliest dawn, and soon after we heard the hoarse cry of an elephant within half a mile of us. I permitted my horses to graze while the dew was on the grass, after which, along with the dogs, I sent them to water with a party of Bakalahari at a fountain reported three miles distant, and in the mean time I regaled myself with coffee and rhinoceros.

It is extraordinary how soon the mind accustoms myself to everything, good or bad. There I sat taking my breakfast, with a troop of princely elephants feeding within a few minutes ride of me, with as much indifference as if I were going woodcock shooting. I certainly did not feel half so anxious about the matter as I usually did when taking my breakfast on a fine May morning, with a southerly wind, before starting to fish my native river. This indifference was probably owing to the reduced state of my system from improper diet and constant toil.

When the Bakalahari returned with the dogs and horses, they reported fresh spoor of bull elephants by the fountain; and at the same moment another party, whom Mutohuisho had dispatched in the direction of the cry, returned to say that it was a herd of bulls which we had heard that morning. This was very pleasing intelligence, for I had fancied that the elephants must be a troop of cows, whose traces we had observed on the preceding evening. Everything being ready, we made for the elephants, and, as we approached them, an old bull rhinoceros was detected standing within forty yards, which, as if aware that I dared not fire on him, kept trotting along the path before me. We discovered the elephants quietly browsing on very unfavorable ground, the greater part of the forest consisting of the ever-recurring wait-a-bits. The troop was composed of three old bulls, two of which carried stumpy and broken tusks.

On the evening of the 20th, after bowling over another elephant with a splendid pair of tusks, I returned to camp, where, to my utter horror, I found my favorite Colesberg dangerously ill. Guessing that it was the distemper, I had him up instantly and bled him freely, but to no purpose. Finding him worse on the morrow, I bled him again, but before mid-day he died in great pain, and shortly after life had departed a copious discharge of white foam issued from his nostrils by which I knew that his illness was the African distemper.

I had also the mortification to observe that "The Immense Brute" was affected, evincing symptoms similar to those of Colesberg, on which I had him caught and bled him freely. About the hour of mid-day we got under way, when I trekked till sundown in a southwesterly course, steering for the mountains of Bamangwato. I formed my encampment beside a little fountain, whose name I never ascertained.

CHAPTER XVIII

Having so far succeeded in the object of my expedition, and both my wagons being now heavily laden with the tusks of elephants and a large collection of the spoils of the case, with a number of other interesting curiosities, I at length resolved once more to turn my face toward the distant dwellings of my countrymen. On the 23rd of September, however, although harassed in my mind, and fearing to lose all my horses if I did not speedily forsake the country, I yielded to my inclination, and the persuasions of Mutchuisho, once more to take the field, and follow the spoor of two bull elephants, reported to have visited a distant fountain. Before starting I gave Johannus my phlegm, and a hasty lesson in the art of bleeding, with instructions to bleed copiously any of my stud evincing the slightest symptoms of distemper. We held an easterly course, and at sundown on the second day I bagged a white rhinoceros and a fine old bull elephant, beside whose carcass I bivouacked as usual. On the forenoon of the 25th I saddled up and held for camp, accompanied by only one attendant.

It was a glorious day, with a cloudy sky, and the wind blew fresh off the Southern Ocean. Having ridden some miles in a northerly direction, we crossed the broad and gravelly bed of a periodical river, in which were abundance of holes excavated by the elephants, containing delicious water. Having passed the river, we entered an extensive grove of picturesque camel dorn trees, clad in young foliage of the most delicious green. On gaining a gentle eminence about a mile beyond this grove, I looked forth upon an extensive hollow, where I beheld for the first time for many days a fine old cock ostrich, which quickly observed us and dashed away to our left. I had ceased to devote my attention to the ostrich, and was straining my eyes in an opposite direction, when Kleinboy called out to me, "Dar loup de ould carle ;" and turning my eyes to the retreating ostrich, I beheld two first-rate old bull elephants, charging along at their utmost speed within a hundred yards of it. They seemed at first to be in great alarm, but, quickly discovering what it was that had caused their confusion, they at once reduced their pace to a slow and stately walk. This was a fine look-out; the country appeared to be favorable for an attack, and I was followed by Wolfe and Bonteberg, both tried and serviceable dogs with elephants. Owing to the pace at which I had been riding, both dogs and horses were out of breath, so I resolved not to attack the elephants immediately, but to follow slowly, holding them in view.

Presently emerging into an open glade, I came full in sight of the mighty game; it was a truly glorious sight; there were nine or ten of them, which were, with one exception, full-grown, first-rate bulls, and all of them carried very long, heavy, and perfect tusks. Their first panic being over, they had reduced their pace to a free, majestic walk, and they followed one leader in a long line, exhibiting an appearance so grand and striking that any description, however brilliant, must fail to convey to the mind of the reader an adequate idea of the reality. Increasing my pace, I shot alongside, at the same time riding well out from the elephants, the better to obtain an inspection of their tusks. It was a difficult matter to decide which of them I should select, for every elephant seemed better than his neighbor; but, on account of the extraordinary size and beauty of his tusks, I eventually pitched upon a patriarchal bull, which, as is usual with the heaviest, brought up the rear. I presently separated him from his comrades, and endeavored to drive him in a northerly direction. There is a peculiar art in driving an elephant in the particular course which you may fancy, and, simple as it may seem, it nevertheless requires the hunter to have a tolerable idea of what he is about. It is widely different from driving in an eland, which also requires judicious riding: if you approach too near your elephant or shout to him, a furious charge will certainly ensue, while, on the other hand, if you give him too wide a berth, the chances are that you will lose him in the jungle, which, notwithstanding his size, is a very simple matter, and, if once lost sight of, it is more than an even bet that the hunter will never again obtain a glimpse of him. The ground being favorable, Kleinboy called to me to commence firing, remarking very prudently that he was probably making for some jungle of wait-a-bits, where we might eventually lose him, I continued, however, to reserve my fire until I had hunted him to what I considered to be a safe distance from the two old fellows which we had first discovered.

At length closing with him, I dared him to charge, which he instantly did in fine style, and as he pulled up in his career I yelled to him a note of bold defiance, and, cantering alongside, again defied him to the combat. It was thus the fight began, and, the ground being still favorable, I opened a sharp fire upon him, and in about a quarter of an hour twelve of my bullets were lodged in his forequarters. He now evinced strong symptoms of approaching dissolution, and stood catching up the dust with the point of his trunk and throwing it in clouds above and around him. At such a moment it is extremely dangerous to approach an elephant on foot, for I have remarked that, although nearly dead, he can muster strength to make a charge with great impetuosity. Being anxious to finish him, I dismounted from my steed, and, availing myself of the cover of a gigantic nwana-tree, whose diameter was not less than ten feet, I ran up within twenty yards, and gave it him sharp right and left behind the shoulder. These two shots wound up the proceeding; on receiving them, he backed stern foremost into the cover, and then walked slowly away. I had loaded my rifle, and was putting on the caps, when I heard him fall over heavily; but, alas! the sound was accompanied by a sharp crack, which I too well knew denoted the destruction of one of his lovely tusks; and, on running forward, I found him lying dead, with the tusk, which lay under, snapped through the middle.

Regaining my horse, I advanced toward this elephant, and when within forty yards of him he walked slowly on before me in an open space, his huge ears gently flapping, and entirely concealing me from his view. Inclining to the left, I slightly increased my pace, and walked past him within sixty yards, upon which he observed me for the first time; but probably mistaking "Sunday" for a hartebeest, he continued his course with his eye upon me, but showed no symptoms of alarm. The natives had requested me to endeavor, if possible, to hunt him toward the water, which lay in a northerly direction, and this I resolved to do. Having advanced a little, I gave him my wind, when he was instantly alarmed and backed into the bushes, holding his head high and right to me. Thus he stood motionless as a statue, under the impression, probably, that, owing to his Lilliputian dimensions, I had failed to observe him, and fancying that I would pass on without detecting him. I rode slowly on, and described a semicircle to obtain a shot at his shoulder, and, halting my horse, fired from the saddle; he got it in the shoulder-blade, and, as slowly and silently I continued my course, he still stood gazing at mo in utter astonishment. Bill and Flam were now slipped by the natives, and in another moment they were barking around him. I shouted loudly to encourage the dogs and perplex the elephant, who seemed puzzled to know what to think of us, and, shrilly trumpeting, charged headlong after the dogs. Retreating, he backed into the thicket, then charged once more, and made clean away, holding the course I wanted.

The weather had hitherto been favorable for the toilsome pursuit of elephant hunting, little rain having fallen since I had first entered the country. At length, however, the rainy season was at hand, and we were constantly visited by the most appalling thunder-storms, accompanied by overwhelming torrents of rain, which filled the hitherto dry nullahs and gravelly water-courses with running streams, and converted the parched forest and arid plains into blossoming verdure and grassy meads. While hunting I was often overtaken by the rains, and on these occasions I still managed to keep myself tolerably comfortable by compelling the natives to erect for me a bothy, or temporary hut. This duty they often proved reluctant to perform; but I invariably managed to gain my point by explaining to them that, if my guns and powder were exposed to the rain, they would die, and then I could kill no more elephants for them.

When attended by a large party, the erection of a good substantial bothy was a simple and easy proceeding, and was accomplished in the following manner: One party, armed with tomahawks, went in quest of long forked poles, which they cut in lengths often feet: a second party gathered green brush-wood; and the third collected a large quantity of long dry grass, which they tore out of the ground by the roots. The poles were set up in a circular position, the forked ends meeting and resting against one another overhead, then the brush-wood was tightly inn laced between the poles, leaving a small low aperture for the door, and the fabric was effectually thatched with the long grass, the conical summit being usually crowned either with the enormous ear or a portion of the hide of an elephant. Such was the bothy which the natives were wont to build for me when overtaken by storms, or when the sky looked threatening, during the remainder of that and all the subsequent seasons that I hunted among the Bechuaqa tribes. But it often happened, when I had lain down for the night with no other roof above me than the vaulted canopy of heaven, that my placid slumbers were rudely disturbed by rain falling like a water-spout on my face. Such events as these were extremely disagreeable, more especially when it came down so heavily as to preclude the possibility of maintaining our usual watch-fires. In weather like this the prowling tyrant off the forest is ever most active in his search for prey, and our ears were occasionally greeted with the deep-toned voices of troops of lions, as, attracted by the smell of our beef, they prowled around our encampments.

I continued hunting to the eastward of Bamangwato until the 8th of October, during which time I added four other noble elephants, besides rhinoceroses and other animals, to my already satisfactory list of game.

The rains having fallen, the country was already adorned with a goodly coating of verdant grass, and my oxen, having done little else than feed and rest themselves for several months, were now full of spirit and in fine condition, and rattled along before my heavily-laden wagons, over rugged hills and through the trackless mazes of the forest, at a rapid and willing pace, and on the evening of the 4th of October I once more formed my encampment at Lesausau, in the Bamangwato Mountains, in the neighborhood of Sicomy's kraal.

Here I was quickly welcomed by Sicomy, who visited me in company with a numerous body of his tribe. He expressed himself much gratified at seeing me return in safety from the dangerous pursuit in which I had been employed, remarking that he was often anxious about me in my absence, for, if any casualty had befallen me, my king, he said, would be certain to seek restitution at his hands. His majesty was pleased to compliment me on my extraordinary success and skill in hunting, and observed that the medicine of the white man must indeed be strong.

In the course of the evening he amused me with the quaintness of his questions, asking me if ray father and mother were alive, how many brothers and sisters I had, if the flocks and herds of my king were extremely abundant, and if his subjects were more numerous than his own. On informing him that our chief was a woman, he seemed much tickled by the disclosure; and when I said that her subjects were as numerous as the locusts, he looked round on his warriors with an evident grin of disbelief, and then inquired of me if all my countrymen could vanquish the elephants as easily as I did. This was a puzzler: so I replied that I could not say; but I knew that the hearts of all my nation were very strong, like the heart of the lion when his cubs are small. The whole assembly was greatly moved by this bright remark, and a general murmur of surprise and admiration extended through the dusky ranks as each man repeated to his neighbor the surpassing courage of my lion-hearted countrymen.

Mollyee and Mollyeon were brothers; they were tall, active-looking savages, with large, bright, sparkling eyes, and a pleasing cast of features. Kapain was a short, thick-set, noisy individual, remarkable for his ugliness, and was the funniest fellow in all Bamangwato. Kuruman was a good-natured boy of about sixteen years of age; his face was prepossessing, resembling that of a girl more than the sex to which he professed to belong. I entertained Sicomy with stewed meat and coffee, and he and his retinue remained that night in my encampment. Before retiring to rest he intimated to me, through Mutchuisho, that he wished to trade with me on the ensuing day, which I said I should be happy to do until the hour of mid-day, when I would positively inspan and leave Lesausau. Accordingly, at an early hour on the morrow sundry fine tusks and some good specimens of native arms and costume made their appearance, which I obtained in barter for beads, ammunition, and other articles. On inquiring of the king what had become of Isaac, he said that he had long since returned to Kuruman in company with a son of "old Seretse," a Bechuana of distinction residing in the vicinity of Kuruman. This individual, whose name, being translated, signifies "mew" is remarkable for his bitterness against the advancement of the Christian religion and for the number of his progeny. Bidding adieu to Sicomy at mid-day on the 5th, I continued my march for Corriebely, which I reached about noon on the following day. I was accompanied, as usual, by a number of the natives, in the hope of obtaining a supply of flesh, elephants being reported to have revisited Massouey. Heavy rains had fallen throughout this district, and the country now presented an entirely new appearance, rank young grass having everywhere sprung up, and the plains and forests displaying a profusion of the richest verdure. It was here that I had concealed a large quantity of lead, in a hole beneath the ashes of my fire, before re-crossing the mountains of Bamangwato. Proceeding to the spot, I had the satisfaction to observe that the ground appeared to have been undisturbed, and, returning to the wagons, I commenced to unlash from the side of one of these a shovel. The natives, who always watched my movements with great attention, at once observed me, and a large party followed me to my former fire-place.

I continued hunting at Massouey till the 12th, when, bidding a long farewell to the land of elephants, I inspanned, and marched upon Lepeby, which I reached at an early hour on the following day, having traveled several hours during the night, availing myself of the bright moonlight. When last I visited this fine fountain the game drank at it in numerous herds, but now not an animal of any kind came near it, with the exception of a few rhinoceroses. This I always found to be the case at the fountains during the summer months, when the game are very independent of water, owing to the more abundant moisture contained in the young grass. In the forenoon I went bird-nesting among the reeds and rushes which grew around the fountain. Hundreds of birds resembling the red pole were busy building their grassy nests, which they ingeniously suspended between the tops of the reeds. In the rushes I found two nests of the water-hen, containing eggs, which, along with the nests, exactly corresponded with those in Scotland. Two beautifully-painted wild geese, an egret, or white heron, and about twenty teal, ornamented the fountain, and were so tame that they permitted me to approach within a few yards of them.

At an early hour on the 16th I trekked for Bootlonamy, which I reached at sundown on the same evening, and drew up the wagons under an impenetrable grove of picturesque mimosas, which were then gayly decked with a profusion of highly-scented yellow blossoms, brightly contrasting with their summer vestment of delicious green. Here I continued hunting for several days, and enjoyed excellent sport, daily securing several fine specimens of the different varieties of game frequenting the district. On one occasion, while hunting, I started a secretary from off her nest, which was built on the top of a very dense green tree, with thorns on the fish-hook principle. With much difficulty I cut my way to the large thorny branch on which the nest was built, and, to proceed further being impossible, from the denseness of the thorns, I cut through this branch with my knife, and by dragging it down I got hold of the eggs, which were the size and shape of a turkey's, and the color of a buzzard's egg.

On the forenoon of the 19th we were visited by a most terrific storm. The thunder was the most appalling I had ever heard, resembling the simultaneous discharge of a thousand pieces of artillery it burst close over my head with a report so sudden and tremendous that I involuntarily trembled, and the sweat ran down my brow. At other times the thunder rumbled on every side, and rolled away with a long-protracted sound, which had not died before fresh explosions burst above and around me. The lightning was so vivid that it pained my eyes; it seemed so near, that I fancied every moment it must strike the wagons, which would certainly have proved extremely inconvenient, as I had three hundred pounds of gunpowder stowed in one of them beneath my bed. About sundown the storm had passed away, having exquisitely purified the atmosphere, while the grateful earth and fragrant forest emitted a perfume of overpowering sweetness. I then sauntered out with my rifle toward where the oxen were grazing, and, falling in with a herd of brindled gnoos, I shot a couple of shaggy old fellows, firing right and left. The storm set in again about 10 P.M. with thunder and lightning, which continued throughout the greater part of the night.

CHAPTER XIX

I had now arrived at a period of considerable importance in my lonely expedition, an event having occurred which caused me a world of trouble and anxiety, yet was nevertheless finally beneficial in its results, as it taught me what difficulties a man may surmount when he is pressed by adversity; and it was also the means of my becoming an accomplished wagon-driver. I allude to my being abandoned by all my colonial servants, with the exception of Ruyter, the little Bushman. I attributed this unmanly and dastardly proceeding mainly to their despair of succeeding in bringing the wagons safely across the sandy deserts intervening between me and the distant missionary station of Bakatla, on account of the broken state of one of the axletrees of my traveling wagon, Kleinboy in one of his drunken fits having driven it against a tree with such violence that one of the wooden arms of the fore axletree was cracked right across, so that little now held the wheel excepting the finch-pin and the iron skein. I remarked on the 22nd that there was something unusual on the minds of my colonial followers, for none of them could look me in the face; and in the evening I spoke harshly to them concerning some ground coffee which I had missed from my canteen.

On the 23rd of October I was lying asleep in my wagon, a little before the day dawned, when Ruyter awoke me to report that my four Hottentots had decamped during the night. He said that each of them had taken with him a large bundle of biltongue or sundried meat, and that they had tried hard to prevail on him to accompany them. This was a rather startling announcement, for I had barely enough of hands to perform the work when they were with me, and the four savages from Bamangwato, like myself, were quite unaccustomed to the laborious and intricate art of wagon leading and driving, and the inspanning and outspanning of oxen. Imagining that the Hottentots would not persevere in so rash and unwarranted a measure, and that they would assuredly change their minds and retrace their steps to their master when they reflected on the step they had taken, I did not endeavor to overtake them, but employed the morning in stowing the wagons, lashing down pots, spades, axes, &c., in their proper places, and overhauling the gear preparatory to marching.

The vley of Bootlonamy being firm and hard, we rattled along it at our wonted pace; but in the evening, as we cleared the vley and entered on the sandy tracts beyond, the oxen, having discovered that their new drivers could not wield the whips with the rapidity and execution of the old, declined to move along the heavy sand beyond the pace they fancied, often halting of their own accord. Eventually, in ascending a sandy ridge, the Bushman's wagon stuck fast in the deep sand, and in trying to drag it out the oxen broke the "dissel-boom," or pole. Finding that the labors we had undertaken were greater than I had calculated upon, I resolved to ride on the morrow in pursuit of the runaways; and accordingly, at daybreak on the following day, leaving the wagons and their valuable contents at the mercy of the savages, I started with the Bushman and a spare horse to endeavor to overtake them. There was no water where the wagons stood, so I instructed Mollyeon to proceed with the cattle in quest of that essential requisite. I held along my old wagon-track, where we traced the footsteps of the Hottentots; and having ridden some miles, we reached the spot where they had slept, and where the ashes of their fire still were smoldering. I followed up their spoor till mid-day, when I accidentally took up the spoor of a party of Bakalahari, which we followed in a westerly direction, imagining that the Hottentots were with them.

Faint, hungry, and thirsty, we now desisted from our fruitless search, and on looking for my matches, I found, to my intense mortification, that I had lost them; and being on this occasion minus my shooting-belt and rifle, we spent the night without a fire, thereby incurring great danger of losing the horses and ourselves by lions. Scarcely had we off-saddled when two huge rhinoceroses came up and stood within twenty yards of us, and would not for a long time be persuaded to depart. Sometime after I observed a dark-looking object prowling around us, and evidently anxious to cultivate the acquaintance either of ourselves or the horses. It was a hyena. Rising from my comfortless couch, I pelted him with stones, when he took the hint and made off. The horses were completely done up, and when knee haltered would not feed. One of them, on being off saddled, lay stretched upon the ground, and after a while, on endeavoring to walk, repeatedly rolled over on his side.

On the 25th I cast loose the horses as soon as it was clear, and ascended to the summit of a pyramidal little hill beside which we had slept, to ascertain from thence whither I had wandered; but the view from this hill did not help to elucidate matters, endless forests stretching away on every side without a mark to assist my memory. I now resolved to seek no longer for my ruffianly Hottentots, but to retrace my spoor to the water I had discovered on the preceding evening, and halt there for a day until the horses should sufficiently recover their strength to carry us back to the wagons. By adhering to the horses' tracks, I reached the water at an early hour, and here I discovered the fresh tracks of the Hottentots on the top of our horses' spoor of the preceding evening. I had, however, resolved not to ride another yard after them; I accordingly off-saddled, and remained there for the remainder of the day. In the vicinity of the water we discovered the spot where the Hottentots had slept during the night. Although possessed of flint and steel, they had not kindled a fire, having nevertheless collected fuel for that purpose previous to our arrival on the preceding evening. This, as I afterward learned from themselves, was to prevent our discovering their position, in case we had returned that evening. I spent most of the day in endeavoring to make fire, which I failed to accomplish for want of tinder. This was extremely annoying, for I had brought along with me both tea and coffee, as also a kettle, and a haunch of springbok.

On the morning of the 26th we cast loose our horses, and proceeded to consume raw meat and water. While thus breakfasting, a pair of superb roan antelopes approached the water, advancing within easy range before they noticed us. We saddled up and rode for the wagons, which we reached in the afternoon, having off-saddled for an hour by the way. I found the wagons as I had left them, as also the savages, who had fortunately discovered a small vley of rain water about two miles to the southward of their position, where they had daily refreshed themselves and the cattle. My situation was by no means an enviable one, and my mind was burdened with anxiety. One of the wagons was fast in deep sand, with the dissel-boom broken, and the fore axle of the other was cracked, so that at any moment it was likely to give way; and if this should happen on the line of march while crossing the desert and far from water, I should have had no alternative but to abandon the wagon to its fate. Moreover, owing to the indo lent disposition of the Hottentots, everything connected with the gear was broken and out of order, while the hatchets appeared to have been used in chopping gunflints, and all their handles were in similar condition.

I arose at dawn on the morning of the 27th, and, having cast loose the horses and oxen, rummaged out my tools, and in two hours I got out the broken dissel boom and put in a new one, which I formed from the stem of a tough mimosa. This being accomplished, I yoked twelve oxen to the wagon which was sticking in the sand, but tried in vain to make them drag it out, for the cunning animals knew that it was fast, and would not exert themselves to attempt to extricate it. After inconceivable trouble and repeatedly shifting the positions of the various oxen in the span, I at length made a fortunate arrangement of the oxen. The brutes for once pulled all together, and once more the wagon was in motion, I then inspanned the other team, and we reached the water without further trouble. As we neared the water I detected a giraffe browsing within a quarter of a mile; this was well, for we required flesh. Toward the end I thought he was going to beat me, and I was about to pull up, when suddenly he lowered his tail, by which I knew that his race was run. Urging my horse, I was soon alongside of him, and with three shots I ended his career. Having obtained for the present both flesh and water, my next look-out was to consider how I was to cross the sandy desert which lay between me and the kraal of Booby. It was very evident that I could not return by the route I had previously held, having already ascertained that that country to ox-wagons was now impassable, all the waters being dry.

On explaining this to my Bamangwato followers, Mollyeon stated that he had once traversed that country in a dry season many years before, and that he and his comrades had obtained water in some deep pits, which had been excavated by Bakalahari in a rocky part of the desert, considerably to the eastward of my former route. He said we should require the greater part of two days to reach this water, our route thither lying across a soft sandy soil, varied in many places by almost impenetrable forest; he, moreover, seemed a little doubtful as to whether he should be able to discover the place, and, when we did, whether the pits might not prove dry. This was certainly a bright look-out, more especially as the next water (which he represented as a perpetual fountain) was two days beyond the uncertain pits.

On the 28th I was occupied about the wagons all the day, putting aside things to rights. I had thoughts of trekking on the following day, and could not divest myself of the most dismal forebodings, for I felt certain that the heavier wagon would again stick fast, or that the cracked axle-tree would come in contact with some tree, and leave me in the desert a hopeless wreck, remote from water or any assistance. I had certainly good reason to be uneasy. On the 29th I waited till the sun was up, that the cattle might drink plentifully, when I immediately inspanned, and commenced my anxious journey. For the first ten or twelve miles we proceeded along a hollow, where the soil was in general tolerably firm; but on leaving this hollow we entered upon a most impracticable country, the wagons sinking about four inches in the soft sand. Though I held on, I had not the slightest hope of getting through it, for every hundred yards required the utmost exertion both of ourselves and oxen; yet I had the best of two days more of it to expect before I could reach the promised water. To increase our difficulties, our progress was presently opposed by an interminable forest, where the trees stood so close together as often to bar the possibility of the wagons passing between them.

On the 30th I inspanned before it was light, and again held on, as on the preceding day, through heavy sand and interminable forest, where it was necessary to keep the axes in constant operation. In the afternoon we reached the promised watering-place, but on springing from the wagon, and running anxiously forward for an inspection of the pits, I had the mortification to find that all they contained was a little mud, in which sundry heterogeneous insects were sprawling. The Bechuanas, however, signified to me that, by clearing out the pits and digging a little, water would make its appearance. Accordingly, having outspanned the jaded oxen, I unlashed the spades, which were vigorously plied, when the water began very reluctantly to trickle in from every side. We thus cleared out the three most likely pits, and in two hours I obtained a cry moderate supply of water for each of the oxen, which I gave them individually out of my large fleshpot. My poor horses did not get a drop; and we now proceeded to inspan, and resume our march beneath a burning sun of unusual intensity. The sand became, if possible, worse than ever, and the wagons repeatedly stuck fast. We held through a jungle of the most virulent wait-a-bit thorns, which reduced my wagon sails to ribbons; and when the sun went down I halted for the night, and cast my wretched oxen for an hour.

On the 31st my vans were again in motion before daylight; and about 4 P.M., to my infinite delight and great relief, I got clear of the desert, and reached a strong perennial fountain situated in a finely-wooded valley on the northern borders of the mountain country, extending to the southward, with little intermission, as far as the chain of the Kurrichane rante. Toward the end of the march it was necessary to descend into a valley, and cross a very awkward watercourse, in which the baggage-wagon was within a hairbreadth of being capsized. Ascending from this valley, we crossed a precipitous ridge, where large disjointed masses of rock threatened the momentary destruction of the wagons. As I was yoking one of the oxen, which had broken his yoke-skey and got out of his place, I received from a vicious ox in front a severe kick on the cap of the knee, which gave me intense pain and laid me prostrate on the ground. I, however, managed to drive the wagon to its destination, where, after lying for a few minutes, the pain increased so much that I lay panting on my bed. Just as I had out-spanned, and before my knee had stiffened, a herd of zebras approached the fountain to drink. This was a God-send at such a moment, our flesh being at an end and the dogs starving. In torture as I was, I managed to make a limping stalk toward them, when I obtained a fine double-shot and brought down a brace of tine old mares.

On the morning of the 2nd I shot a koodoo, which antelope seemed here to be tolerably abundant; and about mid-day, as I sat writing beneath the wagon, I observed a troop of zebras approaching the fountain, followed by a string of koodoos, three of which carried unusually fine horns. While I sat looking at them through my spy-glass, I directed Ruyter to bring up the horses, when we saddled the "Gray" and the "Chestnut Pony," and rode slowly toward them, till they started, when we gave them chase. They took right up the face of a stony ridge, and as they disappeared over its summit the Bushman was riding within a spear's length of the finest buck. Before, however. I could gain the ridge, the "Old Gray" refused to proceed further, when, dismounting, I resumed the chase on foot, but failed to fall in with my after-rider, who eventually brought the koodoo to a stand. Retracing my steps, I directed my attention to my poor "Old Gray," which was evidently attacked with the African distemper. With considerable difficulty I brought him to the camp, where I instantly bled him, but to no purpose, and in another hour the "gallant gray" lay down and "stretched his stiff limbs to rise no more." At night the lion feasted on him, and when he was full the leopard and hyenas finished him.

On the morning of the 8th I left this fountain and held for Booby, which I reached at mid-day on the 5th. On my way thither we one evening fell in with a large herd of elands, out of which I captured a first-rate bull. I was kindly welcomed by Caachy, now the chief of Booby, the former chief having been blown up in my absence as already mentioned. Caachy informed me that my runaway Hottentots had reached his kraal, and were very much exhausted by their march. He had assisted them with corn, and passed them on to Bakatla. They informed this chief that I had dismissed them from my service, having engaged other servants at Bamangwato. I remained at Booby till mid-day on the 7th, and obtained several very fine karosses and other native curiosities in barter from the tribe. The king supplied me liberally with boyahva, or native beer, which I thought most excellent, but found that it possessed a soporific tendency, inducing me on one occasion to lie down and sleep for half the day, while the king and his nobility were waiting to trade with me.

Early on the 13th, while taking coffee, I was met by a party from Bakatla, who had been kindly dispatched by Dr. Livingstone, the resident missionary, on hearing of my abandonment by my colonial servants. The party consisted of a Bechuana, named Mabal, belonging to Kuruman (who assisted Dr. Livingstone in teaching the children of the Bakatlas), and. three of the Bakatla tribe. These men reached me just at the proper moment; for, having inspanned, before we had proceeded three hundred yards the damaged axle-tree broke short across, and the wheel rolling away, the wagon came down on its side. This was a catastrophe I had for some time anticipated, and I was only thankful that it had. been deferred so long. We outspanned, and having unloaded the wagon, we put a support under it, and took out the fore-tell, and I then set about making a false axle-tree of tough thorn-wood. The vertical sun was extremely powerful, and both my ankles gave me severe and never-ceasing pain from wounds inflicted by the cruel wait-a-bits, and inflammation induced by the unvarying animal diet on which I had so long subsisted. In the afternoon of the following day I got the false axle-tree fixed in its proper position, and having loaded up the wagon we were once more ready for a start.

On the 15th we inspanned, and, having passed through the bold mountain gorge, of Sesetabie, we encamped on the margin of a periodical river whose precipitous banks and broad channel of deep soft sand caused me considerable apprehensions of difficulties for the morrow.

On the 16th I unlashed my spades and pickax, and worked hard for several hours cutting down the precipitous banks of the river and 3onstructing a road for the wagons to pass; after which we inspanned and took the stream. I drove my wagon safely through; but, alas not so with the baggage-wagon. Twice it stuck fast in the treacherous sand while crossing the river's bed, but the sturdy oxen pulled it out, and had dragged it more than halfway up the almost perpendicular bank, when the native who led the long team, unrainful that a wagon was behind them, suddenly turned the leading oxen short toward the river's bank, thus rendering it impossible for the driver to steer his after-oxen. The wagon was dragged off the fine road which I had made for it, and after quivering for a moment as if loth to meet its fate, it fell heavily over and rolled down the bank with a most terrific crash, smashing the fine capped tent, and sending the ivory and all my highly-valued trophies flying into the bed of the river in a mass of the most dire confusion.

This was enough to vex any man; but I had now become so seasoned to adversity that I only laughed at the capsize as though the accident had happened to a foe; and having unyoked the oxen, we commenced carrying the heavy ivory and other articles up the bank to the level ground beyond after which we righted the wagon, and a team of oxen dragged it up the bank. I then set to work to repair the tent with green boughs, and before sunset we had again replaced the greater part of the cargo. As the sun went down "The Cow" died from the distemper which had carried off my other two horses. The night set in with thunder, lightning, and rain; jackals and hyenas prowled around us, and soon found the remains of ray lamented charger, on which they feasted till the dawn of day.

The 17th ushered in a lovely morning, and the sky was beautifully overcast with clouds. When I got things dry I finished stowing the wagon, and we then trekked, holding on till the evening, when the axle-tree which I had made burst, and the finch-pin giving way, the wheel rolled off, leaving me once more a wreck. While securing my few remaining horses, I remarked that a handsome little bay horse, named "Hutton," evinced symptoms of the distemper, but I did not bleed him, as it seemed to be of no avail. Heavy rain continued falling throughout the night, and next morning the ground where we had outspanned was a mass of deep mud. At an early hour all hands were busy in again unloading the broken wagon, and before night I had finished another axle-tree and fixed it in its place. The day throughout was dark and gloomy—heavy clouds hung low on the mountain of the eagles, reminding me of the mist I was wont to see in the distant country of the Gael, and our ears were repeatedly saluted with the subdued voices of a troop of lions which were moaning in concert around its base. In the evening the horse called "Hutton" died, and scarcely had night set in when his doleful coronach was wildly reechoed by the shrill voices of a score of jackals, which the lions hearing soon came to their assistance, and presently we heard them feasting on his remains.

On the morning of the 19th we resumed our march, and at a late hour on the evening of the 20th we reached the missionary station at Bakatla, where I was kindly received by Dr. Livingstone and his amiable lady. They had been anxious concerning my fate, and entertained great apprehensions for my safety. Mrs. Livingstone had seen my Hottentots as they passed through Bakatla, where they remained only one day; and that lady represented them as bearing the appearance of men who had been guilty of crime. She had endeavored, but without success, to prevail upon them to rejoin their master and return to their duty. Dr. Livingstone at the time was absent on a visit to Sichely, superintending the erection of a dwelling-house and place of public worship at that chief's kraal, named "Chouaney," whither he intended shortly to remove, there being another missionary, named Mr. Edwards, already stationed at Bakatla, who was then absent on a visit to the colony. Dr. Livingstone informed me that at present there was war between the Baquaines, of whom Sichely is chief, and the Bakatlas, and that the latter were in daily expectation of an attack.

The 23rd was Sunday, when Dr. Livingstone showed me, on comparing notes, that I had lost a day during my sojourn in the far interior. I attended Divine service, and had considerable difficulty to maintain my gravity as sundry members of the congregation entered the church clad in the most unique apparel. Some of these wore extraordinary old hats ornamented with fragments of women's clothes and ostrich feathers. These fine hats they were very reluctant to take off, and one man sat with his beaver on immediately before the minister until the door-keeper went up to him and ordered him to remove it. At dinner we had a variety of excellent vegetables, the garden producing almost every sort in great perfection; the potatoes, in particular, were very fine. Today another of my stud, named Yarborough (so called in honor of a gallant major of the 91st from whom I purchased him), died of the distemper, and was immediately consumed by the starving curs of the Bakatlas.

We were marching quietly along, and were nearly opposite the center of the reeds, when, on emerging from a grove of thorny mokala-trees, casting our eyes to the right, we suddenly beheld a numerous herd of buffaloes grazing on the open plain between us and the vley. Their dark imposing squadrons extended over a great space of ground, and we reckoned that there might have been between six and eight hundred of them. I immediately saddled "Sunday," and rode toward them. As I drew near, they stood gazing at me for a minute, and then, panic-stricken, the whole herd started off together, making for the nearest wood. Pressing my horse, I was soon ahead of them, and by shouting I turned them right about, when they thundered along in a compressed mass, and held for the reeds. Their amazing numbers greatly impeded their progress, and I had no difficulty in keeping alongside of them. I kept on their right flank to enable me more conveniently to fire, and on one occasion, on my riding very near the foremost of the herd, a large division of those behind me suddenly extended to the right and increased their pace, and, on looking over my shoulder, I found myself almost surrounded by their helmeted squadrons.

As I galloped along I endeavored to select the finest head, but among so many it was no easy matter to make a choice, and as soon as I selected one he disappeared among the ranks of his companions. I marked the reeds bowing before them far on my right and left as they splashed and struggled through the marshy vley, and presently they gained the other side, when, emerging from the reeds, they held across the open plain, steering for their strongholds in the woods beyond. As the clouds of dust behind me cleared away, I looked back and beheld a fine old cow stagger for a moment and then fall dead, and near her stood a wounded calf, whose mother had remained beside it, being loth to leave her offspring.

I now returned to Dr. Livingstone, when we brought up the wagon for the fallen buffaloes, and halted for the night. Just as we had outspanned, a blue wildebeest, having observed the oxen, and taking them for buffaloes, fearlessly approached the wagon, when, advancing under cover of one of the oxen, I bowled him over with my rifle. Early on the following morning the reed cutters from Chouaney hove in sight, and were not a little gratified to find so bountiful a supply of their favorite "niama," or flesh, awaiting their arrival. The afternoon was cold and rainy, and at a late hour we outspanned at Chouaney, where we were immediately welcomed by a messenger from Sichely, who expressed himself highly gratified at our arrival, and promised to come and breakfast with me next morning.

CHAPTER XX

At an early hour on the 26th of November Sichely presented himself with a large retinue. The appearance of this chief was prepossessing, and his manner was civil and engaging; his stature was about five feet ten inches, and in his person he inclined to corpulency. His dress consisted of a handsome leopard-skin kaross and on his arms and legs, which were stout and well turned, he wore a profusion of brass and copper ornaments manufactured by tribes residing a long way to the eastward. In the forenoon I accompanied Sichely to his kraal, situated in the center of the town, and alongside of it stood respectively the kraals of his wives, which were five in number. These kraals were neatly built, and were of a circular form, the walls and floors being smoothly plastered with a composition of clay and cow-dung, and secured from the weather by a firm and well-constructed thatch of rank dry grass. Each kraal was surrounded by an area enclosed with a strong impenetrable fence six feet in height. The town was built on a gentle slope on the northern side of a broad extensive strath, throughout the whole extent of which lay wide fields and gardens enclosed with hedges of the wait-a-bits.

The modes in which they propitiate the clouds are various. The one most commonly practiced is by collecting a few leaves of each individual variety of tree in the forest, which they allow to simmer in large pots over a slow fire, while a sheep is killed by pricking it in the heart with a "lemue" or long sewing-needle, while the rain-maker is employed in performing a variety of absurd incantations. The steam arising from the simmering leaves is supposed to reach and propitiate the clouds, and the remainder of the day is spent in dances, which are joined in by all the tribe and kept up till midnight, being accompanied with songs having a long-continued chorus, in which all join, and the burden of which is the power and praises of the rain-maker. It often, however, happens that the relentless clouds decline attending to the solicitations of the rain-maker, and the fields of young corn become parched and withered. Other schemes are then resorted to. A number of the young men sally forth, and, forming an extensive circle, they enclose the rocky face of some mountain-side in which the rock-loving klipspringer is likely to be met with, when, by gradually contracting their circle like our Highlanders of old, they generally manage to catch alive sundry klipspringers, whose voices are supposed to attract rain. The unfortunate little antelopes thus captured are paraded round the kraal, while the rain-maker, by pinching and tormenting them, induces them to scream. But as it often happens that these and all his other machinations prove unavailing, the rain-maker is at times obliged eventually to make a moonlight flitting and cut and run for it, when the services of another of the fraternity are courted.

When the rain-makers fail to fulfill their promises, they always ascribe their want of success to the presence of some mysterious agency which has destroyed the effect of their otherwise infallible nostrums. One of these anti-rain-making articles is ivory, which is believed to have great influence in driving away rain, in consequence of which, in the summer season, they produce it only as the sun goes down, at which time it is brought for the trader's inspection carefully wrapped up in a kaross. I remember on one occasion incurring the censure of a whole tribe, who firmly believed me to have frightened the rain from their dominions by exposing a quantity of ivory at noon-day; and on another occasion the chief of a certain tribe commanded a missionary with whom I am acquainted to remove all the rafters from the roof of his house, these having been pointed out by the rain-maker as obstructing the success of his incantations.

The Griquas, taking advantage of the superstitions of the Bechuanas, often practice on their credulity, and, a short time before I visited Sichely, a party of Griquas who were hunting in his territory had obtained from him several valuable karosses in barter for a little sulfur, which they represented as a most effectual medicine for guns, having assured Sichely that by rubbing a small quantity on their hands before proceeding to the field they would assuredly obtain the animal they hunted.

When Dr. Livingstone was informed of the circumstance he was very much shocked, declaring that in future the natives would fail to believe him when he denounced supernatural agency, having now seen it practiced by his own countryman. I obtained several very fine karosses, as also ivory, ostrich feathers, and sundry interesting curiosities, in barter from Sichely and his tribe; and at noon on the 27th we took leave of Sichely and started for Bakatla. In the evening of the following day I lost another horse of the distemper it was "The Immense Brute;" and next morning the chestnut pony also died. About midnight an immense herd of buffaloes came feeding slowly toward us, and, imagining our oxen to belong to their own party, they continued to advance until we were actually surrounded by them. I then arose in my sleep, and, having remarked in Sichuana to the natives that the buffaloes were very good, I once more lay down, utterly unconscious of what I had done or spoken.

On the afternoon of the 29th we outspanned at Bakatla. A party of Baralongs were then on a visit to Mosielely on a trading excursion for skins for the manufacture of karosses. The headquarters of these men was situated to the westward of Motito, on the borders of the great Kalahari desert. Night set in with a terrific thunder-storm, which prevailed for several hours the lightning was most painful to the eyes, and deafening peals of thunder continually burst above and around us. From the proximity of the explosions, we entertained considerable fears for the safety of the natives in the town, for the lightning appeared repeatedly to strike in that direction; and when the storm had subsided, a messenger from the king came down to the missionary's dwelling-house to report that the kraal occupied by the six strangers had been struck by the electric fluid, and that one of them was killed on the spot, and the other five were more or less affected by the shock. Dr. Livingstone informed me that this melancholy event would entail great alarm and uneasiness upon Mosielely, since all the tribes would blame him for the accident.

On the 11th I took leave of my kind host Dr. Living stone, and, after a steady march of many days, on the 21st of January I reached Kuruman, where I was entertained by Mr. Moffat with his usual kindness and hospitality. The following day was Sunday, when I attended Divine service in the large church morning and evening, and saw sixteen men and women who had embraced the Christian faith baptized by Mr. Moffat. It was now the fruit season, and the trees in the gardens of the missionaries were groaning under a burden of the most delicious peaches, figs, and apples. The vines bore goodly clusters of grapes, but these had not yet ripened. My runaway Hottentots had passed through Kuruman sometime previous to my arrival, and it was reported that disease had overtaken them at the missionary station of Campbellsdorp, where they were now all four stretched upon a bed of sickness, and in a state of the most abject want and misery. Isaac had likewise made his appearance in due course, and he came boldly forward to claim his wages, which I honestly paid him. I left in Mr. Moffat's kind keeping one of the wagons with its contents (which we stowed away in a room obligingly lent me by Mr. Moliat for the purpose), and also the whole of my oxen, with the exception of one span, with which, on the evening of the 7th, I set out for Koning, which I reached at an early hour on the following morning, having marched during the greater portion of the night.

Leaving Koning on the afternoon of the 8th, I resumed my march for Daniel's-kuil. Between Koning and Daniel's-kuil occur two interesting caves, long famous as affording a residence and protection to hordes of marauding Bushmen. The larger of these caves is situated on the west side of the wagon-track; it is of great size, and contains a perpetual fountain of delicious water, and its sides have been adorned by its Lilliputian inhabitants with correct likenesses of most of the game quadrupeds of Africa, as also unicorns, which of course they never saw, and must therefore have heard spoken of by other men. From this cave the Bushmen were wont to sally forth not very long since, and lift fat cattle from the sleek herds of their more industrious neighbors, the Griquas and Bechuanas. Returning with these cattle, their custom was to drive them all into the cave, whence, being well supplied with water, they did not again proceed until the flesh was either rotten or consumed. It was in vain that the exasperated owners of the cattle followed on their traces to the Bushman-cave, for here they well knew it was madness to follow further, as inevitable death would be the result, by the poisoned arrows of their subtle foes within. At length the Bushmen became so frequent and daring in their attacks, that a number of the Bechuanas held "a great talk" on the subject (as they say in America), and ended by resolving to attack the Bushmen, and accomplish their destruction at whatever cost.

Accordingly, when the next robbery was committed, the Bechuanas marched upon the Bushman-cave, armed with large oval shields and battle-axes; and, entering the cave, they steadily advanced under cover of their shields, while the Bushmen's arrows rattled thick upon them like a storm of hail. The Bechuanas thus continued to advance until they came to close quarters, when they cut them down with their battle-axes. The other cave is situated to the eastward of the wagon track; here, on a similar occasion, fire was made use of to smoke out the Bushmen, when those who escaped death by suffocation fell by the battle-axes and assagais of their foes without.

On the 10th I marched from Daniel's-kuil, and early on the 12th I encamped at Campbellsdorp, where I found Mr. Bartlett and Captain Cornelius Kok in great force. Here I at length overtook my runaway Hottentots. Sickness and starvation had done their work upon them, and they were so altered in their appearance that I scarcely knew them. They were now acting as servants to the Griquas who had nursed them in their illness and they were working hard to earn their bread. On inquiring of there why they had forsaken me, they said that they had started in a rash and thoughtless moment, and that, although they almost immediately repented the step they had taken, fear and shame prevented them from returning to their duty. Commiserating their condition, I presented them with the amount of their wages during the time they had remained with me, and, being now quite independent of their services, I allowed them to remain with the masters they had chosen. I here met an extremely plausible individual, a Dutchman, from the Bo-land or Cape district, who was got up in his rig at considerable expense. This fellow was swindling the Griquas right and left, purchasing from thera all their best cattle at extravagant prices, and settling for them with paper notes, which naturally were forged. He represented himself as being one of a wealthy firm in Cape Town, and stated that two of his partners were then purchasing cattle among the Boers to the eastward, from whom they had already collected two thousand head; which cool assertion the Griquas were silly enough to believe, and he left their country for the Bo-land with a large drove of fat oxen. Eventually, however, he was brought to justice, and I afterward heard of his being safely quartered in the jail of Beaufort.

At a late hour on the 13th I outspanned my wagons on the fragrant bank of the lovely

Vaal River by clear moonlight, and on the morrow, the water being then fortunately low, I crossed the river with little difficulty, and on the 20th I took the drift of the Great Orange River, but with very faint hopes that my worn out oxen would succeed in dragging me through its treacherous sands, more especially since two Boers who had crossed an hour previous had deemed it necessary to inspan sixteen tearing, well-conditioned oxen into their light wagons. I was right in my conjecture, for with infinite flogging and shouting I got the wagon half way through, when it stuck fast, and no efforts could prevail upon the oxen to move it a yard further. A Griqua offered to lend me on hire a fresh span of able bodied oxen, when, with the help of these and some of my best, I got safely through, and once more encamped within her majesty's dominions. While the wagon was sticking in the middle of the river, a Boer took the drift from the opposite side with a light new wagon and twelve superb oxen, which bore him through in gallant style. Resuming my march for Colesberg, I trekked on till near midnight, when I lost my way in the dark. The country here was parched and arid, not a blade of grass for the weary oxen, but hopeless sterility stretched far around.

On the 21st I left the Bushman to bring on the wagon, while I walked ahead, under a most terrific sun, to the farm where I had purchased Prince and Bonteberg while en route to the far interior. My costume consisted of a dilapidated wide-awake hat, which had run the gauntlet with many a grove of wait-a-bits, a dusty looking ragged shirt, and a pair of still more ragged looking canvas trowsers, which were, moreover, amputated above the knee, while my face was adorned with a shaggy red beard, which told ensemble imparted to me the appearance of one escaped from Bedlam. As I drew near the farm, its inmates took fright at my wild appearance, and two of the Boers, timidly projecting their heads from the half-closed door, loudly shouted to me to lay down my gun.

On the 26th I marched at dawn of day, and in four hours I entered the village of Colesberg, where I found my old friends, the 91st, replaced by a detachment of the 45th. My first move was to visit the post-office, where I was very much disappointed to find no letters awaiting my arrival. Having off-loaded my wagon, I handed it over to Mr. Arnott, the resident blacksmith, to undergo repairs, of which it stood much in need. My Bechuana followers were extremely struck with the size and appearance of Colesberg, and the movements of the military elicited their unfeigned delight and approbation.

On the 1st of February I left Colesberg, and reached Grahamstown on the forenoon of the

22nd, when I took up my residence with Captain Hogg, of the 7th Dragoon Guards, in my old quarters at the barracks of the Cape Mounted Rifles. The officers of the 7th had brought out with them a pack of fox-hounds, which while they lasted, afforded excellent sport, but, unfortunately, the climate of Southern Africa, especially near the coast, is so very unfavorable for well-bred English dogs, that, although no trouble nor expense was spared in the management of these hounds, and fresh drafts were constantly exported from England, and litters of pups carefully reared in the colony, the pack nevertheless had considerably diminished. These hounds were under the especial surveillance of Captain Hogg, who hunted them in a manner which evinced his consummate skill and judgment in the manly and ennobling pursuit of the chase.

CHAPTER XXI

I continued in Grahamstown until the 7th day of March, when I set out once more on my weary journey for the distant forests of the far interior. Before leaving the town I settled my accounts with the merchants from whom I had obtained supplies, and who evidently seemed to consider my returning to the colony as a very doubtful event. I engaged a discharged soldier of the 91st, named George Martin, in the capacity of head servant. This man hailed from Haddington, and bore an excellent character on leaving the regiment. He was accustomed to the charge of horses, in which he took a great interest. My most important purchases in the sporting department consisted of a valuable double-barreled rifle, with spare shot-barrels by Westley Richards, which I obtained from Captain Hogg, and two right good steeds, one of which was a very superior coal-black gelding, which I purchased of Captain Walpole, of the Engineers, for £20, which was considerably below its value. I named this horse Black Jack; in paces and disposition he very much resembled my lamented Colesberg, and he was altogether one of the finest horses I ever mounted. His end was sudden and severe; for on a subsequent expedition, along with another of ray favorite horses, he was torn to pieces and consumed by a troop of ruthless lions. The other horse which I purchased was a gray; and as it is probable that this horse may be introduced in future pages, under the designation of the "Old Gray," I trust the reader will wit be confounded with the idea of the resurrection of the original "Old Gray."

On the morning of the 9th I reached Fort Beaufort, when I encamped at the mess-house of the 7th. I continued there until the morning of the 10th, when I resumed my march for the interior. In Fort Beaufort I purchased four right good horses from the officers of the garrison one of these was a jet black steed, and was named by his late master Schwartland. This horse was one of the finest shooting-horses in Southern Africa, and understood his work so well that he seemed to follow the game with all the eagerness of a grey hound, and yet he would suddenly halt in full career when I wished to fire, if I merely placed my hand upon his neck. From his back I subsequently shot many elephants and other game, and his name will often appear in after pages. At the farm of Messrs. Nelson and Blane I purchased two more horses, which I called Brown Jock and Mazeppa, and also a span of oxen and some much cows.

On the 2nd of April I entered the village of Colesberg, where I was actively employed in making final preparations for my distant campaign until the 9th. I engaged two Hottentot servants named Boot and Kleinfeldt, the latter individual being one of those who had forsaken my banner at Bootlonamy, and I purchased two more valuable steeds, which increased my stud to ten very superior young horses. I also purchased a number of rough, long-legged serviceable dogs, of a variety of breeds, which, with several other ragged-looking tykes that I subsequently purchased from Boers along the line of march, increased my kennel to about twenty business-like dogs. At sunrise on the 9th we marched out of the village and held on until we reached the Orange River at Boata's Drift, where we outspanned beneath the shade of a grove of willows.

I was now all anxiety to reach my Fountain of Elephants, and pushed on with all speed for Massouey. On the 15th, just as I had reached the Bastard kraal of Rhama, I fell in with ray old servant Carollus, who had absconded from me at Bootlonamy. He was in company with the wagons belonging to Mr. David Hume, the trader, on their return to the colony, but, meeting with his old companions Kleinfeldt and Kleinboy, he resolved to turn about and re-enter my service, which I was not sorry for, as I was short of hands for the distant expedition I was about to make. I also fell in with Captain Arkwright and Mr. Christie, who were proceeding up the country on a similar expedition to my own.

On the 16th of May I halted at Chouaney, at the residence of Dr. Livingstone, who told me that one or two troops of elephants had been frequenting the district. With one of these I fell in on the 20th, when I had an opportunity of testing the sportsmanlike qualities of my new servant Martin. The troop consisted of nine bull elephants, the finest of which I shot, but Martin, after selecting the poorest of the lot, ultimately lost him. We now pressed on as rapidly as possible for my favorite fountain Massouey, which we at length reached on the 29th.

I felt sincere pleasure in revisiting this very interesting spot. I found it well frequented by the elephants. Two troops of cows and three old bulls had drunk there on the preceding night.

When the wagons came up to my old halting-place, I took a hasty breakfast, and then started on the spoor of an enormous old bull. After following him north for about six miles, we lost him in the spoor of a troop of cows; I accordingly followed the spoor of the cows, and soon came up with them. The troop consisted in all of about ten, but there were only three full-grown cows in the troop; each of these three, unluckily, went off in different directions, I rode within twenty yards of the best, and, halting, put two balls close behind her shoulder, and, calling to Martin to finish her, galloped after the second best. I soon got a view of her, and in three minutes had turned her head toward camp, and presently rolled her over with about six shots. Martin and the Bushman not appearing when two hours had elapsed, I rode to camp, where, to my astonishment, I found my servant, who had actually lost my elephant through the most inexcusable want of pluck. I was very much annoyed, and regretted having attacked the troop at all.

At dawn of day Mollyeon and I walked to the fountain to seek for elephants' spoor. A troop of cows, several small bulls, and two well-grown bulls, had drunk during the night, besides an immense number of rhinoceroses, perhaps twenty. I made a hasty breakfast, and then took up the spoor of the two best bulls, with one after-rider. The spoor led nearly southeast. After following it for about six miles, we found ourselves in an elevated part of the forest, which commanded a fine view of the mountains to the east, and here Mollyeon climbed to the summit of a sandal-wood tree to try if he could see the elephants. He could not see those we were spooring; but he saw three other bull elephants, about three parts grown, feeding slowly along, steering about north; after a short and dangerous conflict, I slew the best with five bullets.

On the morning of June 1st, before the sun rose, Mollyeon and I walked to the fountain to see if elephants had drunk. Ten bull elephants had been there, and had all gone off together, holding a .southeasterly course; this was glorious. I started on the spoor with five natives, and Kleinfeldt as after-rider on Dreadnaught. I took eight of my dogs, all led in strings, and rode Schwartland, my best shooting-horse. After following the spoor for about five miles, we found ourselves to leeward of the elephant I had shot on Saturday, and here the elephants had smelled the blood, and started off in great fear, going clean away through open country, steering one point west of south. They got into an old elephant foot-path, and held steadily on for many miles, not halting to break one branch or to allow the ground. The leading native said he did not expect to see them, and I was certainly of the same opinion. At length they got into a thickly-wooded part of the country, and although they were still holding clean away up wind, they had occasionally little to feed. Here I started an oryx. We presently reached the border of a very wide open country, where the spoor took a turn to the east. We proceeded a four hundred yards further, when we had the unexpected satisfaction to behold the mighty squadron drawn up in the open cover, in open order, two hundred yards ahead. Some of them stood motionless as statues, others moved slowly here and there, and browsed upon the trees.

The troop consisted of ten bull elephants: eight of them were about three parts grown; the other two were enormous old elephants, in magnificent condition. We halted and gave the dogs water, and I then rode slowly round the elephants to ascertain which was the best. After riding twice along their front, they all, as if by one accord, turned their faces to me, and advanced leisurely within forty yards, giving me an excellent opportunity of making my choice. At length they saw me, and, sounding the alarm, all made off together in great consternation. I galloped alongside of them to make my final choice, and selected the largest elephant. I had some difficulty in getting him clear of his comrades, some of which were extremely fierce, and were trumpeting along, with their tails and trunks aloft. At length I got him clear; all my dogs had gone off to the right and left after other elephants, and Dreadnaught came galloping up to me, having thrown my after-rider, who did not succeed in recapturing him.

My elephant now, hearing the barking and trumpeting on every side, halted beside a bushy tree, with his head high, and right to me but, presently turning his broadside, I gave it him sharp right and left after the shoulder; and the dogs, hearing the shots, came up to my assistance. The conflict now became fast and furious; I had very pleasant work with this fine old elephant. My horse behaved very well, and the elephant's fury and attention were chiefly directed toward the dogs, who stuck well to him; but he was by far the toughest elephant to finish that I have ever engaged with. I gave him thirty-five balls, all about and behind his shoulder, and discharged at distances varying from fifteen to thirty-five yards, before he would halt and die. At length he reduced his pace to a very slow walk; blood flowed from his trunk and all his wounds, leaving the ground behind him a mass of gore; his frame shuddered violently, his mouth opened and shut, his lips quivered, his eyes were filled with tears; he halted beside a thorny tree, and, having turned right about, he rocked forward and backward for a few seconds, and, falling heavily over, his ancient spirit fled. The natives now came up, and, having promised to go on the spoor of my horse Dreadnaught, I returned to Massouey, having off-saddled for an hour.

No elephants having drank at the fount for some days, on the 5th, I resolved to leave my favorite Massouey. I accordingly marched about 1 P.M. I passed Corriebely an hour before dark there was water enough for the horses. Here I met Mutchuisho with a large party of Bechuanas, sent by Sicomy to endeavor to make me come and trade with him. I halted for an hour after sunset, and then inspanned and trekked on till the moon went down, when I halted near my old outspanning-place, having performed a very long and difficult march.

On the 7th Sicomy made his appearance early, and toward evening bought powder and lead with seven elephants' teeth. Soon after this bargain was concluded he ordered men to take away the teeth, and he threw me back the powder; but on my kicking back the powder, and swearing I would shoot the first man who touched the ivory, he relinquished the idea.

On the succeeding day Sicomy prowled about the wagons all day, and bothered me so that I at last lost my temper, and swore at him. The natives held a consultation for a few minutes, which ended by their saying that they were all going to leave me. I said that I was happy to hear it. They then decamped to a man; but in an hour four of my old acquaintances appeared, and said that the captain wished me to come and see him; but I replied that I was sick, and going to sleep. In another hour he made his appearance; and on asking him what I had done that he had called all his men away, he replied that they had gone away to have a sleep. Presently Arkwright and Christie ride up to my wagons theirs were at hand. On the march they had lost one ox and two horses in pitfalls. At night Arkwright and I watched the water, but did not get a shot.

On the 9th Sicomy brought me ivory. He asked me to go to my hunting-ground, saying that he would trade with me there. He was very anxious to separate the two parties. As soon as possible, therefore, I inspanned, and trekked down the broad straight, steering south, although the natives asserted that I should find no water, and tried to guide me north. After trekking about eight miles, much to the annoyance of the Bamarigwatos, I discovered the residence of the Bahwas, where I halted for the night, having sent a message to Schooey, the old chief, that I would trade with him next day.

The next day the old chief, with his wives and nobility, appeared at an early hour, and by mid-day I had purchased several tusks of elephants; also two very fine karosses of leopard-skin, &c. I then inspanned, and in two hours got clear of the Bamangwato Mountains, when I held about east, through thick forest, halting for the night beside a small fount, where the horses could not drink. On the march pallah were abundant and very tame.

On the morning of the 12th Sicomy came to my fireside, and said he was going to trade with me. A party of Bakalahari had arrived a little before, bearing twenty nine elephants' teeth. After some trouble we set the trading a going, and in about three hours I had purchased ten bull and ten cow elephants' teeth for ten muskets, and seven other cow elephants' teeth for powder, lead, and flints. I then bought two kobaoba knobkerries. At this moment natives came in, and reported elephants to have drunk within a mile during the night. This caused an immense bustle in twenty minutes I was under way, with two after-riders and a party of good spoorers, followed by about a hundred and fifty starving natives. We took up the spoor a mile to the south, and followed it due east until the sun went down, when we halted for the night. While spooring we met the country in flames far and wide, but we crossed the fire, and found the spoor beyond. We saw a troop of eight fat male elands, and a troop of eight giraffes.

Next day we followed the spoor for several miles in an easterly course, when it took a turn to the northwest, through most horrible wait-a-bit thorns. About mid-day we came up with the elephants. The troop consisted of one mighty bull, and two bulls three parts grown. I first shot the best of the two small bulls, and then the old bull. The natives and all my dogs had kept him in view, and one fellow had pricked him in the stern with an assagai. Upon the strength of this, the Bechuanas came up and claimed him as theirs when he fell; but on my threatening to leave their country, they relinquished the idea.

On the 16th and 17th I bagged two first-rate bull elephants in the level forests to the eastward of Mangmaluky.

On the 18th, after breakfast, I rode to Mangmaluky to water my horses. One old bull elephant had been there, but the natives had too much flesh, and would not spoor. I rested all day, expecting my wagons, but they did not appear. At night a panther came within ten yards of my fire, and killed Cradock and disabled Wolf, my two best elephant dogs.

Early in the morning we resumed the spoor, which led us due west along the borders of the desert without a check until sundown. We had now spoored these elephants a very great distance, and the horses had not had water since the morning of the preceding day. I felt compassion for the thirsty steeds, and was on the point of turning, when, lo! a string of Bakalahari women were seen half a mile before us, each bearing on her head an immense earthen vase and wooden bowl containing water. They had been to a great distance to draw water at a small fountain, and were now returning to their distant desert home. This was to us a perfect God-send. The horses and dogs got as much as they could drink, and all our vessels were replenished. The sun being now under, we halted for the night.

At sunrise we resumed the spoor, and after following it for about ten miles, and finding that these elephants had gone clean away into the desert beyond the reach of man, we gave it up, and made for the fountain where the women had drawn the water on the preceding day. On reaching the fountain wo found that four bull elephants had drunk there during the night. It was a soft, sandy soil, and the spoor was beautifully visible. I had never seen larger spoor than that of two of these; they had fed slowly away from the fountain, and we followed on with high hopes of seeing them that day.

At length we got into a more densely wooded country, and presently observed the elephants standing in the forest about one hundred yards off. Having succeeded in securing the dogs, I shifted my saddle to Jock, and rode slowly forward to inspect the mighty game. Two of the elephants were but three parts grown; the other two were very large, but one of them was a great deal taller and stouter than the other. This immense elephant, which was, I think, decidedly the largest I had ever seen, had unfortunately both his tusks broken short off close to the lip; I therefore hunted his comrade, who carried a pair of very beautiful and perfect tusks. At the sixth shot he came to a stand and presently fell. I then dismounted and ran up to him, when he rose to his feet and stood some time, and then walked a few paces, and fell again and died. Ongoing up to him I found that he carried the finest teeth I had yet obtained; they must have weighed one hundred pounds each. He was an extremely old bull, and had been once much wounded with assagais, the blades of two of which were found in his back.

On the 17th I made for camp, and held through a fine open country lying northwest from Corriebely. In following some ostriches I came upon an extremely old and noble black rhinoceros lying fast asleep in some low wait-a-bits. The birds having tried in vain to waken him, I fired from the saddle. The first ball hit him as he lay in the shoulder; the second near his heart, as he gained his feet. In an instant the dogs were round him; he set off downhill at a steady canter, and led me a chase of a mile, when he came to a stand, his shoulder failing him. At this instant I beheld a troop of about twenty fine elands trotting before me on the open slope; I therefore quickly finished the black rhinoceros with two more balls, and then gave chase to the elands. I bagged the two best in the troop, a bull and cow, the latter about the fattest I have ever seen. I brought the bull within one hundred yards of the chukuroo.

At dawn next day I shot, from the spot I had slept on, a springbok, running, through the heart, at one hundred yards. After cutting off the horns of the black rhinoceros, I held on for Letlocbee, and slept at Lebotane, a very strong and perpetual fountain.

On the 19th, at sunrise, I pursued my march to the famous fountain of Letlocbee, to which I removed my camp. On the 24th I left Letlocbee, and marched upon Lotlokanc.

In the forenoon of the next day I rode out to look for koodoos without success. While riding through the forest I came upon the bloody spoor of an elephant; he had been evidently hunted by natives. The elephant was not far away, for, following the spoor a few hundred yards, I came upon about sixty natives, who were hanging the flesh in garlands upon the thorny trees all around. This was an old bull elephant, and was quite lame, when the Bechuanas found him, from a ball wound in the shoulder. On returning to camp, one of my Hottentots, who had been after some strayed oxen, stated that he had come upon a buffalo newly killed by a lion, and that the lion was lying in the bushes close by, watching his prey.

The next day, after breakfast, I rode np the will glen above camp, intending to seek for bastard gemsbok on the other side of the mountains. I had ridden half way up the glen, when lo! the long-wished for lovely sable antelope stood right in my path; a princely old buck he stood about two hundred yards ahead, looking at me. Having heard that dogs can easily catch this antelope and having all my dogs at my heels, I sent them ahead, and fired a shot to encourage them; in half a minute they were at the heels of the potaquaine, and turned him down hill. He crossed the glen before me, and dashed up a very rough and rocky pass in the rocks to my right, the dogs following, but considerably thrown out. I listened to hear a bay, but listened in vain; to follow on horseback was impossible. I therefore galloped round to an opposite point, and listened with breathless anxiety, standing in my stirrups to catch one sharp note from my trusty dogs. Nor did I wait long in a distant hollow in the rocks I could faintly hear my dogs at bay.

My heart beat high; it must be the sable antelope, and the dogs would never leave him. Already I felt that he was mine, and with a joyous heart I urged Mazeppa over the most fearful masses of adamantine rock, and at last came into the hollow, where my dogs were keeping up a furious bay. Some thick bushes concealed the game from my view; I peeped over these, and, to my intense disappointment, instead of the sable antelope, I beheld an old bull koodoo fighting gallantly for his life. I bowled him over with a shot in the heart, and rode to follow two other sab antelopes which I had seen on the face of a rocky hill while galloping round the rocks to seek for my dogs. I had ridden a few hundred yards, when, high above me on the shoulder of a rocky and well-wooded mountain on the opposite side of the ravine, I detected a fourth sable antelope, a fine old buck. I rode into the deep ravine, and, having secured the steeds, I stripped to my shirt, and ascended the bold face to stalk him.

I held for a little to leeward of where I had marked him; the Bushman followed with Boxer on a string. When I gained the summit I proceeded with extreme caution, and at length beheld him through the trees within a hundred yards of me; I crept about ten yards nearer, and then lay till he should move; this he presently did. He walked obligingly forward, and stood broadside in all his glory, with his magnificent meter shaped horns sweeping back over his haunches. I fired. The ball broke his fore leg in the shoulder, and he dropped on his face, but, recovering himself, gained his legs, and limped slowly over the ridge. Boxer immediately appeared, and was beside me just as I peeped over the ridge, and beheld the wounded buck looking back within fifty yards of me. On seeing Boxer he turned about, and as he turned I sent my second ball through his ribs. He then disappeared, and stumbled down the rocky mountain side, with Boxer at his heels. I followed as fast as could be, and found him half way down the mountain, sitting on his haunches at bay, where I finished him with a shot in the heart. This was a magnificent sable antelope in the prime of life; he was very fat, and the flesh was excellent.

On the 1st of September, about 12 o'clock, Mollyee came and told me that my cattle-herd had come upon four wildebeests killed by a troop of lions. I immediately sent for the steeds and rode to the spot, with Martin and the Bushman as after-riders, and accompanied by all my dogs. On reaching the ground, the dogs immediately took up scent, and went beating up the wind. I rode after, hunting them on, and presently I missed Boxer and Alert. Wolf now beat up a scent to windward, on which he afterward went oft' at full speed, and was soon heard at bay with a lion. Just as Wolf started I heard a dog bark to leeward, and, riding hard in that line, I found Lassie barking at a large bush, in which the lions had taken shelter, but were gone. I was followed by poor cripple Argyll, who went boldly in and took up the scent. I lost sight of Argyll in the bushes. I then turned my face as Wolf had gone, and rode hard to seek him; at length he came up to me, quite exhausted with his exertions.

I rode back to seek Boxer, Alert, and Argyll. On coming to the place where Argyll had gone off, I found lions' spoor, and the spoor of the dogs on the top of it. After holding this spoor for a few hundred yards, I met my dogs, who, returning, led me to the game I sought—it was a noble lioness. As I approached I first beheld her great, round face and black-tipped ears peeping over the low bushes. On riding up she obstinately kept her full front to me, although the dogs were barking close around her at length she exposal a raking side shot, and the ball smashed her shoulder. She then charged among the dogs without doing any harm. At my second shot Schwartland was unsteady and spoiled my aim; the ball, however, passed through the middle of her foot from side to side. I beckoned to Martin for my Moore, and, having got it, rode up within a few yards of the lioness and gave her a shot, which crippled her in her other shoulder. She then fell powerless on the ground, and I fired my fourth shot for her heart on receiving it, she rolled over on her side and died. I cut off her head and the ten nails of her two fore feet, and rode to camp, where I found that the rascally Hottentots, taking advantage of Martin's absence, had boned all my rich game broth, replacing it with cold water. It blew a very stiff breeze of wind while I was hunting the lions, which entirely prevented me from hearing the dogs bark. The evening being very cold and windy, I did not watch the water. Lions roared around our camp all night.

CHAPTER XXII

On the afternoon of the 3rd of September I watched the fountain. Toward sunset one blue wildebeest, six zebras, and a large herd of pallahs were all drinking. I am enjoying contemplation for at least fifteen minutes, and, most of them having then slaked their thirst, I sent a ball through the heart of the best headed pallah. I then took a long shot at the blue wildebeest bull, and sent the other ball into his shoulder. I now came to the camp, and ordered the pallah to be paced in front of my hole beside the water, to attract the lions. Having taken my coffee, I returned to the water with Kleinboy and Mollyee. It was bright moonlight. We had scarcely lain down when the terrible voice of a lion was heard a little to the east; the jackals were feasting over the remains of the white rhinoceros of yesterday, and only one or two occasionally came and snuffed at the pallah. Presently a herd of zebras, accompanied by elands, approached the water, but were too timid to come in and drink a troop of wild dogs now came boldly up, and were walking off with the pallah, when I fired into them. They made off, but immediately returning and again seizing my pallah, I fired again, and wounded one of them.

Soon after we had lain down a thundering clattering of hoofs was heard coming up the vley, and on came an immense herd of blue wildebeest. They were very thirsty, and the leading cow very soon came boldly up and drank before me. I sent a ball through her; she ran sixty yards up the slope behind me, and fell dead. Her comrades then thundered across the vley, and took np a position on the opposite rising ground. In two minutes the hyenas and jackals had attacked the carcass of this wildebeest. Soon after this a lion gave a most appalling roar on the hush height close opposite to us, which was succeeded by a death-like stillness which lasted for nearly a minute.

I had listened with intense anxiety for about fifteen minutes longer, when I heard the hyenas and jackals give way on either side behind me from the carcass of the wildebeest, and, turning my head slowly round, beheld a huge and majestic lion, with a black mane which nearly swept the ground, standing over the carcass. He seemed aware of my proximity, and, lowering his head, at once laid hold of the wildebeest and dragged it some distance up the hill. He then halted to take breath, but did not expose a broadside, and in a quarter of a minute he again laid hold of the wildebeest and dragged it about twelve yards further toward the cover, when he again raised his noble head and halted to take breath.

I had not an instant to lose; he stood with his right side exposed to me in a very slanting position; I stretched my left arm across the grass, and, taking him rather low, fired the ball took effect, and the lion sank to the shot. All was still as death for many seconds, when he uttered a deep growl, and, slowly gaining his feet, limped toward the gover, roaring mournfully as he went. When he got into the thorny bushes he stumbled through them as he moved along, and in half minute I heard him halt and growl fearfully as if dying. I had now every reason to believe that he was either dead or would die immediately, and if I did not seek him till the morning I knew very well that the hyenas and jackals would destroy him. I accordingly went up to camp, and, having saddled two horses, I and Martin rode to seek him, taking all the dogs, led in strings by the natives. On reaching the carcass of the wildebeest we slipped the dogs, and they went off after the hyenas and jackals we listened in vain for the deep growl of the lion, but I was persuaded that he was dead, and rode forward to the spot where I had last heard him growl. Lassie, now coming up, commenced barking at a bush in front of me, and, riding round, I had the immense satisfaction to behold the most magnificent old black-maned lion stretched out before me.

The ball had entered his belly a little before the flank, and traversed the length and breadth of his body, crippling him in the opposite shoulder. No description could give a correct idea of the surpassing beauty of this most majestic animal, as he lay still warm before me. I lighted a fire and gazed with delight upon his lovely mane, his massive arms, his sharp yellow nails, his hard and terrible head, his immense and powerful teeth, his perfect beauty and symmetry throughout; and I felt that I had won the noblest prize that this wide world could yield to a sportsman. Having about fifteen natives with me, I sent for rheims and the lechter-uit, and we bore the lion to camp.

On my way from the water to get the horses and dogs, I shot an extremely old bull black rhinoceros with a single ball he dropped to the shot. His horns were quite worn down and amalgamated, resembling the slump of an old oak-tree.

On the 8th, as I and Kleinboy watched the underwater about midnight, we heard a black rhinoceros blowing beside the upper water. We very rashly walked up within about eighteen yards of him, with no other shelter than a small bush. On perceiving us, the borele at once turned his head to me and advanced slowly: Kleinboy, who was on my right and had a good chance, fortunately fired without orders, and the ball entered the shoulder with a fine direction. Borele then charged madly and furiously through trees and bushes, right toward camp, making the most tremendous blowing noise, and halting in a stony open flat close to the wagons he stood, and staggered about for a minute or two, and then fell. On coming up to him, I found him a magnificent specimen, carrying three distinct horns.

After breakfast on the 10th, the oxen having drunk, we inspanned and marched to Bootlonamy, which we reached at sunset.

After a march of three days, during which the cattle and horses nearly died of thirst, we reached Moselakose, a retired fountain in a bold glen or gorge in the first mountain chain before us. As we approached this fine fountain, the poor, thirsty, loose cattle rushed ahead to the water, not a little gratified by the sight.

I found the spoor of game abundant at the water accordingly, out spanned at a considerable distance from it, and at once set about making a hole from which to shoot the game as they came up to drink.

After breakfast on the 10th I rode to the water and again lay in my hole. There were large herds of game standing within a few hundred yards of me when I lay down, and soon after the horses had disappeared they came on from all sides and completely surrounded me. It was of no consequence that they got my wind, and frequent alarms were sounded—the thirsty game to windward would not heed the alarm, and, standing their ground fearlessly, they gave the others confidence. There was standing within shot of me at once about three hundred pallahs, about twelve sassaybies, and twenty zebras. I could only make out two very fair heads in all that vast herd of pallahs, and these were not to be compared with my best Soobie heads; I therefore amused myself by watching the game, and did not fire, having resolved to wait quietly, in the hope of some rarer game appearing, such as koodoo, sable antelope, or wild boar, &c.

A singular circumstance occurred as I watched the waters on the 20th. Having shot a sassayby, he immediately commenced choking from the blood, and his body began to swell in a most extraordinary manner; it continued swelling, with the animal still alive, until it literally resembled a fisherman's float, when the sassayby died of suffocation. It was not only his body that swelled in this extraordinary manner, but even his head and legs, down to his knees.

The 21st was a bitter cold morning, with a strong wind from the southwest. I rode to my hole at the fountain before the morning star appeared. Shortly, becoming impatient of lying still, I rose from my hole to examine what game has drunk during the night, and, to my astonishment, at once discovered the spoor of a mighty bull elephant, which must have drunk there not many hours before. I went in haste to camp, and, having made all ready for a three-days' trip, took up the spoor with two after-riders and six natives. It led us in an easterly course, first through a neck in the mountains, and then skirting them for about five miles through thick cover and over hard adamantine rocks and sharp stones. The elephant had fed as he went along, and we soon came up with him standing in a thicket. When we first caught sight of him he was within twenty yards of us, a bushy tree nearly concealing him from our view. I first observed one of his tusks, and then I had to dispatch Kleinboy to catch the cowardly natives, who were making off at top speed with my dogs on strings. The dogs fought well with him it was very rocky ground, and I gave him one deadly shot before he was aware of our presence. I then hunted him into softer ground, and slew him with the tenth shot.

This fellow made up my fiftieth elephant bagged in Africa, not to mention numbers lost.

On our way to camp, while following an old established elephant and rhinoceros foot-path, I observed a gray mass beneath a bush, with something which looked like a shining black horn stuck out on one side it was within about eight yards of our path. When I got alongside of it I saw that it was a princely old bull buffalo, with a very remarkably fine head. He had lain his head flat on the ground, and was crouching, in the hope that we should ride past without observing him, just as an old stag or a roebuck does in Scotland. I gave the dogs the signal of the presence of game, when, as dogs invariably will do, they dashed off in the wrong direction. The buffalo sprang to his feet, and in one instant he was lost in the thicket.

From the quantity of buffalo's spoor on the north gulf of this mountain range, I made up my mind that there must be some strong water on that side of the hills, as only one or two buffaloes occasionally came to drink at the fountain where I was encamped; the natives all declared that there was none. I, however, on the 22nd, determined to ride thither to explore, and accordingly started with Kleinboy and the Bushman. We held first about west, and then crossed the mountains by a succession of very rocky valleys and ravines. When we had gained the highest part of the rock, which opened to us the forests of the north, a troop of seven doe koodoos and three rhooze-rheeboks started on the opposite side of the ravine. The dogs, observing the koodoos, gave immediate chase; and after a very fine and bold course, they brought one to bay far in the valley below, which Kleinboy shot.

I had, in the meantime, ridden ahead, following an old-established game foot-path, and after proceeding two or three miles I had the satisfaction to discover a beautiful fountain in a deep rocky ravine on the north side of the mountains. Here was fresh spoor of black and white-rhinoceros, buffalo, wildebeest, sassayby, koodoo, klip-springer, &c. A little after this I was met by my after-riders, who had likewise discovered a ravine containing water a little to the east. There they had started two bull buffaloes, three buck koodoos, and a troop of rheebok. I then rode to inspect this water, and took up the spoor of the buffaloes, in the hope of bringing them to bay with the dogs.

On teaching the steeds I rode hard for camp, as the day was far spent. Passing the mouth of another bold ravine, we crossed very well-beaten paths, which led me to suspect that this ravine also contained a fountain. We had ridden about half way to camp when a fine old bull eland came charging up to leeward, having got our wind. I sprang from the back of Mazeppa, and gave him both barrels as he passed me. We then gave him chase through very thick cover, and after a sharp burst of about a mile I shot him from the saddle he carried a very fine head, and was, notwithstanding the lateness of the season, in very good condition.

On the 23rd, in the forenoon, I rode to explore the suspected ravine of the day before, and, having crossed the mountain chain, came upon the fresh spoor of a very large troop of cow elephants leading toward the spot. I at once determined to follow it, and dispatched the Bushman to camp for the dogs and Kleinboy's gun, &c. I rode slowly ahead on the spoor, imagining the elephants at a great distance, when, on gaining a ridge, I came full upon the troop, drawn up within twenty five yards of me. There were perhaps from twenty five to thirty of them. The instant I came upon them they got my wind, and, rumbling, away they went in three divisions into the impenetrable cover.

The ground that I had now reached was one solid mass of sharp adamantine blocks of rock, so that a horse could with difficulty walk on it. I held along the ridge above the cover, and in half a minute I heard one division of the elephants crashing through the cover after me. They came on a little above me, and another troop held the same course a little before me, so that I had considerable difficulty in getting clear of them, and when I did I held for the level ground beneath the dense cover. Here I fell in with one elephant with a calf she had only one tooth. I gave her a shot after the shoulder; and next minute, while trying to head her in the dense cover, she very nearly ran me down in her charge. I, of course, lost her immediately, being without dogs.

I then gave up the elephants in vexation with the ground, and rode to explore the ravine. My wounded elephant, however, happened to take the same course above me in the cover, and I once more fell in with her. She was going slowly along the hill sides, keeping in the thickest cover, with a rocky ground, where my horse would be of no service to me. I might now have got her, but as she had only one tooth I was not anxious about her, so I held up the bold wine.

On the 25th, after breakfast, I started with bedding and provisions to hunt for a few days on the other side of the hills. We visited the first water, and established a place of concealment with rocks and green boughs on the rock. While we were making this bothy a wild boar hove in view, but, observing us, he escaped. We then held on to the further ravine, and on my way thither I nearly rode down a fine old bastard gemsbok, which got away among the rocks. I repaired an old hiding-hole at this water, building it up with fragments of rock. I then sent the steeds to a proper distance, put out my fire, and lay down to watch for the night.

First came a pallah, closely followed by a wild dog. The pallah escaped; the wild dog presently returned, and, observing my retreating men, barked loudly; ten minutes after, about eight wild dogs came up the glen and drank. Night now set in, and the moonlight very faint. Presently an occasional loud displacement of rock and stone announced the approach of large game it was two old bull buffaloes; they came and drank, and went away without approaching within shot. Soon after, fourteen buffaloes came; but before these had finished drinking, they got an alarm, and charged panic stricken up the rugged mountain side. They had winded two lions, which came up to the fountain head, and drank within eighteen yards of me, where they lay lapping loudly, and occasionally halting for four or five minutes, but, from their light color and the masses of rock that surrounded them, I could not see to fire. About ten minutes after they had drunk I fancied that they were still lingering, and on throwing a stone their step was heard retreating among the dry leaves and stones.

Soon after this six old bull buffaloes approached from a glen behind us they walked very slowly, standing long to listen. When the leader came up to within twenty yards of us, Kleinboy and I fired together; it ran thirty yards, and in two minutes fell. His comrades, after considering the matter for five minutes, came on once more : we again took the leader, and he also dropped. His comrades, as before, retreated, but, soon returning, we wounded a third, which we did not get. The moon was now under, and it was very dark; the buffaloes, however, were determined to try it on once more, and coming up a fourth and last time, we shot another old bull. In about ten minutes lions were very busy on the carcass of the first buffalo, where they feasted till morning, taking another drink before they went away. Toward daybreak we wounded a white rhinoceros, and soon after two black rhinoceroses fought beside us, but I was too sleepy to rise.

In the evening of the 28th I shot an old bull koodoo. At night I watched the water near my camp with Kleinboy. After a long time had elapsed, an enormous old bull muchocho or white rhinoceros came slowly on, and commenced drinking within fifteen yards of us, and next minute a large herd of zebras and blue wildebeest. It was long before the muchocho would turn his side; when he did, we fired together, and away he went with zebras and wildebeests concealed in a cloud of dust. Next came an old bull borele; we fired together, and he made off, blowing loudly, after charging round and round, seeking some object on which to wreak his vengeance. Next came another borele, and he got two bullets into his person. The fourth that came was another old bull muchocho; he ran forty yards and fell. And fifth came a cow borele; she fell dead to the shots. Three other rhinoceroses came about me, but I was too drowsy to watch any longer, and fell asleep.

These fountains afforded me excellent shooting for about a fortnight longer, during the whole of which time I watched nightly in my different hiding-holes, and bagged buffaloes, rhinoceroses, koodoos, zebras, and other game. One night, while so engaged, a horrid snake which Kleinboy had tried to kill with his loading-rod flew up at my eye, and spat poison into it. Immediately I washed it well out at the fountain. I endured great pain all night, but next day the eye came all right.

CHAPTER XXIII

On the 16th of October we inspanned, and trekked steadily on for Sichely under a most terrific sun, and halted at sundown without water the country was covered with spoor of all the larger varieties of game, including elephants.

On the 17th I inspanned, and trekked a couple of miles, when I found myself once more on the banks of the Ngotwani, which, except at its source, was this year generally dried up; we, however, found a spot in its gravelly bed where, by digging, we obtained sufficient water for all. The natives in charge of the loose cattle chose to remain behind all night, I having too well supplied them with flesh. Though my remaining stud of six horses and twelve trek-oxen were thus absent all night, I was not anxious about them, trusting to the usual good herding of the natives. When, however, they came up after breakfast, they were minus all the loose oxen, without being able to give any account of them, further than that they imagined that they were with us I accordingly dispatched two of my men on horseback to take up their spoor.

On the 18th I arose before it was clear, and rode up the banks of the river with my dogs to seek for waterbuck, and presently arrived where another considerable river's bed joins the Ngotwani. Near this spot I came upon an old water-buck, the first I had ever seen. He was standing among some young thorn-trees, within sixty yards, and had his eye full upon me. Before I could pull up my horse he was off at a rapid pace, and crossed the river's bed above me. I shouted to the dogs, and fired a shot to encourage them; they had a pretty fair start, and in half a minute the buck disappeared over a rocky ridge, with three or four of my best dogs within thirty yards of his stern. I knew that he would make fur the nearest water; accordingly, I kept my eye down the river, and listened with an attentive car for the baying of the dogs.

On the morning of the 22nd I rode into camp, after unsuccessfully following the spoor of a herd of elephants for two days in a westerly course. Having partaken of some refreshment, I saddled up two steeds and rode down the bank of Ngotwani with the Bushman, to seek for any game I might find. After riding about a mile along the river's green bank, I came suddenly upon an old male leopard, lying under the shade of a thorn grove, and panting from the great heat. Although I was within sixty yards of him, he had not heard the horses' tread. I thought he was a lioness, and, dismounting, took a rest in my saddle on the Old Gray, and sent a bullet into him. He sprang to his feet, and ran half way down the river's bank, and stood to look about him, when I sent a second bullet into his person, and he disappeared over the bank. The ground being very dangerous, I did not disturb him by following then, but I at once sent Ruyter back to camp for the dogs. Presently he returned with Wolf and Boxer, very much done up with the sun.

I fancied it was the hyenas, and fired a shot to scare them from the flesh. All was still; and, being anxious to inspect the heads of the buffaloes, I went boldly forward, taking the native who accompanied me along with me. We were within about five yards of the nearest buffalo, when I observed a yellow mass lying alongside of him, and at the same instant gave a deep growl. I thought it was all over with me. The native shouted "Tao," and, springing away, instantly commenced blowing shrilly through a charmed piece of bone which he wore on his necklace. I retreated to the native, and we then knelt down. The lion continued his meal, tearing away at the buffalo, and growling at his wife and family, who, I found next day by the spoor, had accompanied him. Knowing that he would not molest me if I left him alone, I proposed to the native to go to our hole and lie down, but he would not hear of it, and entreated me to fire at the lion. I fired three different shots where I thought I saw him, but without any effect; he would not so much as for a moment cease munching my buffalo. I then proceeded to lie down, and was soon asleep, the native keeping watch over our destinies. Sometime after midnight other lions were heard coming on from other arts, and my old friend commenced roaring so loudly that the native thought it proper to wake me.

The first old lion now wanted to drink, and held right away for the two unfortunate steeds, roaring terribly. I felt rather alarmed for their safety; but, trusting that the lion had had flesh enough for one night, I lay still, and listened with an attentive ear. In a few minutes, to my utter horror, I heard him spring upon one of the steeds with an angry growl, and dash him to the earth; the steed gave a slight groan, and all was still. I listened to hear the sound of teeth, but all continued still. Soon after this "Tao" was once more to be heard munching the buffalo. In a few minutes he came forward, and stood on the bank close above us, and roared most terribly, walking up and down, as if meditating some mischief.

The first notice I got was his sudden spring to one side, accompanied by repeated angry growls, while I involuntarily made a convulsive spring backward, at the same time giving a fearful shriek, such as I never before remember uttering. I fancied just as he growled that he was coming upon me. We now heaped on more wood, and accept up a very strong fire until the day dawned, the lions feasting beside us all the time, notwithstanding the remonstrances of the little native, who, with a true Bechuana spirit, lamenting the loss of so much good flesh, kept continually shouting and pelting them with flaming brands.

The next morning, when it was clear, I arose and inspected the buffaloes. The three that had fallen were fine old cows, and two of them were partly concerned by the lions. The ground all around was packed flat with their spoor; one particular spoor was nearly as large as that of a borele. I then proceeded to inspect the steeds: the sand around them was also covered with the lion's spoor. He had sprung upon the Old Gray, but had done him no further injury than scratching his back through the skin: perhaps the lion had been scared by the rheims, or, on discovering his spare condition, had preferred the buffalo.

On the 24th we marched at dawn of day, and held up the Ngotwani, halting at the fine large pool of water where I had shot the three cow buffaloes two nights previously. I had left Ruyter and some natives to look after my flesh, and these reported lions to have surrounded them all night, coming boldly up within a few yards of them, and only retreating when burning brand were sent flying at their heads.

The 26th was a cool, cloudy morning, and looked like much rain. I was in the saddle long before the sun rose, and rode down the river to seek water-buck, accompanied by all my dogs. I had not ridden far when the dogs dashed up the wind, and started a large herd of cow buffaloes, to which I gave chase. They led me a long gallop right round camp, and ended by taking down wind up the Ngotwani, and sought shelter in the thorny thickets along its banks. Here, as a troop of them charged past me, I dismounted and shot one fine old cow; she brought up in a thicket, but took two more balls before she fell.

The dogs were now coursing up and down the river's bank after an old cow with her two calves of this and last year. At length all three took into a deep pool some hundred yards long, and swam up and down and from side to side, followed by all the dogs. I wounded the old cow, but would not finish her then, and I next shot the two calves, one of which sank to the bottom, but soon after floated. I then came home to my camp for the natives to draw the flesh. Returning, we found the old cow still there, but standing in deep muddy water. She carried a very fine head, but, unfortunately, a bullet had splintered the point of one of the horns. While we were cutting up the veal "the old cow" to the side and got away.

The next day was deliciously cloudy, with some slight showers of rain. In the evening Sichely came down to seeing, bringing my four lost oxen, which he had at length made up his mind to restore. Three of Sichely's men engaged to accompany me to the colony, their wages to be three guns and two cows.

I now proceeded slowly by way of Lotlokane, Motito, and Campbellsdorp, and encamped on the Vaal River on the 11th of November. Here I was obliged to wait for several days, owing to the great body of water coming down rendering a passage impossible.

On the 16th, however, the river having subsided, I inspanned my two wagons, and took the drift with my heaviest wagon, drawn by fourteen oxen. I led the team on horseback, and, several Griquas assisting us, we took the drift very high, and got a little more than half way through, when two of the oxen became entangled in the gear, and, being dragged along, my drive or foolishly halted the wagon. The result of this foolish management was, that the oxen instantly turned right-about-face, and stood with their heads up water, the stream being too powerful for them to stand still otherwise. We spent a fruitless hour of very harassing work, trying to right the oxen, which was, however, impossible, and at length we were obliged to cut away the trek-tow and met the oxen ashore.

The day was now waning away, and both men and oxen were very much knocked up. It was most distressing work, and it was greatly aggravated by the cruel, sharp stones which composed the river's bed, and the virulent, invisible double gee-thorns with which the banks were strewed. I began to despair of getting the wagon out that day; and from the appearance of the weather toward the sources of the river for some time past, we had every reason to expect a flood at any moment. It was a dismal prospect, and my heart was ill at ease. Late in the day we made lose my strong new buffalo trek-tow, and bent it on to the dissel-boom, and then, bringing in the oxen, we managed to fasten the tow on to this one. I also placed several men on the wheels. This time we very nearly succeeded; the wagon started and proceeded several yards, when one of the tows gave way, and we were again left in the lurch.

I could not help thinking of Robinson Crusoe when he visited for the last time the wreck of his ship. I rested but little that night, and had good reason to be anxious; for if the river should come down at all, it would be impossible to do anything with the wagon next day, and I could not expect anything but to see a tearing flood. If this had happened I should have been utterly ruined, for nearly all my worldly property was contained in the wagon. I sent a messenger to Mr. Hughes, requesting him to assist me in my troubles with men and oxen next day, although it was the Sabbath.

I had the gratification to find at day-dawn that the river had fallen a little during the night, and had just finished my breakfast when four Griquas came up, bearing a long stout rope, which Mr. Hughes had forwarded for my use. These men informed me that he had sent men out in different directions to seek for three span of his oxen to be brought to my assistance. We then set about getting the gear in order, and very soon two spans of the oxen appeared with another party of Griquas. We next made fast one end of the rope to the dissel-boom, and to the other end of this rope we fastened the large buffalo trek-tow, which reached slanting across the strong current to shallower water where the oxen could stand. We then brought in two span of oxen, and fastened the end of their tow on the buffalo, and put the oxen in motion.

The river had at this moment increased about six inches, and was now stronger than on the preceding day; moreover, it was still increasing. This put me at once in great consternation; my hopes, which a little before were very high, now sank, and I expected in a few hours, perhaps, to see my wagon overwhelmed and swept away. This, however, was not the case; the river did not increase much more, and in our second attempt we were successful. The trek-tows were on this occasion knotted together, the oxen all trekked fair and together, and the heavily-laden wagon, with its precious contents, was rescued from a watery grave. We hailed its rescue with continued cheers the oxen held stoutly on, and dragged the wagon without a check right out to the shallow water on the border of the river. We then shortened the gear, and, having inspanned two after-bullocks, drove the wagon right out of the river's bed, and outspanned on the top of the high bank.

The next move was to get the other wagons through. The Griquas at first made some demur, saying that it was Sunday; but I very soon got rid of that objection by telling them that I would prepare some food and coffee for them, when they set to work with a good will, and in two hours more the other three wagons were brought safely through, and were high and dry.

On the 8th we entered the village of Colesberg. All the forenoon I was busy off-loading two of the wagons. We spread out the curiosities in the market-ground, making no end of a parade it was truly a very remarkable sight, and struck all beholders with astonishment

On the 13th I left Colesberg, and set out on my way to Grahamstown, passing on the 17th the Thebus flats. On the march I saddled up, and, leaving the wagons, rode across the country for Hendric Strydom's farm, where I had commenced ray sporting career in South Africa. As I rode across the flats I found springbok and black wildebeest still abundant. On reaching the residence of my former friend, I found the blackness of desolation pictured there. The house was falling to pieces, and the grass grew rank where the pot was wont to boil. In a melancholy mood, I then turned ray face for the farm where I had ordered my wagons to halt; and, as I rode along, I mused on the fleeting and transient nature of all human condition. On the 25th I reached Fort Beaufort, where I dined with some old acquaintances at the mess of the 7th.

On the 29th we marched to the Fish River at dawn of day. Here I found about sixty wagons waiting the falling of the river to get through. Some of us set to work to clear away a bank of mud on the opposite side, after which a good many wagons, lightly laden, crossed the river; but on attempting to bring through my large wagon, she stuck fast, and was at length extricated with the help of another span. We saved her just in time, for the river was increasing fast when we got her out, and in another half hour was running a rapid torrent, at least ten feet deep. I found several very jolly farmers, English and Scotch, lying on the opposite side; in particular, one Annesley, of whom I had heard a great deal. This man was a regular "brick," a thorough Scotsman from the borders. He came up to me at once, and asked me to come and have a glass of whisky with him he was accompanied by his family; his eldest daughter was a very line girl

By the 1st of February the river had fallen most rapidly. After some world in clearing away the mud on both sides, wagons began to cross, and a great rumpus was kept up during the remainder of the day. I got my second wagon through about 11 A.M. Soon after I had got through good old Annesley took the drift, and on approaching the opposite side his wagon had the most fearful capsize in deep water, seriously damaging a quantity of very valuable property. In an instant we were all at his assistance, and in a very short time we got out his wife and family and damaged cargo, and righted his wagon for him. I brought him over dry clothes, and spent about three hours in assisting him in his difficulty. I then inspanned and trekked on to Boatasberg, where I halted about midnight, with good moonlight.

On the 2nd I marched into Grahamstown, where I sold my ivory well, the ivory and ostrich feathers realizing in the market somewhere about £1000.

CHAPTER XXIV

I remained in Grahamstown for some weeks, being undecided as to my future plans. At last, however, I decided upon making another elephant-shooting expedition. I accordingly started for the far interior on the 11th of March, and, having resolved to try a short cut through the territories of the chief Mahura, I crossed the Vaal River on the 5th of May, far to the eastward of my former track.

Early on the 7th we entered upon the broad straight through which the Hart River flows. Here we discovered a small fountain, where we halted for the night. We marched early on the 8th, holding up the strath parallel with the Hart River. Presently we came upon the largest pack of wild dogs I had ever seen there were about forty of them. They went off very leisurely, and when my dogs chased them they turned about and showed fight. We were in motion most of the day; very large herds of cattle were to be seen pasturing on all sides.

On the 12th we marched before breakfast to within three miles of Mahura. Having taken breakfast, I rode ahead with Ruyter, and called on Mr. Ross, the resident missionary. We walked together to the town, and visited Mahura and his brother; the expressions of neither of these men were at all in their favor. I told Mahura that I wanted an ox with very large horns, which he promised to provide. He asked me if we were still at war with the Tambookie tribes. He also mentioned that ten men of the Bastards had been shot by Mochesse's natives. Mr. Ross informed me that Mahura was at present meditating war upon a tribe to the northeast, and also that Mochuarra, the chief at Motito, meditated an attack upon Sichely.

Mahura was sitting in the missionary's house : accordingly, I rode thither, and arrived along with these men. On my words being reported, he was at first exceedingly wroth, and said that, in consequence of what I had said, he would not permit me to proceed through his country. I only smiled at these threats; and he eventually cooled down, and took leave of us apparently in good humor. In the evening he returned and took tea with Mr. Ross and myself, and then accompanied me to my camp; he rode on horseback in a large white great-coat, accompanied by his brother and two other mounted attendants. I showed him all my rifles, with which he expressed himself much pleased; having drank his fill of coffee, he took a friendly leave, promising to visit me early next day.

True to his word, Mahura came and breakfasted with me, after which I obtained six karosses from him in barter for ammunition. I then presented him with a whip-stick and two pounds of powder, and walked down to the missionary's house, ordering my men to inspan. Mahura promised to come thither and take leave of me, but did not keep his word. About midday I marched, holding a spoor of three wagons some months old, said to lead me into my old course at Great Chooi.

On the 20th we reached the bank of the Meritsane, two miles below my old spoor. On the march we saw for the first time spoor of the black rhinoceros, also pallah and koodoo on the mountain, and hartebeests on the open country.

On the 22nd we marched at early dawn, and, having proceeded about four miles, left the main road to Bakatla, and held across the country to our right for my old outspanning-place at

Lotlokane; two hours more brought us thither. I did not find the vast herds of game congregated here as usual, water being everywhere abundant the grass over the whole country was remarkable, being much higher than my oxen.

On the 27th we trekked to Chouaney, which we reached at sundown, and remained there to trade next day. I obtained from Sichely two natives to accompany me to the Limpopo, their pay being a musket each. I got also from the chief twelve elephants' teeth, several very fine karosses, native arms, and other curiosities.

About mid-day we marched, and slept near the Ngotwani, along whose banks my course lay for the Limpopo. The country through which the Ngotwani twines is soft and sandy, and in general covered with dense thorny jungle, which greatly impeded our progress, having constantly to cut a passage before the wagons could advance. Several lions commenced roaring around us soon after the sun went down.

On the evening of the next day I had a glorious row with an old bull buffalo he was the only large bull in a fine herd of cows. I found their spoor while walking ahead of the wagons, and, following it up, came upon a part of the herd feeding quietly in a dense part of the forest. I fired my first shot at a cow, which I wounded. The other half of the herd then came up right in my face, within six yards of me. They would have trampled on me if I had not sung out in their faces and turned them. I selected the old bull, and sent a bullet into his shoulder. The herd then crashed along through the jungle to my right, but he at once broke away from them and took to my left. On examining his spoor, I found it bloody. I then went to meet my wagons, which I heard coming on, and, ordering the men to outspan, took all my dogs to the spoor. They ran it up in fine style, and in a few minutes the silence of the forest was disturbed by a tremendous bay. On running toward the sound, I met the old fellow coming on toward the wagons, with all my dogs after him. I saluted him with a second ball in the shoulder; he held on and took up a position in the thicket within forty yards of the wagons, where I finished him. He carried a most splendid head.

On the 8th of June we made the long-wished-for fair Limpopo an hour before sunset. I was at once struck with this most interesting river the trees along its banks were of prodigious size and very great beauty. At the very spot where I made the water, a huge crocodile lay upon the sand on the opposite side; on observing me he dashed into the stream.

The next day I rode ahead of the wagons with Ruyter, and hunted along the bank of the river. I immediately shot a water-buck. This animal and pallah were very abundant. As I advanced I found large vleys along the river side, a favorite haunt of the water-buck. After breakfast I again rode forth with fresh horses with my Bushman. We still found water-buck and pallah very abundant. I presently gave chase to a herd of the former to try their speed ; but as they led me into the midst of a labyrinth of marshy vleys, I gave it up.

At that instant the Bushman whispered, "Sir, sir;" and looking to my right, two princely old buffaloes stood in the jungle within forty yards of me. They got my wind, and started before I could get ready to fire. They held along the river bank ahead of me but not requiring them I did not give chase. After this I carao upon a huge crocodile basking on the sand, which instantly dashed into the stream. I now got into a vast labyrinth of marshes of great extent. Several species of wild duck and a variety of water-fowl were extremely abundant and very tame, hundreds passing before my eyes at once; Guinea-fowl, three sorts of large partridge, and two kinds of quail being likewise numerous.

I presently wounded a noble old water-buck as he dashed past me in marshy ground. In following him up I met an old buck pallah, which I shot dead on the spot with a ball in the middle of the breast. Following on after the wounded water-buck, along the high bank of the river, which was, however, concealed from my view by the dense cover, I suddenly heard a loud splash, and, coming suddenly clear of the cover, beheld the lovely water-buck standing broadside on an island in the middle of the river. Before I could dismount to fire, he dashed into the water and swam to the opposite bank. I grasped my trusty little Moore and waited till he won the terra firma, when with one well-directed shot I dropped him on the spot. A very strange thing then occurred; the buck, in his death-pangs, slid down into the river, and, continuing his struggles, swam half way across the river back to the island, where he lay upon a sand-bank.

On the 16th I rode ahead of ray wagons at day dawn thick mist was rolling along the Limpopo. Presently I saw two crocodiles in the stream below me. A little after I had the pleasure to find, for the first time, the spoor of sea-cows or hippopotami. I had never before seen it, but I knew it must be theirs; it was very similar to the spoor of borele, or black rhinoceros, but larger, and had four toes instead of three. Before returning to my wagons I tried to ride down a waterbuck, which I turned off from the river, but in this I failed, though I managed to keep close to him in the chase, and eventually to knock him up along with ray horse.

I again sallied forth with the Bushman and fresh steeds, and, directing the wagons to take the straight course, followed the windings of the river. Presently, poking over the bank, I behold three enormous crocodiles basking on the sand on the opposite side. I was astonished at their awful appearance and size, one of them appearing to me to be sixteen or eighteen feet in length, with a body as thick as that of an ox. On observing us they plunged into the dead water by the side of the stream. The next minute, one of them popping up his terrible head in the middle of the stream, I made a beautiful shot, and sent a ball through the middle of his brains. The convulsions of death which followed were truly awful.

At dawn of day on the 12th a noise was heard for about twenty minutes up the river, like the sound of the sea, accompanied by the lowing of buffaloes. It was a herd crossing the river. I rode thither to look at them, and was retracing my steps to camp, when, within three hundred yards of my wagons, I beheld an old bull buffalo standing contemplating my camp, with my followers looking at him in great consternation. They set the dogs after him, when he took away up the river. As the ground was extremely bad for riding, being full of deep holes, and all concealed with long grass, it was some time before I could get away after the dogs; and when I had ridden a short distance, I met them all returning, their feet being completely done up with the long march from the colony.

I now turned my face once more for camp, when I heard one of my dogs at bay behind me. Galloping up to the spot, I found my dog "Lion" standing balking at an old water-buck in an open flat. The buck, on observing me, made away for the river, and, joining a herd of does, they dashed into the stream, and were immediately upon the opposite bank. I was in a sequestered bend of the river, where the banks for several acres were densely clad with lofty reeds and grass, which towered above my head as I sat on my horse's back. Beyond the reeds and grass were trees of all sizes, forming a dense shade this is the general character of the banks of the Limpopo, as far as I have yet seen. I was slowly returning to my camp, in anything but good humor at my want of success with the game I had just been after, when, behold, an antelope of the most exquisite beauty, and utterly unknown to sportsmen or naturalists, stood broadside in my path, looking me full in the face. It was a princely old buck of the serolomootlooque of the Bakalahari, or bush-buck of the Limpopo. He carried a very fine, wide-set pair of horns. On beholding him I was struck with wonder and delight. My heart beat with excitement. I sprang from my saddle, but before I could fire a shot this gem of beauty bounded into the reeds and was lost to ray sight. At that moment I would have given half what I possessed in this world for a broadside at that lovely antelope, and I at once resolved not to proceed further on my expedition until I had captured him, although it should cost me the labor of a month.

The antelope having entered the reeds, I gave my horse to my after-rider, and with my rifle on full cock and at the ready, proceeded to stalk with extreme caution throughout the length and breadth of the cover; but I stalked in vain; the antelope had vanished, and was nowhere to be found. I then returned to my steed, and rode slowly up the river's bank toward my camp. I had ridden to within a few hundred yards of the wagons, and was meditating how I should best circumvent the serolomootlooque, when once more this lovely antelope crossed my path. I had been unwittingly driving him before me along the bank of the river. He trotted like a roebuck into the thick cover, and then stood broadside among the thorn bushes. I sprang from my saddle, and guessing about his position, I fired and missed him; he then trotted along a rhinoceros's footpath, and gave me a second chance. Again I fired, and before my rifle was down from my shoulder the serolomootlooque lay prostrate in the dust. The ball had cut the skin open along his ribs, and, entering his body, had passed along his neck, and had lodged in his brains, where we found it on preparing the head for stuffing. I was not a little gratified at my good fortune in securing this novel and valuable trophy; he was one of the most perfect antelopes I had ever beheld, both in symmetry and color. I had him immediately conveyed to camp, where I took his measurement, and wrote out a correct description of him for the benefit of naturalists. I christened him the "Antelopus Roualeynei," or "bush-buck of the Limpopo."

On the 14th, after a very early breakfast, I proceeded with three after-riders, two double-barreled rifles, and about a hundred rounds of ammunition, to the spot where I had yesterday found the hippopotami; but they had taken alarm, and were all gone. The spoor leading up the river, I rode along the banks, examining every pool until my steed was quite knocked up, but found not a single sea-cow. The spoor still led up the river; they had made short cuts at every bend, sometimes taking the direct line on my side, and sometimes on the other. Finding that I must sleep in the felt if I followed on, I dispatched Ruyter to camp for my blankets, coffee-kettle, biscuit, &c., and fresh steeds. I searched on foot, and penetrated every thicket and every dense jungle of reeds that overhung the river, until at last, faint with hunger and fatigue, I sought some game on which to make a luncheon, and had the good fortune to fall in with a young doe of the "Antelopus Roualeynei," which I shot, and in a few minutes she was roasting on a mighty fire.

Ruyter, at this moment coming up, brought a welcome supply of biscuit and coffee, and reported my yellow horse "Flux," about my very best, to have died of horse-sickness. After luncheon I continued my search for hippopotami, and just as the sun went down I started an old fellow from beneath some tall reeds, which hung over a deep broad pool. On hearing me approach he dived with a loud splash, and immediately reappeared with a blowing noise a little further up the river, and within twenty yards of the bank. Having looked about him, he again dived, and continued his course up the river, which could be traced from the wave above. I ran in front of him, and when he came up the third time I was standing opposite to him, ready with my rifle at my shoulder. I sent the bullet into his brain, when he floundered for one moment at the surface, and then sank to the bottom. There he most probably only remained for half an hour; but in a few minutes night set in, and I had thus the extreme mortification to lose ray hippopotamus, the second one which I had shot. We slept beneath a shady tree; at midnight a few drops of rain fell, and I feared a drenching; it, however, passed away. In the course of the day we saw several very large crocodiles, three of which I shot. One of these lay upon an island; I shot him dead on the spot; he did not gain the water.

CHAPTER XXV

On the 17th of June, having found a good drift, I crossed the Limpopo with my wagons, and drew them up in a green and shady spot. I then rode a long way down the eastern bank in quest of hippopotami, and late in the evening I found one, which I did not molest, trusting to find him next day.

On the 18th a dense mist hung over the river all the morning. Ordering the wagons to follow in an hour, I rode ahead to seek the sea-cow of the previous night, but after a long search I gave it up as a bad job, and, kindling a fire to warm myself, awaited the wagons, which presently came up. Here I halted for two hours, and then once more rode ahead to seek hippopotami. The river became more promising for sea-cow. At every turn there occurred deep, still pools, with occasional sandy islands densely clad with lofty reeds, and with banks covered with reeds to a breadth of thirty yards. Above and beyond these reeds stood trees of immense age and gigantic size, beneath which grew a long and very rank description of grass, on which the sea-cow delights to pasture.

I soon found fresh spoor, and after holding on for several miles, just as the sun was going down, and as I entered a dense reed cover, I came upon the fresh lairs of four hippopotami. They had been lying sleeping on the margin of the river, and, on hearing me come crackling through the reeds, had plunged into the deep water. I at once ascertained that they were newly started, for the froth and bubbles were still on the spot where they had plunged in. Next moment I heard them blowing a little way down the river. I then headed them, and, with considerable difficulty, owing to the cover and the reeds, at length came right down above where they were standing. It was a broad part of the river, with a sandy bottom, and the water came half way up their sides.

As I approached Behemoth her eye looked very wicked. I halted for a moment, ready to dive under the water if she attacked me; but she was stunned, and did not know what she was doing; so, running in upon her, and seizing her short tail, I attempted to incline her course to land. It was extraordinary what enormous strength she still had in the water. I could not guide her in the slightest, and she continued to splash, and plunge, and blow, and make her circular course, carrying me along with her as if I was a fly on her tail. Finding her tail gave me but a poor hold, as the only means of securing my prey, I took out my knife and cut two deep parallel incisions through the skin on her rump. Lifting this skin from the flesh so that I could get in my two hands, I made use of this as a handle; and after some desperate hard work, sometimes pushing and sometimes pulling, the sea-cow continuing her circular course all the time, and I holding on at her rump like grim Death, eventually I succeeded in bringing this gigantic and most powerful animal to the bank. Here the Bushman quickly brought me a stout buffalo rheim from my horse's neck, which I passed through the opening in the thick skin, and moored Behemoth to a tree. I then took my rifle and sent a ball through the center of her head, and she was numbered with the dead.

At this moment my wagons came tip within a few hundred yards of the spot, where I outspanned, and by moonlight we took down a span of select oxen and a pair of rheim chains, and succeeded in dragging the sea-cow high and dry. We were all astonished at her enormous size; she appeared to be about five feet broad across the belly. I could see much beauty in the animal, which Nature has admirably formed for the amphibious life it was destined to pursue.

We were occupied all the morning of the 19th cutting up and salting the select parts of the sea-cow; of the skull I took particular charge. She was extremely fat, more resembling a pig than a cow or a horse. In the evening I rode down the river, and shot a brace of water-bucks, after which I left the river-bank and rode to the summit of an adjacent hill, from which I obtained a fine view of the surrounding country. Many bold blue mountain ranges stood to the north and northwest; to the east and southeast were also mountain ranges; while to the south a very remarkable light colored rock, in the form of a dome, shot high above the level of the surrounding forest.

The next day, at dawn, I rode down the river side to seek serolomootlooques, and ordered my wagons to follow in a couple of hours. After riding a few miles, I observed a serolomootlooque of surpassing beauty standing on the top of the opposite bank of the river; he stood with his breast to me, and from the broad belt of reeds on this side of the water it was impossible to get nearer than a hundred yards of him. Taking a deliberate aim, I fired off-hand, and heard the ball tell upon him. Here the river was deep, requiring swimming, and I had fears of the crocodiles. I sent the Bushman across, however, on horseback, who immediately discovered blood, and presently came upon the buck, and found his forearm smashed in the shoulder. I went over, and, starting the buck in the cover, put a bullet in his ribs. He then got into some thick reeds, when I took up a position on one side, and ordered Ruyter to beat up the cover. The buck broke near me, when I sent a third bullet right through and through his shoulder; and the tough old buck still scorning to fall, I quickly fired my other barrel, and most unluckily cut his lovely horn off at the base. The buck now charged headlong into a thick bush, and died. His head, before I destroyed it, was perhaps the finest along the banks of the Limpopo; the horns were of extraordinary length, and had a most perfect set and tarn.

On the 21st I rode some distance down the river with Ruyter in quest of sea-cow and serolomootlooques; we found fresh spoor of the former, and I shot one doe of the latter. Ruyter drove her up to me by beating the reeds; he also started a fine old buck, which did not break cover. As I rode along I saw six crocodiles and a great number of monkeys of two varieties; also several deadly serpents, one of them a cobra, very similar to the Indian cobra. Bees were very abundant along the Limpopo, the gigantic old hollow trees affording them abundant homes. My natives brought me some fine honey while I was taking my breakfast; they found it in an old ant-hill. I was astonished to observe along the banks of the river enormous trees, from three to four feet in diameter, cut down by the Bakalahari only for the sake of the honey which they contain. The Bakalahari fell them with immense trouble and perseverance, with little tomahawks of their own formation.

The ant-hills along the Limpopo and throughout this part of Africa arc truly wonderful ; it is common to see them upward of twenty feet high and one hundred feet in circumference. They are composed of clay, which hardens in the sun like a brick; they have generally one tall tapering spire in the middle of the fabric, the base of the spire being surrounded with similar projections of smaller height. The natives informed me that we were opposite to the tribe Seleka, whom they tried to persuade me to visit, but I resolved to stick to the Limpopo.

On the 22nd we came upon the Macoolwey, a large, clear running river, joining the Limpopo from the southeast here I bagged a princely water-buck.

At dawn of the succeeding day I rode forth to try to cross the Limpopo and hunt for serolomootlooques, but failed to find a drift. I then rode some distance along the bank of. the Macoolwey seeking a passage ; but I was still unsuccessful. I then retraced my steps to the Limpopo, determined to get through, cost what it might, as the banks looked very promising for serolomootlouques. I discovered a drift, but deep. I resumed to camp for fresh horses, and rode forth with two after riders, and a pack-horse carrying bedding, as I had resolved to hunt for serolomootlooques over the river for a couple of days. We got safely through, and held up the stream. I sought every turn of the water on foot, the boys leading my horse, but failed to fall in with a buck serolomootlooque. I therefore retraced my steps down the river to a spot where buffaloes had drunk on the preceding evening, and there spent the night.

In the morning I rode down to a likely cover for serolomootlooques opposite the drift. Here I started one old buck, but did not fire; he went off barking exactly like a roebuck, which they very much resemble in form, gait, voice, and habit. Following on after this buck, I started two does, one of which I shot. Here I left one of my after-riders with two of the steeds, while I and Ruyter rode down the bank of the Limpopo to explore. I found the river wearing quite a different appearance below its junction, being very much broader—nearly as large, indeed, as the Orange River. Crocodiles of enormous size were to be seen at every turn, and I shot four huge fellows. We then fell in with a large rock serpent, or "metsapallah," about eleven feet long, which I shot with a hall through the head, and brought to camp slung round my neck.

On the 27th I rode down the river at dawn of day, and ordered my wagons to follow in two hours. While riding along the river's bank, some distance beyond the limits of yesterday's ride, opposite to a broad sand-bank densely covered with reeds, I heard a loud plunge, which was immediately followed by the welcome blowing sound of sea-cows. I instantly divested myself of my leather trowsers, and went down into the reeds, where I came suddenly upon a crocodile of average size, lying in a shallow back stream; and on his attempting to gain the main river, I shot him with a bullet in the shoulder he lay dead on the spot. This was the first crocodile which I had managed to lay my hand is upon, although I had shot many. The sound of my rifle alarmed the sea-cows; some took up, and some down the river. I was unfortunate with them, shooting two and losing them both. As I was seeking the wounded hippopotami, my wagons came up. Soon after breakfast, the chief Seleka, with a number of his aristocracy, paid me a visit; and in the afternoon I rode down the river, ordering my wagons to follow, and found the fresh spoor of a mighty old bull elephant.

I rode forth at sunrise on the 28th, ordering my wagons to follow in two hours. Seleka had sent men down the river, before it was clear, to seek sea-cows; and they soon came running after me to say that they had found some. I accordingly followed them to the river, where, in a long, broad, and deep bend, were four hippopotami, two full-grown cows, a small cow, and a calf. At the tail of this pool was a strong and rapid stream, which thundered along in Highland fashion over large masses of dark rock.

On coming to the shady bank, I could at first only see one old cow and calf. When they dived I ran into the reeds, and as the cow came up I shot her in the head; she, however, got away down the river, and I lost her. The other three took away up the river, and became very shy, remaining under the water for five minutes at a time, and then only popping their heads up for a few seconds. I accordingly remained quiet behind the reeds, in hope of their dismissing their alarms. Presently the two smaller ones seemed to be no longer alarmed, popping up their entire heads, and remaining above water for a minute at a time; but the third, which was by far the largest, and which I thought must be a bull, continued extremely shy, remaining under the water for ten minutes at a time, and then just showing her face for a second, making a blowing like a whale, and returning to the bottom.

The next day, after proceeding a few miles, I killed a very fine buck of the serolomootlooque. I again rode down the river's bank, with two after-riders, to seek hippopotami, the natives reporting that they were to be found in a pool in advance, where another river joined the Limpopo. After riding a short distance, I found the banks unusually green and shady, and very much frequented by the sea-cow; and presently, in a broad, deep, and long still bend of the river, I disturbed the game I sought.

They were lying in their sandy beds among the rank reeds at the river's margin, and on hearing me galloping over the gravelly shingle between the bank and the reeds, the deposit of some great flood, they plunged into their native strong-hold in dire alarm, and commenced blowing, snorting, and uttering a sound very similar to that made by the musical instrument called a serpent. It was a fairish place for an attack; so, divesting myself of my leather trowsers, I ordered my after-riders to remain utterly silent, and then crept cautiously forward, determined not to fire a shot until I had thoroughly overhauled the herd to see if it did not contain a bull, and at all events to secure, if possible, the very finest head among them.

The herd consisted of about fourteen hippopotami; ten of these were a little further down the stream than the other four. Having carefully examined these ten, I made out two particular hippopotami decidedly larger than all the others. I then crept a little distance up the river behind the reeds, to obtain a view of the others. They were two enormous old cows, with two large calves beside them. The old ones had exactly the same size of head as the two best cows below; I accordingly chose what I thought the best of these two, and, making a fine shot at the side of her head, at once disabled her. She disappeared for a few seconds, and then came floundering to the surface, and continued swimming round and round, sometimes diving, and then reappearing with a loud splash and a blowing noise, always getting slowly down the river, until I re-attacked and finished her a quarter of a mile further down, about an hour after.

I held up the river to see what the other sea-cows were doing, when, to my particular satisfaction, I beheld the body of the other huge sea-cow which I had shot in the brain floating in the pool where I had shot her, and stationary within about twenty yards of the other side. I then held down the river to the tail of the pool, where the stream was broad and rapid, and less likely to hold crocodiles, and here, although cold and worn out, I swam across to secure my game. The wagons now came up, and two of my Hottentots swam over to my assistance; but, just as we were going in to secure the sea-cow, she became disengaged from the invisible fetters that had held her, and which turned out to be the branch of a gigantic old tree that some flood had lodged in the bottom of the pool. The sea-cow now floated down the middle of the river; when she neared the tail of the pool, we swam in and inclined her course to shore, and stranded her on a fine gravel bank.

This truly magnificent specimen was just about the same size as the first, and apparently older, but her teeth were not quite so thick. Ordering the natives at once to cut off her huge head, and having seen it deposited safely on the bank along with that of her comrade, I held for my wagons, having to cross the Lepalala to reach them. I was very cold and worn out, hut most highly gratified at my good fortune in first killing, and then in securing, too out of the four best sea cows in a herd of fourteen.

CHAPTER XXVI

On the 1st of July I inspanned at sunrise and marched to the town of the Baseleka, which I reached in about four hours, having crossed the Lepalala on the way. I outspanned on the bank of the river. Seleka's town is built on the top and sides of a steep and precipitous white quartz rock, which rises abruptly, and forms a very remarkable feature in the green forest scenery which surrounds it. In the evening Seleka brought down four fairish bull elephant's teeth, which I bought for four muskets.

On the morrow I took an early breakfast, and then held east with Seleka and about a hundred and fifty of his men to seek elephants, they having heard from the Bakalahari of the position of a troop of bulls. This day I might reckon as the beginning of my elephant hunting this season. As the country appeared to me well adapted for the sport, and as I regretted not a little that my men and a good stud of horses should be idle at the wagons while they might be bringing me in fifty pounds once or twice a week, I armed and mounted John Stofolus and Carey, both of whom vaunted much of their courage and skill. I instructed them, in the event of our finding, to select a good elephant, and, if not able to kill him, at least to hold him in view until I had finished mine, which I promised to do as quickly as possible, and then to come to their assistance.

We had not proceeded far from the white rock when we entered a forest frequented by elephants, and we very soon came upon the fresh spoor of a troop of about ten fine bulls. The spooring was conducted very properly, the old chief taking the greatest care of the wind, keeping his followers far back, and maintaining silence, extending pickets in advance, and to the right and left, and ordering them to ascend to the summits of the tallest trees to obtain a correct view of the surrounding forest. Presently the mighty game was detected. Old Schwartland was led alongside of me, and my dogs were all in couples, eight in number. I quickly mounted, and, riding slowly forward, obtained a blink of one of the elephants. I called to the natives to slip the dogs, and then dashed forward for a selection. I chose the last, and gave him a shot as he passed me; and then, riding hard under his stern, I yelled like a demon to clear him from his comrades and to bring the dogs to my assistance.

The natives were now fighting with an immense old Dull hearing them, I rode in their direction, and came upon Carey stationary in the forest. Here the dogs took up the scent of an elephant, and I followed them, but they eventually dropped it. I then tried to retrace my steps to the dead elephant, which I did by chance, having lost my way in the level boundless jungle and wandered far. I found a few natives, who reported their captain and most of his men to be still engaged with the elephant, and they said that Carey had joined them in the chase. I off-saddled for a little, but, hearing the cries of the natives in the distance, I saddled old Schwartland, and rode onward till I found the natives and Carey quite done up, and on the point of dropping the game. The elephant, although red with blood, and resembling a porcupine by the number of the assagais, was little the worse for all that he had received. I then attacked him, and, with eight or ten shots, ended his career.

Next morning, Bakalahari coming up and reporting to have heard elephants during the night, old Seleka and I went in quest of them. We were joined by the gallant and vaunting John Stofolus, who had slept at the wagons, and swore that he had lost his way in a long chase after an elephant. Both he and Carey expressing regret for their previous mismanagement, and vowing to prove themselves men this day, I allowed them to accompany me. We soon took up the spoor of one old bull, which led us into a forest thoroughly plowed up and broken with bull elephants. Here this fine fellow joined a glorious squadron of from twenty to thirty mighty bulls. When we discovered their position I dashed forward, shouting to the dogs, and was instantly in the middle of them. Then followed a wondrous scene. The elephants, panic-stricken, charged forward, leveling the forest before them, trumpeting, with trunks and tails aloft, as the dogs mingled with them.

Looking back over my shoulder, I beheld elephants come crashing on behind and within a few yards of me. I then pressed forward, overtook about ten bulls that were inclining to the west, rode under their sterns, chose the best, and, yelling at the top of my voice, separated him from his comrades, and brought my dogs to my assistance. In a few minutes he had many mortal wounds. Not hearing my trusty John and Carey fire, and the elephant's course being right toward camp, I ceased firing and drove him on before me. Presently these worthies came up to me, having been after a most splendid bull—the cock of the troop—which I, in my haste, had ridden by. They had fired two or three shots, and then left him. I now saw that all my hunting this season must depend on my own single hand, as my followers, instead of a help, were a very great hindrance and annoyance to me. If I had been alone that day I should most certainly have taken more time, and have selected the elephant they had lost, which the natives said carried extremely large and long teeth.

On the 11th we marched at dawn of day, holding northeast, and halted on the bank of the Limpopo. There the wagons remained, while I hunted of the river, bagging two first-rate bull elephants and one hippopotamus. One of these elephants I shot across the Limpopo, under the mountains of Guapa. I fought him in dense wait-a-bit jungle from half past eleven till the sun was under, when his tough old spirit fled, and the venerable monarch of the forest fell, pierced with fifty-seven balls. On the 17th I inspanned and trekked about five miles down the stream, when I halted beside a long, deep hippopotamus hole, in which were two bulls and one cow, but it being late I did not trouble them.

The next day I rode down the river to seek sea-cows, accompanied by my two after-riders, taking, as usual, my double-barreled rifles. We had proceeded about two miles when we came upon some most thoroughly beaten, old-established hippopotamus paths, and presently, in a broad, long, deep, and shaded pool of the river, we heard the sea-cows bellowing. There I beheld one of the most wondrous and interesting sights that a sportsman can be blessed with. I at once knew that there must be an immense herd of them, for the voices came from different parts of the pool; so, creeping in through the bushes to obtain an inspection, a large sandy island appeared at the neck of the pool, on which stood several large shady trees.

The neck of the pool was very wide and shallow, with rocks and large stones; below it was deep and still. On a sandy promontory of this island stood about thirty cows and calves, while in the pool opposite, and a little below them, stood about twenty more sea-cows, with their heads and backs above water. About fifty yards further down the river again, showing out their heads, were eight or ten immense fellows, which I think were all bulls; and about one hundred yards below these, in the middle of the stream, stood another herd of about eight or ten cows with calves, and two huge bulls. The sea-cows lay close together like pigs; a favorite position was to rest their heads on their comrades' sterns and sides. The herds were attended by an immense number of the invariable rhinoceros birds, which, on observing me, did their best to spread alarm throughout the hippopotami. I was resolved to select, if possible, a first-rate old bull out of this vast herd, and I accordingly delayed firing for nearly two hours, continually running up and down behind the thick thorny cover, and attentively studying the heads. At length I determined to go close in and select the best head out of the eight or ten bulls which lay below the cows. I accordingly left the cover and walked slowly forward in full view of the whole herd to the water's edge, where I lay down on my belly and studied the heads of these bulls. The cows, on seeing me, splashed into the water, and kept up a continual snorting and blowing till night set in.

After selecting for a few minutes, I fired my first shot at a splendid bull and sent the ball in a little behind the eye. He was at once incapacitated, and kept plunging and swimming round and round, wearing away down the pool, until I finished him with two more shots. The whole pool was now in a state of intense commotion. The best cows and the bulls at once became very shy and cunning, showing only the flat roofs of their heads, and sometimes only their nostrils. The younger cows were not so shy, producing the whole head; and if had wished to make a bag, I might nave shot an immense number. This, however, was not my object; and as there was likely to be a difficulty in securing what I did kill, I determined only to fire at the very best.

On the 20th I again rode down the river to the pool, and found a herd of sea-cows still there; so I remained with them till sundown, and bagged two very first-rate old sea-cows, which were forthcoming next day. This day I detected a most dangerous trap constructed by the Bakalahari for slaying sea-cows. It consisted of a sharp little assagai or spike most thoroughly poisoned, and stuck firmly into the end of a heavy block of thorn hood about four feet Ions and five inches in diameter. This formidable affair was suspended over the center of a sea-cow path, at a height of about thirty feet from the ground, by a balk cord which passed over a high branch of a tree, and thence to a peg on one side of the path beneath, leading across the path to a peg on the other side, where it was fastened. To the suspending cord were two triggers so constructed that, when the sea-cow struck against the cord which led across the path, the heavy block above was set at liberty, which instantly dropped with immense force with its poisonous dart, inflicting a sure and mortal wound. The bones and old teeth of sea-cows which lay rotting along the bank of the river here evinced the success of this dangerous invention. I remained in the neighborhood of the pool for several days, during which time I bagged no less than fifteen first-rate hippopotami, the greater portion of them being bulls.

At dawn of day on the 28th we inspanned and marched up the river to the drift. All hands worked hard in cutting down the bank on the opposite side, the Bakalahari assisting us; and in the afternoon we got the cap-tent wagon, which was very lightly laden, through the river with twelve oxen. The baggage wagon stuck fast in the mud, and remained there all night, with the fore-wheels half way up the bank, and the after-chest under the water; and although we put twenty oxen to it, we could not get it out.

The next day our first work was to reduce the bank on which the wagon stood, after which, with considerable difficulty, we got it out with twenty of my best oxen. The whole day we were busy drying the innumerable contents of the fore and after chests of each wagon, almost everything being thoroughly saturated, and I sustained considerable loss in fine powder, percussion caps, biscuit, tea, coffee, sugar, and a number of other articles, some of which were damaged and some entirely destroyed.

I marched at dawn of day on the 30th. Seleka and his men and my hired Baquaines had done all in their power to prevent my proceeding further; but as they could not conceal the waters from me, my course being to follow the Limpopo, I was perfectly independent of them. They remained by me until I crossed the Limpopo, and then all turned home. I was now once more without natives, and held down the northwestern bank of the river, but very soon

Bakalahari joined us, and their numbers increased as we held on. I had the good luck this day to bag five more first-rate hippopotami.

The next day, after assisting my men to get out some of the sea-cows, I rode down the river with two after-riders to explore. Having ridden a few miles, came upon a troop of twelve, the best of which I disabled and killed the next day. This was a most splendid old cow, and carried tusks far superior to any we had yet seen; in the afternoon I bagged six more.

The next day the sun had been up two hours, and my horses could not yet be found. I entertained no apprehensions, however, from the lion, but rather suspected some plot between Seleka and my natives to drive my cattle back, and so force me to retrace my steps. I therefore ordered John Stofolus and Hendric to take bridles and a supply of meat, and to follow up the spoor wherever it might lead; and being anxious to see which way it went, I took a rifle and followed in quest of it myself. Observing a number of vultures to the west, and hearing the voices of natives in that direction, I proceeded thither at top speed. To my utter horror, I found my two most valuable and especially favorite veteran shooting-horses lying fearfully mangled and half consumed by a troop of ruthless lions. They were "Black Jock" and "Schwartland," the former a first-rate young horse, worth £24, the latter aged, but by far my most valuable steed, being perhaps the best shooting-horse in Southern Africa; he knew no fear, and would approach as near as I chose to elephant or lion, or any description of game. From his back I had shot nearly all my elephants last year; and so fond was I of this horse, that I never rode or even saddled him until we had found elephants, when I used him in the fight, and then immediately off-saddled.

With a sickening heart I turned from this most painful scene, and, utterly dejected, I returned to camp. As there was much to do about the wagons, and as two of my men were absent seeking the lost horses, I did not immediately go in quest of the lions; this I, however, did in the afternoon, taking all my dogs, but I failed to find them. A large party of the natives from the southwest, the Bamalette, reached me late in the day their object was flesh, and to endeavor to persuade me to come and trade with them. They had fallen in with three of my steeds ; the others were found by my men near the drift where I had last crossed the river. I formed a very strong kraal for my cattle, and made all fast at sundown. Very soon after, the troop of lions came up to my camp on the spoor of the horses, fancying that they could repeat the tragedy of last night; they fought with my dogs in the most daring manner, off and on, until near dawn of day, driving them in to the fireside. The cattle were very restive, and nearly broke away, but the kraal was good and saved, them.

In the morning, ordering my wagons to follow, I rode down the river, followed by at least two hundred natives, to secure the hippopotami shot two days previous Six of these were forthcoming, and we set about getting them to the side they lay upon the rocks in the middle of the river. One of these proved to be an out-and-outer, a tearing old bull, with tusks which far surpassed anything I had yet seen, and quite perfect; I was very much gratified with this fine trophy. There were also two of the cows which carried immense and perfect tusks. When the wagons came up, I found myself minus another steed a fine young mare had fallen into a Bakalahari pitfall, and had been suffocated.

On the 5th I rode down the river and fell in with a large herd of about thirty hippopotami they lay upon some rocks in the middle of a very long and broad pool. I wounded seven or eight of these in the head, and killed two, a bull and a cow, both of which we found next day. At night the lions prowled around our camp, and fought with the dogs until the morning: they came boldly in between the fires of the natives, who lay around my camp.

The next day I ordered my wagons to come on, and rode ahead to the pool where I had last shot. When the wagons came up, I detected the head Bakalahari of the kraal beside which my mare had been killed he was talking with my cattle herds, with whom he seemed to be on very intimate terms. This killing of my horse was either intentional or most culpably careless, as the pits were left covered, and the cattle driven to pasture in the middle of them; I accordingly deemed it proper that this man should be made an example of; so, calling to my English servant, Carey, to assist me, we each seized an arm of the guilty chief, and I then caused Hendric to flog him with a sea-cow jambok; after which I admonished him, and told him that if the holes were not opened in future, I would make a more severe example as I proceeded. The consequence of this salutary admonition was, that all the pitfalls along the river were thrown open in advance of my march, a thing which I had never before seen among the Bechuana tribes. In the afternoon I rode down the river a few pools, and found a very fine herd of about thirty hippopotami.

CHAPTER XXVII

I resolved now to case for a time hunting sea-cows, and to trek ahead in good earnest. I accordingly took considerable trouble in stowing the wagons properly. We then trekked down the river until sundown. I rode ahead of the wagons to explore, and was struck with astonishment at the number of the hippopotami. They seemed to increase the further I trekked down the river; every pool had its herd; they were extremely fearless, allowing me to approach within fifteen yards of them. In the morning I found myself minus my hired natives these ruffians, fearing to receive a chastisement similar to that of the chief of the Bakalahari, which they felt they deserved, thought it best to get out of the way in time, and had cut the service. The chief Matsaca brought me ivory, which I obtained in barter for muskets and some ammunition.

On the 8th we trekked at dawn of day, and after proceeding a few miles came upon the Lotsane, one of those gravelly-bedded rivers, with only water in occasional spots, such as are met with in the Bamanajwato country. Here was much spoor of elephant; mid the natives pressing me to halt and hunt, I outspanned and got everything ready for a trip from the wagons.

The next morning I smarted with a party of natives to seek elephants. We held along the banks of the Lotsane for several miles, holding a northwesterly course; after which we left the river and held southwest and at last followed down to the Limpopo, and so home to camp, without finding a single fresh spoor. Here I found my old friends from Bamangwato, Mollyeon and Kapain, with a party. I was glad to see these men, as I knew they would assist me in my hunting, and they could also converse with me.

On the 10th, at dawn of day, I rode down the river, and ordered my wagons to follow. I found sea-cows more and more abundant; every pool had its herd the margin of the river on each side was trampled down by elephants, rhinoceroses, buffaloes, &c. Having ridden about six miles, I found the fresh spoor of a troop of bull elephants. I off-saddled, and in an hour the wagons came up, when I took up the spoor, accompanied by Carey, Hendric, and Ruyter. After following the spoor for some miles, the natives lost it. A little distance ahead of us was a rocky hill, to the summit of which I ascended. This spot commanded a good view of the adjacent forest. I at once detected an immense herd of elephants. They were drinking in a wide open spot on a gravelly-bedded river which falls into the Limpopo, called by the natives Suking.

On the following day I shot another bull elephant and a white rhinoceros; and on the afternoon of the 12th, returning to camp weary and worn, I came unexpectedly upon a bull elephant of unusual size, standing in the shade on the margin of the Limpopo. He took refuge in an extensive jungle of impracticable wait-a-bits, where it was impossible to do anything on horseback, and I was therefore obliged to hunt him on foot. I slew him with thirty bullets after an extremely severe and dangerous combat of about two hours. I afterward felt much the worse for this severe exertion.

On the 14th I dispatched Hendric to bring on the wagons, which came up in the afternoon. Night set in warn, calm, and still, with a good moonlight. Elephants, sea-cows, and panthers kept up a continued music above and below us along the river until I fell asleep.

On the 15th I felt very ill, but in the forenoon I went down to the river, where I shot two sea-cows. In the evening, feeling worse, I bled myself, but strong fever was on me all night.

Next morning I marched, halting at sundown on the Mokojay, a gravelly-bedded periodical river, where elephants occasionally drank.

On the 18th, at dawn of day, I took leave of Mollyeon and Kapain of Bamangwato, as they would not follow me farther. We then inspanned, and held down the Limpopo. I regretted to observe that the spoor of elephants did not seem to increase in the same ratio as I had allowed myself to imagine. We were in an extremely remote and secluded corner of the world, quite uninhabited; yet the elephants, though frequenting it, were decidedly scarce. I felt extremely weak and nervous from the fever and the quantity of blood which I had lost, in so much that I started at my own shadow, and several times sprang to one side when the leaves rustled in the bushes. I walked along the bank of the river with my gun loaded with small shot, intending to shoot a partridge for my breakfast. Presently I came upon the fresh dung of bull elephants, and at the same moment my people at the wagons saw two old bull elephants within two hundred yards of them and the wind being favorable, they walked unsuspiciously. After a very short chase I succeeded in killing both.

On the 29th we arrived at a small village of Bakalahari. These natives told me that elephants were abundant on the opposite side of the river. I accordingly resolved to halt here and hunt, and drew my wagons up on the river's bank, within thirty yards of the water, and about one hundred yards from the native village. Having outspanned, we at once set about making for the cattle a kraal of the worst description of thorn-trees. Of this I had now become very particular, since my severe loss by lions on the first of this month; and my cattle were, at night, secured by a strong kraal, which enclosed my two wagons, the horses being made fast to a trek-tow stretched between the hind wheels of the wagons. I had yet, however, a fearful lesson to learn as to the nature and character of the lion, of which I had at one time entertained so little fear; and on this night a horrible tragedy was to be acted in my little lonely camp of so very awful and appalling a nature as to make the blood curdle in our veins. I worked till near sundown at one side of the kraal with Hendric, my first wagon-driver—I cutting down the trees with my ax, and he dragging them to the kraal. When the kraal for the cattle was finished, I turned my attention to making a pot of barley-broth, and lighted a fire between the wagons and the water, close on the river's bank, under a dense grove of shady trees, making no sort of kraal around our sitting-place for the evening.

The Hottentots, without any reason, made their fire about fifty yards from mine; they, according to their usual custom, being satisfied with the shelter of a large dense bush. The evening passed away cheerfully. Soon after it was dark we heard elephants breaking the trees in the forest across the river, and once or twice I strode away into the darkness some distance from the fireside to stand and listen to them. I little, at that moment, deemed of the imminent peril to which I was exposing my life, nor thought that a blood-thirsty man eater lion was crouching near, and only watching his opportunity to spring into the kraal, and consign one of us to a most horrible death.

Suddenly the appalling and murderous voice of an angry, blood-thirsty lion burst upon my ear within a few yards of us, followed by the shrieking of the Hottentots. Again and again the murderous roar of attack was repeated. We heard John and Ruyter shriek "The lion! the lion!" still, for a few moments, we thought he was but chasing one of the dogs round the kraal; but, next instant, John Stofolus rushed into the midst of us almost speechless with fear and terror, his eyes bursting from their sockets, and shrieked out, "The lion! the lion! He has got Hendric; he dragged him away from the fire beside me. I struck him with the burning brands upon his head, but he would not let go his hold. Hendric is dead! Oh God! Hendric is dead! Let us take fire and seek him!" The rest of my people rushed about, shrieking and yelling as if they were mad. I was at once angry with them for their folly, and told them that if they did not stand still and keep quiet the lion would have another of us; and that very likely there was a troop of them. I ordered the dogs, which were nearly all fast, to he made loose, and the fire to be increased as far as could be. I then shouted Hendric's name, but all was still.

The next morning, just as the day began to dawn, we heard the lion dragging something up the river side under cover of the bank. We drove the cattle out of the kraal, and then proceeded to inspect the scene of the night's awful tragedy. In the hollow, whore the lion had lain consuming his prey, we found one leg of the unfortunate Hendric, bitten off below the knee, the shoe still on his foot; the grass and bushes were all stained with his blood, and fragments of his pea-coat lay around. Poor Hendric! I knew the fragments of that old coat, and had often marked them hanging in the dense covers where the elephant had charged after my unfortunate after-rider. Hendric was by far the best man I had about my wagons, of a most cheerful disposition, a first-rate wagon-driver, fearless in the field, ever active, willing, and obliging his loss to us all was very serious. I felt confounded and utterly sick in my heart; I could not remain at the wagons, so I resolved to go after elephants to divert my mind. I had that morning heard them breaking the trees on the opposite side of the river. I accordingly told the natives of the village of my intentions, and having ordered mv people to devote the day to fortifying the kraal started with Piet and Ruyter as my after-riders. It was a very cool day. We crossed the river, and at once took up the fresh spoor of a troop of bull elephants. These bulls unfortunately joined a troop of cows, and when we came on them the dogs attacked the cows, and the bulls were off in a moment, before we could even see them. One remarkably fine old cow charged the dogs. I hunted this cow, and finished her with two shots from the saddle. Being anxious to return to my people before night, I did not attempt to follow the troop. My followers were not a little gratified to see me returning, for terror had taken hold of their minds, and they expected that the lion would return, and, emboldened by the success of the preceding night, would prove still more daring in his attack. The lion would most certainly have returned, but fate had otherwise ordained. My health had been better in the last three days: my fever was leaving me, but I was, of course, still very weak. It would still be two hours before the sun would set, and, feeling refreshed by a little rest, and able for further work, I ordered the steeds to be saddled, and went in search of the lion.

I took John and Carey as after-riders, armed, and a party of the natives followed up the spoor and led the dogs. The lion had dragged the remains of poor Hendric along a native foot-path that led up the river side. "We found fragments of his coat all along the spoor, and at last the mangled coat itself. About six hundred yards from our camp a dry river's course joined the Limpopo. At this spot was much shade, cover, and heaps of dry reeds and trees deposited by the Limpopo in some great flood. The lion had left the foot-path and entered this secluded spot."

Several of the dogs were extremely afraid of him, and kept rushing continually backward and springing aloft to obtain a view. I now pressed forward and urged them on; old Argyll and

Bles took up his spoor in gallant style, and led on the other dogs. Then commenced a short but lively and glorious chase, whose conclusion was the only small satisfaction that I could obtain to answer for the horrors of the preceding evening. The lion held up the river's bank for a short distance, and took away through some wait-a-bit thorn cover, the best he could find, but nevertheless open. Here, in two minutes, the dogs were up with him, and he turned and stood at bay. As I approached, he stood, his horrid head right to me, with open jaws growling fiercely, his tail waving from side to side.

On beholding him my blood boiled with rage. I wished that I could take him alive and torture him, and, setting my teeth, I dashed my steed forward within thirty yards of him and shouted, "Your time is up, old fellow." I halted my horse, and, placing my rile to my shoulder, waited for a broadside. This the next moment he exposed, when I sent a bullet through his shoulder and dropped him on the spot. He rose, however, again, when I finished him with a second in the breast. The Bakalahari now came up in wonder and delight. I ordered John to cut off his head and forepaws and bring them to the wagons, and, mounting my horse, galloped home, having been absent about fifteen minutes. When the Bakalahari women heard that the man-cater was dead, they all commenced dancing about with joy, calling me their father.

On the 6th of September, there being no flesh in camp, I galloped up the river side to slay a hippopotamus, and presently heard a troop of them chanting behind me I had ridden past them and not observed them. With these I was unlucky I wounded six or seven, but did not bag one; they became very shy and cunning after the first shot, only protruding their noses. At mid-day I returned to camp and drank tea, after which I galloped down the river to a favorite sea-cow pool about a mile below my wagons I was accompanied by natives carrying my rifles. I found an immense herd of at least thirty hippopotami lying upon the rocks in the middle of the river. I shot the best bull and two fine old cows, and wounded a fourth. The bull and the two cows soon floated, and all three rested together on a ledge of rocks in the middle of the river. I then sent for John and Adonis, and with the assistance of the Bakalahari we got them into shallow water, where we could work upon them.

I was occupied most of the next day in superintending the cutting up of the flesh of the sea-cows, and reducing the same to biltongue, which we hung in garlands upon ox-rheims stretched- between the trees, surrounding them by a strong kraal of thorn trees.

In the evening a large party of Seleka's Bechuanas arrived at my camp. On the 8th one of my horses died of horse-sickness; it was, of course, my favorite, being my best shooting-horse. On reaching camp after my last hunting excursion, "Lion," my very best dog, was reported consumed by a huge crocodile, who frequented the spot where we drew water for such little pleasing varieties the African hunter must make up his mind; they are mere occurrences of every day.

I saddled up at an early hour, and went in quest of elephants with Seleka's men. We crossed the Limpopo, and then held east through the forest for the strong fountain called Seboono. I was unlucky here, however, as I also was next day, although we hunted by a splendid fountain in a more southerly direction. When under the mountains I met with the famous fly called "tsetse," whose bite is certain death to oxen and horses. This "hunter's scourge" is similar to a fly in Scotland called "kleg," but a little smaller; they are very quick and active, and storm a horse like a swarm of bees, alighting on him in hundreds and drinking his blood. The animal thus bitten pines away and dies at periods varying from a week to three months, according to the extent to which he has been bitten.

On the 10th the chief Pocoolway arrived with a large retinue he was a short, stout man, of a prepossessing expression, and both in appearance and manner much reminded me of a certain Scottish earl.

After three or four days' unsuccessful hunting, I resolved on the 14th there being good moonlight, to try what might be done with the elephants by night-shooting at the fountains, and I determined to make Carey shoot with me, he using the big rifle of six to the pound, and I my single-barreled two-grooved of eight to the pound. In the forenoon we were occupied making very hard bullets and sorting our ammunition, &c., &c., for a week's expedition, and at mid-day we started, followed by about sixty natives. We crossed the Limpopo, and held about east, right away through the forest, for the fountain which I had visited on the 8th. On our line of march we found no fresh spoor: the day was extremely hot, and the shuffling Bechuanas chose to lag behind in the forest until they lost me entirely, with the exception of three or four, who kept up with Piet my after-rider, carrying my gun, and leading "Filbert" and "Frochum," two of my best dogs. Not one of these men knew the country, and they had no Bakalabari with them to act as guides. When I reached the small fountain which lies west of the famous fountain for which I was steering, I told Piet to come on with the natives, and that I would ride ahead to the large fountain. I then galloped ahead, and made the fountain on its lee side. On slowly emerging from the thorny thicket through which I rode, I was astonished to behold two superb old bull elephants standing before me in the open space between the cover and the fountain. Both of them carried enormous tusks; one bull, however, was much taller and stouter than his comrade; I had very rarely seen his match, and his tusks at once took my eye as being perhaps the finest had ever beheld. Here, then, was I standing, without on or dogs, and with a very jaded steed, beside, as I afterward had good reason to believe, the very best elephant in all that district, and in perhaps many of the surrounding parts. I would have given any thing at that moment for my gun and dogs.

Fortunately, at this very moment the elephant made a furious charge after me, accompanied by a tremendous trumpet, which at once sealed his fate. They all heard it, and "Cooley" and "Affriar," two right good dogs, were instantly released from the couples and flew to my assistance, followed by Carey and the natives. Right glad was I when I saw black Cooley come up to help me. I at once felt that the elephant was mine, being certain that further assistance was at hand, and, with revived spirits, I yelled with all my might. In two minutes up came Carey on horseback, but without a gun. I called out to him, "For God's sake, Carey, bring me a gun here is the finest elephant in Africa I have held him at bay and fought with him for yearly two hours." Carey rode back and brought me his single-barreled smooth bore, carrying twelve to the pound, and gave me eight bullets out of his belt, expressing immense regret that my gun was not forthcoming. Carey had always an absurd idea that his gun could not kill an elephant: today, however, it was in other hands. "My good fellow," I said, "it is all right; the elephant is ours."

I then opened my fire on him from the saddle put my seventh bullet through his heart: on receiving it, he made a short charge, and stood trembling for a few seconds, when he fell forward on his breast and so lay; but evincing a desire to alter his position, which was a very good one for cutting out the teeth, I dismounted, and, going close up to him, I put two bullets into his ear, when he expired. The tusks of this elephant equaled my expectations; one of them, as usual, was more perfect than its fellow. I had never seen their match but once. On reviewing the whole afternoon's work, I considered myself extremely fortunate in capturing this noble prize, and felt most gratified with the satisfactory termination of my exertions. Piet and his party heard my shots, and they presently came up to us; coffee and other good things were soon spread out on a sheep-skin, and a comfortable sofa being quickly constructed of soft grass, covered with a kaross, I lay down to rest, the happiest of the happy.

The 15th was an extremely hot day. Carey and I were occupied all the morning cutting out the tusks of the big bull elephant; we took particular care not to let the blood fall upon them. In the evening we made hiding-places beside the fountain from which to shoot elephants, and when the sun went down we returned thither and took np our positions for the night. Unfortunately, the dead elephant lay directly to windward of the southern margin of the fountain, on which side were all the best elephant foot-paths. The consequence was that every elephant as he came up got the wind of the natives, and turned right about. Late in the night a troop of eight or ten bull elephants walked slowly across the vley with their heads to the north. I rushed forward to get before them in the wind, and running down the edge of the thorn cover, I got within thirty yards of the last bull, which was the best in the troop. Observing me move, he stood with his tusks up and his head directed toward me in a very suspicious manner for two minutes, when his fears died away, and he turned to me his left side. I then gave him a deadly shot, which brought blood from his trunk, as I ascertained next day. Returning from firing at him, I met Carey; his pluck had failed him, and he had dropped behind. On upbraiding him for not standing by me, he swore stoutly that he had stuck in the mud I as we had to cross a bog below the fountain in running for the shot. I thought this was good, and I said to myself, "I have got a name for you at last." But Carey was a good servant, and very attentive to me throughout my expedition.

The next morning I and Mutchuisho took up the spoor of my wounded elephant. He had gone off very slowly, with blood running from his truck. We had not been long on the watch before three enormous old bull elephants came; and, after much hesitation, and walking once or twice round the water, they came in and commenced drinking. I lay close to the edge of the fountain in a little hollow. The elephants came in to drink on the north side of a run which led away from the fountain, and I lay on the south side of it. Suddenly the finest bull of the three walked boldly through the run and came straight forward to where I lay. If I had remained still he would have walked upon me; but when he came within six or eight yards I gave a loud cough, upon which he tossed his head aloft and gave me a broadside, exposing his left side. I then gave him a shot from the bio two grooved rifle, and he dashed off with his two comrades in immense consternation, holding for the Limpopo.

The next day one of my steeds died of "tsetse." He had been bitten under the mountain range lying to the south of this fountain. The head and body of the poor animal swelled up in a most distressing manner before he died. His eyes were so swollen that he could not see, and in darkness he neighed for his comrades who stood feeding beside him.

CHAPTER XXVIII

On the 17th of September I resolved to leave the fountain of Seboono, as it was much disturbed, and to proceed with a few Balvalahari to a small yet famous water about six miles to the southeast. We accordingly saddled up and held thither. On reaching this fountain, which is called by the natives "Pallaa," I found the numerous foot-paths leading to it covered, as I had anticipated, with fresh spoor of elephant and rhinoceros. I then at once proceeded to study the best spot on which to make our shooting-hole for the night. It would be impossible to prevent some of the game from getting our wind, for the foot-paths led to it from every side. The prevailing wind was from the east, so I pitched upon the southwest corner of the fountain. The water was not more than twenty yards long and ten broad. The west side was bounded by tufous rock, which rose abruptly from the water about five feet high. The top of this rock was level with the surrounding vley, and here all the elephants drank, as if suspicious of treading on the muddy margin on the other three sides of the fountain. I made our shooting-box within six or eight yards of the water, constructing it in a circular form, of bushes packed together so as to form a hedge about three feet high. On the top of the hedge I placed heavy dead old branches of trees, so as to form a fine clear rest for our rifles; these clean old branches were all lashed firmly together with strips of thorn bark. All being completed, I took the Bakalahari and our steeds to a shady tree, about a quarter of a mile to leeward of the fountain, where we formed a kraal and off saddled.

This day was particularly adapted to bring game to the water, the sun being extremely powerful, and a hot dry wind prevailing all the afternoon. I told Carey that we were certain of having a good night's sport, and I was right, for we undoubtedly had about the finest night's sport and the most wonderful that was ever enjoyed by man.

A little before the sun went down, leaving our kraal, we held to the fountain, having with us our heavy-metaled rifles, karosses, and two Bakalahari. We also had two small guns, my double-barreled Westley Richards, and Carey's single-barreled gun. As we approached the fountain, a stately bull giraffe stood before us; the heat of the day had brought him thither, but he feared to go in and drink; on observing us, he walked slowly away. Two jackals were next detected. Guinea-fowl, partridges, two or three sorts of pigeon and turtle-dove, and small birds in countless thousands, were pouring in to drink from every act, as we walked up to our hiding-place and lay down. In a few minutes the sun was under; but the moon was strong and high (it being within three nights of the full), and the sky was clear, with scarcely a cloud.

Soon after Borele departed four old bull elephants drew near from the south. They were coming right on for the spot where we lay, and they seemed very likely to walk over the top of us. We therefore placed our two big rifles in position, and awaited their forward movement with intense interest. On they came, with a slow and stately step, until within twenty yards of us, when the leading elephant took it into his head to pass to leeward. We let him come on until he got our wind; he was then within ten yards of the muzzles of our heavy-metaled rifles; on winding us, he tossed his trunk aloft, and we instantly fired together. I caught him somewhere about the heart, and my big six-pound rifle burst in Carey's hands, very nearly killing us both. The elephant, on being fired at, wheeled about, and retreated to the forest at top speed. I now directed "Stick-in-the-mud" to make use of his single barreled twelve to the pound in the event of more elephants coming up; and thanking my stars that the old Dutch rifle had not sent us both to the land of the zeal, I sat down and watched the dark masses of thesis that cut the sky on every side, in the hope of seeing a mass as high and wide come towering forward into the open space that surrounded the fountain.

Nor did I watch long in vain, for very soon three princely bull elephants appeared exactly where the first came on, and holding exactly the same course. They approached just as the first had done. When the leading elephant came within ten yards of us, he got our wind and tossed up his trunk, and was wheeling round to retreat, when we fired together, and sent our bullets somewhere about his heart. He ran two hundred yards and then stood, being evidently dying. His comrades halted likewise, but one of them, the finest of the three, almost immediately turned his head once more to the fountain, and very slowly and warily came on. We now heard the wounded elephant utter the cry of death, and fall heavily on the earth. Carey, whose ears were damaged by the bursting of the big rifle, did not catch this sound, but swore that the elephant which now so stealthily approached the water was the one at which we had fired.

It was interesting to observe this grand old bull approach the fountain he seemed to mistrust the very earth on which he stood, and smelt and examined with his trunk every yard of the ground before he trod on it, and sometimes stood five minutes on one spot without moving. At length, having gone round three sides of the fountain, and being apparently satisfied as to the correctness of everything, he stepped boldly forward on to the rock on the west, and, walking up within six or seven yards of the muzzles of our rifles, turned his broadside, and, lowering his trunk into the water, drew up a volume of water, which he threw over his back and shoulders to cool his person.

We now returned to the fountain, and once more lay down to watch. Rhinoceroses, both black and white, were parading around us all night in every direction. We had lain but a short time when I detected a single old bull elephant approaching from the south by the same path which all the others had held. This elephant must have been very thirsty, for he came boldly on without any hesitation, and, keeping to windward, walked past within about eight yards of us. We fired at the same moment; the elephant wheeled about, and, after running a hundred yards, reduced his pace to a slow walk. I clapped Carey on the shoulder, and said "We have him." I had hardly uttered the words when he fell over on his side; he rose, however, again to his feet. At this moment the same presuming borele who had troubled us in the early part of the night came up to us again, and, declining as before to depart by gentle hints, I thought it a fitting moment to put an end to his intrusion, and accordingly gave him a ball behind the shoulder. On receiving it, he galloped off in tremendous consternation, and passed close under the dying elephant, who at the moment fell dead with a heavy crash, and broke one of his hind legs under him in the fall.

About an hour after two more elephants came towering on from the east. When they came up they stood for a long time motionless within forty yards of the water; and at length the finer of the two, which was a very first-rate old bull, and carrying immense tusks, walked boldly forward, and, passing round the north side of the fountain, commenced drinking on the rock just as the crippled bull had done. We both fired together, holding for his heart; the bullets must have gone nearly through him, for we had double charges of powder in our weapons. On receiving the shots he dropped a volume of water from his trunk, and, tossing it aloft, uttered a loud cry and made off, steering north; but before he was out of our sight he reduced his pace to a slow walk, and I could quite plainly hear, by the loud, painful breathing through his trunk, that he was mortally wounded; but whether the natives were too lazy to seek him, or having found him would not tell me, I know not, but I never got him. We shot another bull elephant shortly after this; he too uttered a shrill cry, and went off holding the same course the last one did; that was, however, all that I ever say of him.

On the 19th I proceeded with Carey and Piet, and a few Bakalahari, to a small fountain lying one mile to the south here we made two shooting-boxes of boughs of trees. There were three pools at which the game drank, the largest not being more than twelve feet in breadth. I and

Carey at night shot one fine bull elephant and four rhinoceroses, wounding two others, which escaped. On the night following we also wounded two elephants, which got away.

The next night I put in practice a novel experiment I had long entertained—that of hunting elephants by moonlight with dogs and horses, as in the day, being very much annoyed at wounding and losing in the last week no less than ten first-rate old bull elephants. I communicated my idea to "Stick-in-the-mud," and we hastily proceeded to saddle my steed. I led my dogs, eight in number, through the forest to leeward of where a bull who had come to the fountain to drink had gone in, and when I saw that they had got his wind I slipped them. They dashed forward, and next minute I followed the baying of the dogs and the crash and the trumpet of the elephant. He rushed away at first without halting, and held right for the mountains to the southwest. When, however, he found that his speed did not avail, and that he could not get away from his pursuers, he began to turn and dodge about in the thickest of the cover, occasionally making charges after the dogs. I followed on as best I could, shouting with all my might to encourage my good hounds. These, hearing their master's voice beside them, stuck well by the elephant, and fought him better than in the day. I gave him my first two shots from the saddle; after which I rode close up to him, and, running in on foot, gave him some deadly shots at distances of from fifteen to twenty yards.

The elephant very soon evinced signs of distress, and ceased to make away from us. Taking up positions in the densest parts of the cover, he caught up the red dust with his trunk, and, throwing it over his head and back, endeavored to conceal himself in a cloud. This was a fine opportunity to pour in my deadly shafts, and I took care to avail myself of it. When he had received about twelve shots, he walked slowly forward in a dying state, the blood streaming from his trunk. I rode close up to him, and gave him a sharp right and left from the saddle he turned and walked a few yards then suddenly came down with tremendous violence on his vast stern, pitching his head and trunk aloft to a prodigious height, and, falling heavily over on his side, expired. This was an extremely large and handsome elephant, decidedly the finest bull I had shot this year. Afraid of taking cold or rheumatism, for I was in a most profuse perspiration, I hastened back to my fireside, having first secured all the dogs in their couples. Here I divested myself of my leather trowsers, shooting- belt, and veldt-schoens, and, stretched on my kaross, I took tea, and wondered at the facility with which I had captured this mighty elephant.

Feeling fatigued, I intended to lie down and rest till morning. Just, however, as I was arranging my saddles for a pillow, I beheld another first-rate old bull elephant advancing up the vley from the south. I at once resolved that he, too, should run the gauntlet with the dogs. In immense haste, therefore, I once more pulled on my old leathers, and buckled on my shooting-belt, and ran down into the rank long grass beside the fountain to meet him, armed with the large two-grooved rifle, having directed Carey and Piet to come slowly up with the dogs and my horse and gun as soon as they were ready. The elephant came on, and food drinking within thirty yards of me. When I saw Carey coming on with the dogs and steed, I fired, but my rifle hung fire. The shot, however, gave the dogs good courage, and they fought well. The elephant took away at a rapid pace toward the other fountain where the Bechuanas lay, and at first led me through very bad wait-a-bit thorn cover, which once or twice nearly swept me out of the saddle. Presently he inclined to the west, and got into better country; I then rode close to him, and bowled him over with four shots.

While, however, I mourned the loss of these wounded elephants, I reckoned that I had been favored with immense good fortune in many instances during the past week. Ever intent upon embellishing and increasing my princely collection of African hunting trophies, I placed great value upon any specimen I happened to shoot which I thought worth adorning it. Thus I neglected my real interest; and instead of devoting my attention to rendering my expedition profitable, I allowed this very necessary part of the business to remain quite a secondary consideration. Thus, when I shot an ordinary bull elephant, I was accustomed to say to myself, "Ah! a good bull; tusks at least fifty pounds each; 45 6d a pound; bring me in £22 105. Capital day's work; help me to pay for the two horses that died last week, or the four that are bitten with 'tsetse,' and must die in a week or two." But if, on the other hand, I shot an elephant with a pair of tusks of unusual size, perfection, or beauty, I at once devoted them to my collection, and valued them at a ten-fold price. This, then, was one thing in which I reckoned I had been extremely fortunate—I had secured the finest tusks in all that nest of patriarchal old bulls which I had so sadly cut up in one short week, and which, perhaps, the summers of a century had seen roaming through these bundles forests in peaceful security.

The night-shooting being at an end, on the 23rd I retraced my steps to the dead elephants, to assist Carey in superintending the cutting out of the ivory, and in escorting the same along with our supply of fat and flesh to the wagons. Early in the afternoon we had got all ready for a start. The Bechuana captains who were there, and had appropriated my elephants and rhinoceroses, and nearly all the fat, then brought up about fifty men, who shouldered my impedimenta, and we marched for camp. Carey went in front, I rode in the middle, and my after-riders brought up the rear. This long line of naked savages thrilling the mazes of the forest, and bearing home the spoils of a few days' hunting, formed a truly interesting and unusual picture. Every man that was there carried something of mine some led the dogs, some carried the guns and extra ammunition, some cooking vessels, axes, sickles, water-calabashes, provisions, rhinoceroses' horns, the elephant's teeth, and an immense supply of flesh and fat, &c., &c. We made the Limpopo as the sun went down, which we crossed all right, and brought everything safe to camp. I made other excursions from this encampment in quest of elephants, in which I was very successful; but, as they did not differ in their details from the many already described, I shall not run the risk of wearying my reader with an account of them.

On the 30th one of those minor accidents occurred which the hunter in these parts must be prepared continually to encounter. As I awoke that morning, I heard a scream which denoted that "Prince," a most worthless dog, was consumed by a crocodile. There were several of these terrible animals frequenting the still deep stream beside which we lay. They seemed ever to be on the look-out for prey, and I have not the slightest doubt they would have taken one of us if we had ventured in.

On the 2nd of October, in the morning, we packed the cap-tent wagon, and stowed carefully away in grass my favorite tusks, which I intended to keep as specimens.

The next afternoon, while making for the fountain called Satoque, accompanied by Kapain and a party -from Bamangwato, I observed a number of crows and vultures and came across the spoor of a party of Bakalahari. I at once felt convinced that one of my wounded elephants lay rotting near me, but, the sun being nearly under, I did not then wait, resolving to seek it at another time; Kapain promised to send two of his companions early next morning to see if I had not surmised correctly. These men next day arrived, bearing some putrid fat which they had got from the Bakalahari; and I at once said, "Oh, you have found my dead elephant?" They answered, "Yes, but the tusks are stolen." They also said that they had not seen any others of their tribe, but that they had cut that fat out of the elephant. Kapain then promised me to do his best to recover the ivory for me; but I found out, very soon afterward, that he was playing me false. Next day I shot an old bull elephant.

The chief whom I wanted sat in the forum with most of his men; so, dismounting from my horse, I walked up to them, and sat down on the ground in native custom, and, taking snuff myself, handed it round. While I was doing this, John and Carey, armed, occupied the two places of exit from the forum. I sat silent for a little, and then said, "My heart is very bitter with the chief of this village. You were hungry, and I killed much flesh and fat for you. I told you that many of my elephants were lying dead, and that I wanted their teeth. You promised me to watch the vultures, and bring me the teeth. I have traced your spoor home from one of these elephants. Why did the tusks not come to my wagons? I do not want to shed your blood, but I require the teeth to be laid immediately before me."

They all immediately exclaimed, "The teeth are forthcoming, they are forthcoming wait a little, chief of the white men. We saw the vultures, and hid the teeth for you." I was delighted to hear this, but I pretended still to be very angry, and answered, "My heart is still very bitter, for you should have brought the teeth at once to me, and not caused me to come with guns to seek my teeth." The chief then at once dispatched five or six active men to bring the teeth; and Bechuana beer and porridge were placed before me. In an hour the men returned, bearing the tusks of my lost elephant. I was right glad to see them; they were immense teeth, and very finely arched, and almost perfect. I then chose some skins of koodoo and blue wildebeests out of their kraals for packing my ivory in the wagons, for which promised them beads after which returned to camp, the natives going before me, bearing the teeth and skins. These men had drawn the tusks, and concealed them somewhere close to the carcass of the elephant. Here they would most probably have been concealed until I had left the country, when they would have forwarded them to their chief. Just as we reached the drift we met a string of natives returning from my last elephant, bearing flesh and fat. This was a fine opportunity for a seizure. I selected several large bundles of the flesh and some fat, and marched the same to camp on the shoulders of the Bakalahari, along with the ivory. When Kapain saw us arrive at camp, he was utterly confounded, and began to abuse the Bakalahari; thereupon I bundled him out of the kraal. In the afternoon we packed the ivory in the baggage-wagon; it had hitherto lain loose in the kraal. There were fifty-three tusks of bull, and seventeen tusks of cow elephants. Three pairs of these bulls' teeth I intended to keep in my collection; in the cap-tent wagon were seven pairs of picked bulls' tusks, and two pairs of cow elephants' tusks, all of which I likewise devoted to my collection.

CHAPTER XXIX

On the morning of the 8th of October we packed the wagons, and about mid-day inspanned and left the Bakalahari village, where we had lain for nearly six weeks. The old chief of these Bakalahari looked extremely down-hearted when he saw ns preparing to depart, and could hardly refrain from crying. I had come there and found them starving; but ever since my arrival they had more good flesh and fat than they could eat. I had also employed the women to stamp my barley and Bechuana corn, and had always rewarded them liberally with beads, which they made into native ornaments, and with which they adorned their persons. The old chief was distinguished by a snake-skin, which he wore round his head. I gave him some presents at parting, and we then trekked, holding up the river, but at a considerable distance from it, the Limpopo having at this part a very considerable bend. In the evening we came again upon the river, and halted at our old kraal, where I had been troubled with lions on the 5th of August. On the march I lost "Argyll," my best dog, of whom I have often made mention in former expeditions, he having weathered my two campaigns in the Bamangwato country. He was strangled on the trap of the wagon, where he was coupled along with the other dogs. I now resolved to leave the Limpopo, and explore the country in a northwesterly direction I was accompanied by a large body of Sicomy's men. These scoundrels would not give me any information her as to water or elephants, excepting in one direction which suited themselves, invariably answering my questions with, "There is no water in that direction; there are no elephants there."

On the 15th, at sunrise, we inspanned, and held on until late in the afternoon, steering for the mountain of Guapa, where I had seen sable antelope on the 16th of July. We halted for the night without water; during the night rain fell. On the march we saw is poor of eland; my troop of dogs took away after a herd of zebras, one of which broke Filbert's shoulder with a kick, so I was obliged to shoot him. This was a sad loss to me; Filbert was the best dog I had left.

Next day, at dawn, we marched, holding for a vley close under the blue mountain in advance. Having proceeded some miles we fell in with springboks, zebras, blue gnoos; and soon after, to my surprise, an old bull kookama or oryx, carrying a superb pair of horns, started away before the wagons. My dogs were fresh and hungry they were instantly slipped and dashed forward on the scent of the oryx. Unluckily, a wild dog sprang up right in their path, to which they at once gave chase, and thus I lost this most splendid antelope.

I walked ahead of the wagons with my rifle, and soon started two pairs of ostriches. I was going down wind, and kept starting the game. I next sent away a herd of zebras and brindled gnoos; next a sounder wild boar; next a troop of giraffes; and, close to the vley where I intended to halt, I wounded a koodoo, which left a bloody spoor, that I did not choose to follow. The vley to which I had been trusting proved dry. We outspanned here for an hour, however, and then held round the western extremity of this fine mountain range; and as the sun went down, I halted my wagons on its south side, opposite the mouth of a bold and well-wooded ravine, which contained a strong fountain. On the march I rode ahead of my wagons on the spoor of two old bull buffaloes, which our wagon whips had started; these had gone out of my course, so I did not follow far. Returning, I came to a black rhinoceros, which I wounded, but did not get. As I neared the ravine where I intended to halt, I stalked in close upon a second black rhinoceros, which, on receiving two deadly shots, charged madly forward and subsided in the dust. A few minutes after firing at Borele I was following a troop of pallahs close under the green, rocky-mountain, when, lo! a herd of the lovely sable antelope caught my attention. These were quietly browsing on a shoulder of the mountain among the green trees far, far above me. I instantly threw off my leathers, and proceeded to stalk in upon them. An old doe detected me, however, and, instantly sounding the alarm, the herd, which consisted of eight—three coal-black bucks and five does—dashed off, and took through a wild, rocky ravine.

As it was too late in the day to follow them further, I turned my face toward my horses, which I had left at the base of the mountain; and, straining my eyes along the level forest beneath me to seek my wagons, which were now due, I detected them far out from the mountain, steering to go past the fountain. I then fired a signal shot, which brought them up. This unlucky shot started away two bull elephants which were feeding in the thorn cover close beneath me. I drew up my wagons in an open spot more than half a mile from the fountain, wait-a-bit thorns forbidding our nearer approach.

The 17th was a very cool and cloudy day; I took an early breakfast, and then held northeast, close in under the mountain range, accompanied by Kapain and a party of Bakalahari, to seek elephants.

We fell in with immense herds of zebras and buffaloes, numbering between three and five hundred in each herd, and toward evening with a numerous herd of elephants, when I killed one of the finest after an easy chase.

After several unsuccessful stalks for sable antelope, I at length met with the success my perseverance deserved. Returning in the afternoon of the 20th homeward, I suddenly observed a herd of about ten of them in thick cover on the mountain's ridge. I commenced ascending the rugged acclivity as fast as I could, for the daylight would be gone in a very short time. When had got within two hundred yards of them, I found it almost impossible to get in any nearer, as I must cross a stony flat in sight of several of the ever-wary does; it was, moreover, now so late that I could not well see the sights of my rifle. I had almost resolved not to disturb them, and to return to camp on second thoughts, however, I resolved to give it a trial. I made a successful stalk, and crossed this dangerous rocky flat unobserved. There was no moss nor heather under my knees, but a mass of sharp, adamantine fragments of rock, yet this I did not heed.

They now charged for the southern ridge of the mountain, and disappeared over it at a tremendous pace. I quickly loaded, and proceeded to take up the spoor, and at once had the satisfaction to find great spouts of blood all along the spoor of the patriarchal old black buck. This gave me high hopes of success; I waited a few minutes, and whistled for the Bechuanas, who immediately came up to me with "Bles" and "Affriar," two right good dogs. When the wounded buck had proceeded a short distance down the mountain's face, he left the herd and slanted away by himself. In a few minutes, however, I espied her to about three hundred yards from me, under a low tree on the rocky mountain side, with drooping head and outstretched tail, which he kept constantly whisking from side to side, and was evidently extremely sick. As he exhibited no intention of going further, and as the wagons were near, I thought it would be a fine opportunity to give all the dogs blood; so I dispatched Ruyter to camp to fetch them, and remained stationary and watched the wounded potaquaine. After standing in one spot for some time, he made a few tottering steps, then lay heavily down in the grass as if dead, and nothing was visible but his side.

This was most satisfactory there, on the side of his native rugged mountain, lay the ever-wary, the scarce, the lovely, long-sought sable antelope, and a most noble specimen—perhaps the finest buck in all the district. His ever-watchful eye was now sunk in the long grass; and as he was lying beside a little ravine, and a stiff breeze was blowing, I could, if I had chosen, have crept in within thirty yards of him, and shot him dead on the spot; but, so far from doing this, I rather lamented that he was thus badly wounded, for I feared that he would not have life enough left to show a good fight when the dogs came up. It has been truly said that there is many a slip between the cup and the lip, and the truth of this old saying I was about most bitterly to experience. In half an hour the Bushman came on with three Bechuanas, leading all my best dogs. I went up to the potaquaine. He had arisen, and was looking at us as we came on; when I approached within a hundred and fifty yards of him, he disappeared over the ridge.

I pressed forward in the most perfect confidence of an immediate bay; but, when I obtained a view of the open forest around the mountain's base, nor dog nor potaquaine could I see, neither could I hear a sound. I thought the chase must have led up wind, so I held on at mv best pace along the rugged mountains side.

I gained shoulder after shoulder, and opened fresh ground, but nothing living could I see, nor could I hear a sound. To make matters worse, it was blowing half a gale of wind. Most thoroughly confounded, I now in haste retraced my steps to the natives. These useless creatures I found sitting just where I had slipped the dogs. In vain I asked them whither they were gone; they only put me wrong, and lost me the day; for they declared that they had watched the ground below to leeward, and that no dog had gone in that course. They had, however, gone that way, and were at that moment baying a fresh buck very near me, but the unlucky wind prevented me from hearing them. I hastily retraced ray steps once more up wind, and, after proceeding a little further than I had been before, I saw "Alert," a very uncertain animal which I had long possessed, returning toward me.

The dogs have then gone up wind, I thought to myself, and they have the buck at bay in advance. Next moment, however, to my utter amazement, I beheld my wounded potaquaine standing in the forest below me, and not a single dog near him. I was now sure that my dogs had fallen in with some other bucks which I was not aware of, and were gone I knew not whither. After waiting an hour for them, I endeavored to stalk in on the potaquaine: it was bad ground, and he saw me and made off. He went but a short distance, however, and stood again in a drooping attitude beneath a tree; the Bechuanas tried to drive him to a position which I took up, when he left the ground, and I never saw him again.

When I returned to my camp, my people told me that the dogs had bayed a buck for a long time under the mountain, within hearing of the wagons, and that the sounds had died away, as if they had pulled him down and killed him. On hearing this, I at once saddled up two steeds, and rode in that direction to seek my dogs, but saw nothing of them, and, night setting in, I returned to camp. Next day three of the dogs returned; they were covered with the blood of the potaquaine they had killed, and one of them was wounded by his horns. I, however, never found the remains of either this buck or the one I had shot, nor did I see more of my three good dogs which were missing; no doubt they had all been found by the natives, and stolen by them.

At earliest dawn next day I held down wind with Ruyter, and presently found the fresh spoor of a herd of sable antelope which had got my wind, and were off. I then inclined my steps in the direction in which their poor led, and presently observed them among the trees within three hundred yards of us, some lying and some standing. One of the old does soon observed us. We sat gently down in the grass, however, and I crept away back, and made a very fine stalk upon the herd in very difficult ground. I was obliged to do a hundred and fifty yards of it on my breast. A wary old doe kept sentry, and prevented my approaching within a hundred yards. I therefore took this doe, and shot her with a bullet in the shoulder. I then sent Ruyter for the natives, and at once dispatched the head to camp to be stuffed.

In the evening I fell in again with this same troop of potaquaines on the northern range of the mountain. They heard me coming on before I was aware of them, and held up the wind over very rocky ground and through thick cover. I followed on in their wake like an old stag-hound, keeping close to them, and always halting when they halted; thus they did not observe me, and at last I got close in upon them. I could then have had a fine shot at several of the does, but I wanted the old black buck. I aimed for his heart, but an unlucky branch intervened, and, altering the line of my ball, lost me this most noble animal. I, however, fired a snap shot at him with my left barrel, and sent a bullet through his flank. The herd then dashed down the mountain side, making a tremendous rumpus among the loose masses of rock, the old buck leaving a bloody spoor. I did not disturb them further then, the sun being under, but returned to my home beneath the greenwood tree.

I followed the old buck up next day, but without success, and on the 31st I determined to return to my wagons. Accordingly, at dawn of day I rolled up my bedding, and, directing my

Bechuanas to go and call Bakalahari to carry my flesh and impedimenta to camp, I held a southwesterly course across the mountains with Ruyter and a Bechuana boy. This morning richly repaid me for all my toil and exertions in following the sable antelope throughout these stony and rugged mountains. Having proceeded about a mile down the wind, on looking over a height which commanded a fine view of well-wooded, undulating table-land below me, I had the sincere pleasure to behold a beautiful herd of sable antelopes feeding quietly up the wind within a quarter of a mile of me. The herd consisted of seven does and one coal-black magnificent old buck. Even at the distance at which they then were, I could very plainly see that this buck was a most superb specimen; his horns seemed almost too large for him, and swept back over his shoulders with a determined and perfect curve.

Presently, however, I observed a wary old doe, which had fed away among the trees apart from her comrades, standing looking at me. My position was a very awkward one; but I dared not alter it, as this would have lost me the day; so I remained motionless as the rocks over which I crept, and presently her patience was exhausted, and she ceased to suspect me, and held on to her comrades. I now made up my mind that it was impossible to do anything with them where they then, were, and that it would be best to watch them from a distance until they should move into some more uneven ground, where a stalker would have some chance with them.

Having thus resolved, I beat a retreat, and returned to the ridge above, where I had at first made them out Here I again sat, and with a longing heart watched the movements of these loveliest of Afric's lovely antelopes. I was struck with admiration at the magnificence of the noble old black buck, and I vowed in my heart to slay him, although I should follow him for a twelve month. The old fellow seemed very fidgety in his movements, and while the does fed steadily on, he lagged far behind, occasionally taking a mouthful of grass, and then standing for a few minutes under the trees, rubbing his huge, knotted, cimeter-shaped horns upon their branches. At length the does had fed away a hundred and fifty yards from him, and he still lagged behind. This was the golden moment to make a rapid stalk in upon him, while his ever-watchful sentinels were absent. I saw my chance, and stole rapidly down the rocky hill side and gained the level on which the herd were pasturing. He was now obscured from my view by the bushy, dwarfish trees which adorned the ground; the next move was to get my eye upon him before he should observe me I stole stealthily forward and detected him. He was still feeding very slowly on after the does, and seemed quite unsuspicious. I then instantly cast off my shoes and shooting-belt, and, watching the lowering of his noble horns, my eye fixed tiger-like upon him, stalked rapidly in. My heart beat with anxiety as I advanced, and was almost within shot; twenty yards nearer, and I would fire. Again he lowered his head to crop the young grass; I seized the moment, and the twenty yards were won.

Here was a young tree with a fork, from which I had resolved to fire. The potaquaine stood with his round stern right to me. I took a deadly aim and fired the ball entered very near his tail, and, passing through the length of his vitals, rested in his breast. He staggered about for a second, and then, bounding forward about sixty yards, halted, and looked back to sec from whence the deadly shaft had sped that had thus so unceremoniously disturbed his morning meal. The sights of my rifle were still fixed upon him, and just as he pulled up and exposed to me his full broadside, a second bullet left the ringing steel, and crashed through the very center of the old fellow's shoulders.

On receiving this second shot, the sable antelope wheeled about and held after the does, and I knew from his movement, though his pace was good, that he had got the ball in his shoulder and could not go very far. I then walked leisurely back to seek my shoes and shooting-belt, and, having found them, was loading my rifle, when the Bushman, who had been watching my stalk from the height above, joined me, and said that the buck had run but a short distance, and had lain down under a tree. I stole carefully forward, and immediately observed him lying as if still alive, his noble head not laid on the ground, but in an upright posture. Fancying him still alive, and having too often been tricked with wounded antelopes, I then gave him a third bullet, but the dark form of this lovely habitant of the mountain quailed not to the shot; the spirit of the sable antelope had fled. I was transported with delight when I came up and saw the surpassing beauty and magnificence of the invaluable trophy I had won. This potaquaine was very old, and his horns were enormous, fair set, perfect, and exquisitely beautiful. I cut off his head, and, leaving men to convey the flesh to camp, held thither in advance, escorting my hard-won trophy. On my way to camp, coming down the footpath from the fountain, to my dejectment I found the untamable Mazeppa stretched to rise no more, and half consumed by hyenas and vultures he bad died of horse-sickness. The redaction of my stock by the fell hand of death during this week was, alas not confined to Mazeppa only; the pony I bought of my cousin, Colonel Campbell, died of "tsetse," a valuable fore-ox died of some severe sickness, and "Fox," a very good dog, died of the African distemper; three of my very best dogs had also mysteriously disappeared the day they chased the potaquaine.

We remained in the neighborhood frequented by the sable antelope for several days longer, but I did not succeed in killing another, although with other game of every kind I met with great success.

CHAPTER XXX

On the 15th of November we inspanned, and left the mountains of Linguapa. Kapain and his Bechuanas held for Bamangwato; Seleka's Bechuanas held for their chief; and we held a southwesterly course for the impopo, which we reached in less than three hours.

Next day we trekked at dawn, and having marched a few miles we were joined by Bakalahari, who reported having seen elephants on the preceding day. A little after this I shot a water-buck close to the river, when I outspanned.

During the day "Matsaca," chief of the Bamalette, visited me with a retinue he brought a kaross for me, for which I was to cut him on the arm and shoulder, and anoint him with medicine to make him shoot well with the gun which he had bought of me. In the evening I walked a short distance down the river's bank, and shot a lovely fawn of the serolomootlooque, and a buck pallah with a very handsome head.

On the 17th I went in quest of elephants, accompanied by the Bamalette men. We continued along the bank of the river for several miles, when we took up the spoor of three or four enormous old bulls. On our way I wounded a white rhinoceros, which I did not follow to secure. The elephants had fed very slowly away from the river, and before we had followed the spoor an hour we were close upon them. The Bechuanas chose to leave the spoor, and, making a cast to windward, they started the elephants. My dogs being much distressed with the sun, and I not being aware that the game were started, we at this very moment unfortunately sat down and rested for half an hour, which of course lost me the day. When I discovered that the elephants had moved off, I turned my face for camp, and before proceeding far I started an ostrich off her nest the nest contained twenty eggs, which I directed the Bechuanas to bring to camp.

In the course of the day I saw the fresh spoor of about twenty varieties of large game, and most of the animals themselves, viz., elephant, black, white, and long-horned rhinoceros, hippopotamus, camelopard, buffalo, blue wildebeest, zebra, water-buck, sassayby, koodoo, pallah, springbok, serolomootlooque, wild boar, duiker, steinbok, lion, leopard. This district of Africa contains a larger variety of game than any other in the whole of this vast tract of the globe, and perhaps more than any district throughout the world; for besides the game which I have just noted, the following are not uncommon, viz., keilton, or two-horned black rhinoceros, eland, oryx, roan antelope, sable antelope, hartebeest, klipspringer, and grys steinbuck the reitbuck is also to be found, but not abundantly.

We inspanned on the 18th before it was day, and trekked up the Limpopo for about three hours. In the forenoon Matsaca arrived from the carcass of the borele he brought with him a very fine leopard's skin kaross, and an elephant's tooth; these were for me, in return for which I was to cut him to make him shoot well. This I did in the following manner opening a large book of natural history, containing prints of all the chief quadrupeds, I placed his forefinger successively on several of the prints of the commonest of the South African quadrupeds, and as I placed his finger on each, I repeated some absurd sentence and anointed him with turpentine. When this was accomplished I made four cuts on his arm with a lancet, and then, anointing the bleeding wounds with gunpowder and turpentine, I told him that his gun had power over each of the animals which his finger had touched, provided he held it straight. Matsaca and his retinue seemed highly gratified, and presently took leave and departed: I afterward trekked up the river till sundown.

On the succeeding day we marched with the dawn, and held up the river. In the forenoon Bechuanas from Seleka visited me, bearing a tooth of a bull elephant, for which they wanted a gun; the tooth, however, being small, I would not give them one for it, although I might have done so at a fair profit. I found the game extremely abundant, counting no less than twenty-two rhinoceroses, nine of which were in one herd, feeding on the open plain. The wind was as foul as it could blow, and kept continually starting the game. At length, late in the afternoon, I got within shot of four white rhinoceroses. The old bull stood next to me; so, resting my six-pound rifle on the trunk of a tree which an elephant had overthrown, I took him on the shoulder and smashed his forearm; he ran for thirty yards, and then rolled over on his back. He, however, regained his legs and ran a hundred yards further, when his leg failed him, and, coming up on his spoor, I finished him in a few minutes. The wagons now camo up and I halted them on the river's bank, opposite to the rhinoceros.

On the 21st much rain fell throughout the day, rendering the country unfit for trekking, A birth and a death occurred among my cattle. In the afternoon a loud rushing noise was heard coming on like a hurricane this was a large troop of pallah pursued by a pack of about twenty wild dogs. They passed our camp in fine style within a hundred yards of us, and in two minutes the wild dogs had caught two of the pallahs, which my Bechuanas ran up and secured. A pallah, in passing my camp, cleared a distance of fifty feet in two successive bounds, and this on unfavorable ground, it being very soft and slippery.

For many succeeding days my difficulties with respect to bringing on the wagons continued to increase. The rain still poured down, rendering the country impossible to travel, and my oxen died daily of the tsetse bite. In this condition my progress was slow and painful in the extreme, and I waited anxiously the expected succor from Mr. Livingstone. At length I came fairly to a stand, not having sufficient oxen left to draw one wagon. I formed my camp in a shady bend of the river, and fortified it with a high hedge of thorny trees, and in a few days more all my cattle had died with the exception of two young oxen, which I inclined to think would survive the bite of the fatal "tsetse."

On the 7th of December I resolved to have some fishing; accordingly, I routed out some old salmon fishing tackle, and sallied forth with one of the wagon whip-sticks for a rod, and some string for a line. I baited my hook with a bit of the blue wildebeest, and put on a cork for a bob. I cast in my bait in a quiet bend of the river, and anxiously watched the cork, which very soon began to bob. I then conjured up many forms in my mind, and wondered whether it would be a fair fish, such as I might expect in my own land's rivers, or something more like a young crocodile. I was not fated to live long upon conjecture, however, for next moment underwent the cork, and, striking sharply, I threw over my head a fine gray fish about a pound weight, and in appearance like a haddock, with a broad mouth and eight or ten feelers. My Bushman said the Boers, about the Orange River knew this fish, and loved to catch and eat it. Presently my perseverance was rewarded by a second fish of the same kind as the first ; and after this I hooked a very heavy fish, which I lost. I doubt not but most excellent sport might be obtained in the Limpopo.

In the evening Carey and I cut down a very dense thorn-tree to inspect the nest of a secretary The summit of the tree was very wide, dense, and level, and from the terrible nature of the thorns it was utterly inaccessible without the aid of the hatchet. When the tree fell, out from its nest rolled a young secretary, and immediately disgorged its last meal, which consisted of "four lizards of different sorts, of which one was a chameleon, one locust, one quail, and a mouse."

A few days after this I sent out John and Carey into different arts to seek game, and each killed a pallah; but the sky threatening rain, they did not wait to escort their venison, but left natives to bring it on, A considerable time having elapsed, and the Bakalahari not appearing, I dispatched John and some of the natives in my service to look after them, and it was well I die so for, on reaching his pallah, John found the Bakalahari whom he had left to convey it to camp in the act of bolting with the half of it, having cunningly (as he thought) hacked the other half with a sharp stone, and dirtied the flesh with the entrails, thinking to persuade us that it had been done by a leopard or hyena.

On the morning of the 16th, as I was preparing my breakfast, I suddenly beheld a civilized-looking native approach me he wore a shirt, a pair of leather trowgers, and a sailor's red night-cap, and carried a gun and shooting-belt. The instant I beheld him I said aloud, "Natives from Sichely—the oxen are at hand." It was even so my messengers had found Mr. Livingstone at home, who, on hearing of my distress, had at once, in the noblest manner, dispatched men with his whole stock of trek-oxen to my assistance. These I had now the inexpressible satisfaction to behold reach me in saloty. We inspanned at once, and commenced our march and continued to make good way for several days; and on the 26th we reached Kolubeng, the new residence of Sichely. In the morning that chief brought me two young oxen, which I all but purchased for an old saddle and two pounds of powder; but we split upon the cup of powder being level and not piled.

A day or two after, I ascended the rocky hill above the town with Mr. Livingstone, to obtain a view of the surrounding country. I came upon a very high heap of well-bleached moldering bones of many varieties of game, amassed and piled here by a mighty Nimrod now no more, who had in days of yore chosen this hill for his habitation. Mr. Livingstone pointed out to me a range of tabular hills to the southeast, near the sources of the Kolubeng, throughout which he informed me the sable antelope was to be met with. In the evening Sichely came to trade with me, when I obtained several young oxen in barter from him.

On arriving at Sichely's I dispatched natives to Bakatla to fetch two spans of oxen which I had left on my way into the interior in charge of Mr. Edwards, and with these, on the 3rd of the new year, we again inspanned and tried to make a start with twelve oxen in each wagon they, however, finding the wagons extremely heavy, would not move them, nor could we prevail upon them to take to their wonted work, as they ought to do, until every ox had been most unmercifully flogged with both wagon-whips and jamboks. Our course for Bakatla was southwesterly, but, owing to the position of the mountains, we were obliged to make a very zigzag and circuitous march. We halted at sundown. The country here is the most pleasing I have seen in Africa—beautifully wooded, undulating plains, valleys, straths, and conical and tabular mountains of most fascinating appearance, invariably wooded to their summits, stretching away on every side.

We marched steadily for several days, and on the 7th reached Bakatla, which was looking extremely beautiful, being surrounded by very green fields of Bechuana corn. Here we remained a few days while I obtained fresh oxen, and then, pushing on, gained the River Molopo. Early on the 14th I drew up my wagons on its northern bank, and in the forenoon sallied forth to seek for reitbuck, which are here abundant. At this hour of the day, however, it was of little use to seek for them, as they were lying concealed in the endless dense reeds which enclose the Molopo, in some parts extending to a breadth of half a mile, their height averaging from twelve to twenty feet and upward. I found plenty of spoor, including the fresh spoor of lions, which along the Molopo are always abundant. The day was excessively hot, and there was a most painful, oppressive feeling in the atmosphere to an extent which I had rarely experienced. In the afternoon dark masses of clouds arose along the horizon on every side, and constant thunder bellowed in the distance: a little before the sun went down the sky above and all around looked extremely threatening, and I directed my people to prepare for a tempestuous night.

At this time I observed a reitbuck grazing beyond the dense reeds on the other side of the Molopo, and I at once held for him, with my little Moore rifle, accompanied by my Bushman. We had some difficulty in penetrating the dense reeds, and on gaining the other side a change in the direction of the wind started off the reitbuck. I then observed two other reitbuck, a buck and a doe, coming out to graze some distance to windward, and commenced a stalk in upon them. Having proceeded about half way, I suddenly observed two huge yellow lionesses about a hundred and fifty yards to my left, walking along the edge of the reeds, holding a course parallel to my own. The reitbucks smelled the lions and lay down. I got very near them, but they started off, and bounded. straight away from me: I fired and missed the buck.

Ruyter came toward me, and I ran forward to obtain a view beyond a slight rise in the ground to see whither the lionesses had gone. In so doing I came suddenly upon them, within about seventy yards; they were standing looking back at Ruyter. I then very rashly commenced making a rapid stalk in upon them, and fired at the nearest, having only one shot in my rifle. The ball told loudly, and the lioness at which I had fired wheeled right round, and. came on lashing her tail, showing her teeth, and making that horrid, murderous deep growl which an angry lion generally utters. At the same moment her comrade, who seemed better to know that she was in the presence of man, made a hasty retreat into the reeds. The instant the lioness came on I stood up to my full height, holding my rifle, and my arms extended, and high above my head. This checked her in her course; but on looking round and missing her comrade, and observing Ruyter slowly advancing, she was still more exasperated, and, fancying that she was being surrounded, she made another forward movement, growling terribly. This was a moment of great danger. I felt that my only chance of safety was extreme steadiness; so, standing motionless as a rock, with my eyes firmly fixed upon her, I called out in a clear, commanding voice, "Holla! old girl, what's the hurry? Take it easy; holloa! holloa!" She instantly once more halted, and seemed perplexed, looking round for her comrade. I then thought it prudent to beat a retreat, which I very slowly did, talking to the lioness all the time. She seemed undecided as to her future movements, and was gazing after me and snuffing the ground when I last beheld her.

Accordingly, in the morning I drove up my wagons and very soon his highness made his appearance, and requested me to get ready some coffee. Presently about a dozen fine young oxen were brought up, which he said were to purchase powder, and after coffee we proceeded to trading. I selected one young ox, and offered him six pounds of powder for it. He then desired to see the powder, and on my measuring it out he said that I must add two more. From his manner it appeared to me that he did not intend to deal with me even if I gave him what he asked; so I said I would let him have one pound more, and if he did not like to take it we could not deal. He then, with the greatest nonchalance, said, "Lay by your powder," and commenced talking on some other subject. Being very anxious to obtain some good specimens of the large-horned oxen of the Kalihari, and Mahura being by report in possession of some, which he had lifted from the Bawangketse, I told him that if he would bring them up I would give him a good price for them.

He said that he had cattle with large horns, and that he would send to one of his outposts for two oxen which would frighten me to look at.

In the evening the cattle came; these were two immensely tall, gaunt, hollow-sided, very remarkable-looking animals, and carried truly enormous horns. The head of one of them was very handsome; the horns were very wide and fair set, going out quite horizontally for some distance on leaving the head; their width, from point to point, might have been about eight feet. This ox was roan-colored on his face and along the top of his back. The other was red; his horns were thicker than those of his comrade, and were of good length, with very good points, but their sweep was not graceful. They were neither of them so thick as the horns of my red Wangketse ox, Rob Roy, which I left with Fossey, nor by any means so handsome; yet, nevertheless, they were both very remarkable heads, and perhaps such another pair I might never again fall in with. I told Mahura that I possessed finer specimens, but I would be happy to have a deal with him. He then showed me two fine bull elephant tusks, for which I offered him cash; but he said he had no understanding in cash, and that he would keep them until he saw something he stood in need of. His drift was to get one of my valuable double rifles out of me.

Next day Mahura brought me the two large-horned Kalihari oxen, and after coffee he asked me if I was going to buy. I asked him what he wanted for the oxen, when he said powder. I said that I would take them both, and give him eight pounds of powder for each. On hearing my offer he only laughed, and, turning round, ordered his herds to drive the cattle back to the post. I asked him what he v/anted for them this he would not state, but remarked, "You were wont to ride by the Motito road. They may well now say, 'Alas! we have lost that good trader; now may Mahura rejoice that that good man has gone to trade with him." The meaning of this speech was, that Mochuara, the chief at Motito, had presented me with an ox earring very large horns, and that, in return, I had given him a gun. I now considered that I had already been too long with this ruffian, and I accordingly called for my oxen and marched for the Vaal River, distant a day and a half. We held on until sundown, having halted for an hour at mid-day.

We resumed our march at daybreak on the 28th, and held on through boundless open plains. As we advanced, game became more and more abundant. In about two hours we reached a fine fountain, beside which was a small cover of trees and bushes, which afforded an abundant supply of firewood. Here we outspanned for breakfast it was a fine cool morning, with a pleasant breeze. The country was thickly covered with immense herds of game, consisting of zebra, wildebeest, blesbok, and springbok. There could not have been less than five or six thousand head of game in sight of me as I sat at breakfast. Presently the whole of this game began to take alarm. Herd joined herd, and took away up the wind; and in a few minutes other vast herds came pouring on up the wind, covering the whole breadth of the plain with a living mass of noble game.

Bakalahari now hove in sight, running at intervals across the plain, bearing parasols of black ostrich feathers, which they brandished on high, to press on the panic-stricken herds. These fellows must have had good wind, for they held on at a steady trot, exactly like wild dogs (only that the wild dogs gallop and do not trot), and did not allow the game to get very far in advance. It was evident that they were driving it to a range of pitfalls in advance; but being without steeds, and in extreme pain from a swelled ankle, I was unable to follow them up and ascertain their success, as I wished is have done. My ankle became daily worse. I applied leeches to it at Mahura's, which helped me a little, but the number was too small to be of great benefit. I was now entirely unable to set my foot to the ground. Carey thought it was erysipelas, and I was very apprehensive that it would end in something extremely serious.

On the 29th we again set out, and in about three hours we reached the fair, long-wished-for, yet much dreaded Vaal River. I say much dreaded, because, from the constant rains which had continually been falling this season, I had made up my mind that it was not improbable I might have to lie for many months upon the banks of this often impassable river. On this occasion, however, to my great satisfaction, and quite contrary to my expectations, I found the river low, and the drift, which I had never seen before, very good, and free from rocks or very large stones, the descent from our side was easy, but the ascent from the drift on the opposite side was steep and muddy; and some smart showers of rain, which had been falling during the last two hours, had rendered it so slippery that I deemed it best to outspan, and defer taking the drift until the ground should dry a little in the afternoon, when I got my wagons through in safety, taking one at a time with twenty steady oxen.

We now made the Vet River, which flows into the Vaal a little above the drift, and followed its course toward Colesberg. This we found to be an excellent road, but inclining too far to the east. Our march led us through vast herds of game, which I have before spoken of as frequenting the northern boundaries of the colony. On the 20th of February I crossed the Great Orange River at Aleman's Drift, and entered Colesberg next day. I found most of my old friends still here, and also my redoubtable friend old Murphy, as wild and as jolly as ever.

I hired the old barracks for my residence during my stay in Colesberg, and immediately set about sewing up my trophies in canvas, and stowing them away in cases. This was accomplished in about fourteen days.A fortnight more was spent in preparing for another hunting expedition. I purchased a new wagon from a Mr. Emshe for £100, and a fresh stud of sixteen horses, a mule, and a span of oxen from various parties in town, and subsequently I increased my stud to twenty.

CHAPTER XXXI

On the 19th of March, 1848, I left Colesberg with three wagons "well manned and stored," for my fifth and last cruise in the far interior. I was joined by a Mr. Orpen (a mighty Nimrod), who, notwithstanding my representing to him the dangers and hardships of an elephant hunting expedition in their blackest colors, kindly agreed to favor me with his help and company on my lonely trip. My sojourn in Colesberg reduced me considerably, and I was glad once more to breathe the fresh air of the country. We got clear of Colesberg at about 9 A.M., and commenced our march over the country I have so often marked with my wheel tracks, and which my reader must now be fully acquainted with. On my way I completely recruited my oxen and stud, and prepared myself to take the field with an immense pack of stout, serviceable dogs. I also engaged as after-rider a Bushman named Boor.

The game became plentiful in about ten days after we left Colesberg, but when we came to the Vet River I beheld with astonishment and delight decidedly one of the most wonderful displays which I had witnessed during my varied sporting career in Southern Africa On my right and left the plain exhibited one purple mass of graceful blesboks, which extended without a break as far as my eyes could strain the depth of their vast legions covered a breadth of about six hundred yards. On pressing upon them, they cantered along before me, not exhibiting much alarm, taking care, however, not to allow me to ride within at least four hundred yards of them. On, on I rode, intensely excited with the wondrous scene before me, and hoped at length to get to windward of at least some portion of the endless living mass which darkened the plain, but in vail. Like squadrons of dragoons, the entire breadth of this countless herd held on their forward course as if aware of my intention, and resolved not to allow me to weather them.

On the 22nd of April, after some trouble, we crossed the Vaal River, and on the 25th reached Mahura's. I rode ahead of the wagons, and found the old ruffian busily engaged with some of his nobility in reducing with adzes a thorn-wood tree, which was to serve as a beam in a new dwelling-house he was about to erect. He was astonished to see me return so soon, and expressed much satisfaction thereat. I asked Mahura if he had still the two large-horned oxen which I had seen when last here; he replied, they were still forthcoming. In half an hour the wagons arrived, and I drew them up outside the town. The chief shortly afterward made his appearance, and had coffee with us.

For many days back our oxen had been looking very spare, and fallen off in condition, and one or two exhibited symptoms of the tongue sickness at the Vaal River. We now had the intense mortification to discover that nearly the whole of them were attacked with either tongue or hoof sickness. This discovery cast a sad gloom over our prospects. I was unacquainted with the nature of either of the maladies, and the Hottentots declared that an ox required months to recover from either of them, and that they often proved fatal. In this state of things, I deemed it prudent to begin to purchase young oxen from Mahura and his tribe, and gave him to understand that I was willing to do so. The chief replied that his people would be unwilling to bring their oxen, because, when I had last passed through his country, they had brought oxen for barter, and I had purchased none of them; he, however, promised to acquaint them with my wishes. In the afternoon, my wagons having outspanned at a great distance from the water, I inspanned, and trekked down to the Hart stream, which I crossed, and drew up on its opposite bank.

Next day the chief, instead of coming to trade as he had given me to understand he would, held a hunting party with a number of his people on the old Scottish principle of the ring, a common and successful mode of hunting among the South African tribes. On this occasion, however, the ring was mismanaged, and the game broke through. In the evening one large ox was brought for barter, but we did not agree about the price. Our oxen now presented a most woeful appearance, the greater part of them being very lame, and nearly all more or less ailing. This was a most start ling fact, and, as the Bechuanas did not seem disposed to bring oxen for barter, it threatened to oppose an insurmountable barrier to our progress either backward or forward.

Two hours having elapsed after breakfast the following morning, and the chief not having made his appearance according to promise, Mr. O. and I went up to the palace to ask him what were his intentions in respect to the trading. He replied that he could not force his people to bring me oxen, but that he had intimated my wishes to them. I then remarked that he would do me a friendship if he would set his people the example by first dealing with me himself, as I knew that I should then have no difficulty with them. The chief, after some demur, told me that oxen would be brought for barter, and requested me to go before him to the wagons, and get ray coffee-kettle under weigh. In the evening I obtained one good-looking ox from one of his men for ammunition. When Mahura left I presented him with some sugar for his coffee and a whip stick.

The chief again made his appearance, accompanied by his interpreter and several of his people, early next day, bringing stout young cattle to barter for guns and ammunition. Having taken coffee, the chief called me aside, and, pointing out to me two good-looking young oxen, said they were his, and that he wanted powder for them. I asked him how much he would require, and he replied that he had brought a measure, and that if I would fill it with powder I could have the two oxen. When I beheld the wooden measure I thought the chief was going to drive a hard bargain with me. On filling it, however, with powder, I found that it held about eighteen pounds, and as this was not an exorbitant price for two good oxen, I was very glad to get them, and I told the chief I was satisfied with his measure. He and all his people seemed to think they had got a bargain, and, the example now being set, the trading went on rapidly, and by sundown I had purchased twenty-two oxen, twenty of which were quite fit for work. In the forenoon Mr. O. and I went to look at the cattle (which we allowed to remain night and day in the veld), and had the satisfaction to find a decided improvement in them. The chief was in high spirits all day, and on leaving me in the forenoon he said he would give me a fat cow to kill for my people, and that he would bring me a large-horned ox to purchase.

We marched again at sunrise, and at about 10 A.M. I drew up my wagons beside the large pan where I had been storm-stayed for a week last season. On the march I shot a springbok; and observing vultures, Mr. O. and I rode toward them with a troop of the dogs, in the hope of falling in with a lion, but were disappointed. In the afternoon, directing the wagons to follow, I rode ahead with Boor, and on reaching the next large pan drew the cover lying to the south of it, expecting to find a lion. When the wagons came up I formed my camp beside the thorn-grove, and, observing a herd of blue wildebeests making for my cattle, I proceeded to waylay them, and fired two long shots. Next minute Boor came up to me, and said that on my firing he had observed a lion stick his head up in the long grass in the vley opposite to me. I felt inclined to doubt the veracity of his optics. I sent him. back, however, with instructions to bring eight dogs; but Boor thought the whole pack would be better, and returned with thirty.

I then rode direct for the spot where the lion was supposed to be. Booi was correct; and on drawing near, two savage lionesses sat up in the grass and growled fiercely at us. An unlucky belt of reeds, about sixty yards long and twenty broad, intervened between me and the lionesses, and on perceiving their danger they at once dashed into this cover then followed the most woeful cutting up and destruction among my best and most valuable dogs. The lionesses had it all their own way. In vain I rode round and round the small cover, endeavoring to obtain a peep of them, which would have enabled me to put a speedy conclusion to the murderous work within. The reeds were so tall and dense, that, although the lionesses were often at bay within eight or ten yards of me, it was impossible to see them. At length one came outside the cover on the opposite side, when I fired a shot from the saddle. My horse was unsteady; nevertheless I wounded her, and, acknowledging the shot with angry growls, she re-entered the reeds.

A number of the dogs, which had gone off after a herd of blue wildebeests, now returned, and, coming down through the long grass, started a third lioness, which came growling down into the cover and joined her comrades. This was the signal for my united pack to make a bold sally into the center of the lions' den, when they were savagely met by the three lionesses, who rushed furiously up and down, knocking the dogs about with just as much facility as three cats would have disposed of the same number of mice. For several minutes nothing was to be heard but the crashing of the reeds, the growling of the lions, and the barking and shrieking of the mangled pack it was truly a most painful moment to my feelings. Carey, who had come up to assist, remarked to me that "there was an awful massacre going on among the dogs;" and he was right. Night now setting in put an end to this horrid work, and, with feelings of remorse and deep regret at my folly in not having at once called off my poor dogs, I wended my way to camp. On numbering the slain, three of my best hounds were found to have forfeited their lives in the unequal contest, and seven or eight more were very badly wounded, exposing the most fearful gashes, from which several of them never recovered. While I was occupied with the lions my followers were forming a kraal for the cattle.

Before the day began to break next morning lions were heard roaring to the west accordingly, I rode in that direction with Booi and a detachment of dogs, still resolved to follow the king of beasts, notwithstanding the disasters of the former day. Having ridden about a mile, we reached the end of a long piece of cover, averaging a hundred yards in breadth, where I at once discovered the fresh spoor of a troop of lions. The dogs took it up and followed on at a wary pace, the hair bristling on their backs. On reaching the end of this cover a second one appeared several hundred yards to my right, while a little to my left was a small vley, and here I observed a jackal steal away, while a crow sounded his ominous voice in advance.

These signs bid fair for the proximity of lions, and I remarked to Booi that we must be upon them; it was so. Next moment I observed a yellowish form on a parish spot two hundred yards ahead, which we knew must be the lion, and thither we rode at top speed. On observing us he raised his noble head, but quickly again laid it flat on the ground, intending to crouch in the hope that we should pass him by unnoticed. Within twenty yards of him lay a noble lioness, with two half grown young lions. On seeing that our course was direct for where they lay, they bounded up and charged for the cover to our right, the old lion displaying more cowardice than either his royal spouse or the young lions, and taking the lead at the best pace that he could muster. I did not wait for my rifle, but shouting to my dogs I pressed forward and tried to cut off his retreat. I was even with him and the lioness, and within twenty yards, when they reached the cover, which they sullenly entered. The dogs seemingly were apprehensive of following too near such dangerous game, probably warned by the fate of their comrades on the preceding day.

Our dogs kept up an incessant barking during the night, and we imagined that lions were prowling around our camp. In the morning, however, we discovered that we had been favored with the presence of far less illustrious, yet more presuming visitors. A pack of audacious hyenas had visited our fireside, and, not content with cracking and swallowing the bones which they found there, they had eaten our table-cloth, which consisted of the skin of a sable antelope, and carried off the lid of our canteen and two large camp-stools, which I lately had made to order in Colesberg. One of these we had the good fortune to recover, minus the rheims; the other will probably be found in after years, and preserved as a Bechuana or Bushman relic.

On the 12th I drew up my wagons on the north bank of the famous Meritsane. Here I had the pleasure to find that, owing to a large tract of the country having been burned by the Bakalahari some months previously, and favored by the rainy season, a rich and verdant crop of young grass had sprung up, giving the undulating plains a fresh and vernal appearance. I was delighted on beholding this, for I knew that it would have the effect of attracting the game hither from all the surrounding parts, and I confidently hoped to fall in with elands, as they are generally met with by the foremost hunters in the vicinity of the Meritsane. Having breakfasted, I saddled up three of my fleetest steeds, and, accompanied by two after-riders, rode forth in a northern direction, and carefully sought for eland's spoor. Presently I crossed the old Kuruman road, and immediately discovered fresh spoor, similar to that of elands, but, in my opinion, a little too large. In a buffalo country I should have at once pronounced it to be the spoor of buffaloes, but these for many years had not frequented the Meritsane, and were not to be expected nearer than the Molopo. Even in the days of Harris, twelve years ago or upward, buffaloes had forsaken the Meritsane. As I rode on, the spoor became more abundant, and very soon fresh dung disclosed to me that a very large herd of buffaloes had lately pastured there.

The spoor of zebras, blue wildebeests, hartebeests, and sassaybies was extremely abundant, and of all these I fell in with very considerable herds. I had resolved, however, not to disturb the country, for fear of starting any elands which might be there, and rode past, leaving them unmolested. After proceeding for many miles, I had the mortification to ascertain that only a very few elands now frequented these parts, and after a fruitless search for these few I turned my face for camp, and resolved to fire into whatever game I might fall in with. I yached a large herd of blue wildebeests and a herd of hartebeests, and was very unfortunate, wounding several, but failing to secure one. This was to me most particularly annoying, our flesh in camp being completely exhausted, and my large pack of dogs famishing. I resolved, therefore, to march next morning for Lotlokane, and hunt in advance of the wagons.

The next day I rode forth with one after-rider, resolved to do my best to supply the deficiency in camp. I directed the wagons to follow, and outspan at the Plat Rocks, half way to Lotlokane. I had proceeded out a short distance when I had the satisfaction to be« hold a magnificent herd of buffaloes quietly pasturing within half a mile of me on the opposite bank of the Meritsane. This was a first-rate look-out, and exactly what I stood in need of, considering the present low state of my commissariat. I returned to meet the wagons, where I saddled another steed, named Brown, which was steady under fire, and once more rode forth, accompanied by Mr. O., with two after-riders, and a large detachment of the dogs, resolved to deal death among the buffaloes. We rode to leeward of the herd to give the dogs their wind, and then galloped in upon them. At first, bewildered, they stood gazing at us until we were within thirty yards of them, when, seeing their danger, a panic spread throughout the whole herd, and, wheeling about, they crashed along through the underwood in a dense mass, impeding one another's progress.

In two minutes I was alongside of the herd, and, dismounting, fired right and left into two old cows; one of these immediately dropped to the rear of the troop, and, staggering for a few seconds, fell over and expired. The herd now left the river and doubled back, passing through a belt of low cover. I halted a moment to load. Following on, I came right upon the other buffalo that I had wounded, standing with a comrade in a dense bush. I observed her before she could charge me, and three more shots laid her low. The reports of Mr. O's gun now sounded ahead, and, galloping forward, I observed him to my right actively engaged with four old buffaloes, which stood at bay in a large bush in the open country the herd had vanished.

Three of the buffaloes which we had shot having been left in the veld, I deemed it more than probable that a lion might be found on some one of them if sought for at early dawn; accordingly, having substituted a bowl of warm milk for coffee, I rode forth with an after-rider and a troop of my dogs to seek the king of beasts. On gaining the first buffalo, I found that my natives had left a flag of peace flying over him, which had guarded him from the attacks of the beasts of prey. Upon the second buffalo, however, a hundred vultures were feasting merrily; but, as I approached the third, the sudden rush of a flight of vultures over my head toward the buffalo told me that some occupant which had hitherto kept them aloof had that moment quitted the carcass, and on galloping forward and clearing an intervening rising ground, I had the satisfaction to behold a huge and shaggy lion trotting slowly off toward the cover along the banks of the river, within two hundred yards of me.

I instantly rode for him at top speed to get my dogs clear of the carrion, and, if possible, to bring the lion to bay before he should gain any bad cover. We came up with him just as he gained a small belt of reeds on the river's bank. The lion sprang into the river's bed and stood at bay. Riding up within fifteen yards, I disabled him with a shot in the shoulder, and then, springing from my horse, which was unsteady, went up to within twelve yards on foot, and finished him with my second shot, which he got behind the shoulder. This was a fine old lion, with perfect tusks and a very beautiful coat of hair. Leaving Booi to protect him from the vultures, I rode to camp, and dispatched men with instructions to flay him with the utmost care. In the afternoon I inspanned, intending to march, but continued showers of rain prevented me. Next day, however, we reached Lotlokane.

As morning dawned on the 16th a lion roared to the north within a quarter of a mile of us, and shortly after two other lions moaned to the east. I rode in quest of them with dogs and an after-rider. Hartebeests, zebras, and pallahs were standing about in all directions, and, leading my dogs away, I failed to find the lion. In the forenoon, anxious to obtain a gemsbok, I saddled up my three fleetest steeds, and rode in a northerly direction, with two after-riders, taking with me a light single-barreled gun. I started several fine steinboks, which are here abundant. Having ridden a few miles, T entered upon a magnificent level park, thickly adorned with groves of thorn-trees, on which were grazing large herds of blue wildebeests, zebras, hartebeests, and springboks. Knowing that eland and gemsbok are generally to be found in the vicinity of herds of other game, I resolved to ride in a semicircle to windward of these, and carefully examine the ground for the game I sought.

Here I remained for many days, making successful excursions with Mr. Orpen across the river in search of elephants. On these occasions, however, and likewise upon all subsequent encounters with the elephants, I had the mortification to remark, that on coming up with them, my followers invariably yielded to a natural impulse, and thus throughout the entire expedition the whole brunt of the elephant hunting lay upon my shoulders, not a single elephant being bagged or even wounded by any individual in my establishment except myself.

On our return from one of these expeditions we came upon a heart-sickening sight. The Bamalette tribe, through whose district we were now hunting, had been attacked and put to flight by Sicomy a few months before, when a large number of them were massacred, in consequence of which they had deserted their former town and ensconced themselves in an elevated ravine in the mountains. We visited their deserted town and the ground over which they had been pursued and slain. We were horrified to behold the bleaching bones and skulls of those who had fallen; the wolf and jackal had feasted on their remains, and laid the long grass flat round each skeleton, and the blood was still visible upon the stones. Hair and torn fragments of karosses lay scattered around.

On the 12th I had another hard day in the mountains after elephants, and at night I watched a fountain and shot an old lioness. She came and drank within ten yards of me; the ball entered the center of her breast, and rested in the skin in the middle of her back.

On the 13th I dispatched men to camp with the skin of the lioness, and held south for Charcbe, which I found still deserted by the elephants. In the evening the natives were all busy cooking the flesh of the lioness, which was excessively fat, and esteemed by them a particular delicacy.

On the 25th of July, at sunrise, we inspanned and held down the river, leaving three more of my stud behind me, two dead and the other dying of tsetse. At sundown we halted about twenty miles down the river. While on our march next morning we came across the fresh spoor of a troop of bull elephants, when I immediately outspanned. I was proceeding to follow up the elephants' spoor, when I was met by a party of Bakalahari, who informed me that other elephants had drunk on the opposite side, and some miles higher up the river, during the night. I resolved to go there in quest of them. We crossed the Limpopo at a most rocky drift, where the horses were in danger of breaking their legs, and, holding up the river, took up the spoor of three old bulls.

We rode down the river for several mornings hunting after hippopotami, a great number of which we killed. As the tusks of some of these were very fine, we chopped them out of the jaw-bones, a work of considerable difficulty. On the 17th I was attacked with acute rheumatic fever, which kept me to my bed, and gave me excruciating pain. While I lay in this helpless state, Mr. Orpen and Present, who had gone up the river to shoot sea-cows, fell in with an immense male leopard, which the latter wounded very badly. They then sent natives to camp to ask me for dogs, of which I sent them a pair. In about an hour the natives came running to camp and said that Orpen was killed by the leopard. On further inquiry, however, I found that he was not really killed, but fearfully torn and bitten about the arms and head. They had rashly taken up the spoor on foot, the dogs following behind them, instead of going in advance. The consequence of this was, that they came right upon the leopard before they were aware of him, when Orpen fired and missed him. The leopard then sprang on his shoulders, and, dashing him to the ground, lay upon him growling and lacerating his hands, arms, and head most fearfully. Presently the leopard permitted Orpen to rise and come away. Where were the gallant Present and all the natives, that not a man of them moved to assist the unfortunate Orpen? According to an established custom among all colonial servants, the instant the leopard sprang he discharged his piece in the air, and then, dashing it to the ground, rushed down the bank and sprang into the river, along which he swam some hundred yards before he would venture on terra firma. The natives, though numerous and armed, had likewise fled in another direction.

CHAPTER XXXII

Both Orpen and myself were now reduced to a state of utter helplessness—he from his wounds, which were many and dangerous, and I from the fever, though I was slowly recovering. It was of no use, therefore, to remain longer in the low-lying district about the Limpopo, so I resolved to march on steadily to Sichely's country. We accordingly marched on the 27th of September, and on the 2nd of October encamped on the bank of the Limpopo, a little above its junction with the Lepalala. Here Seleka's men requested me to halt a day, as their chief wished to trade with me, which I agreed to do.

Next morning Seleka arrived with a considerable retinue, bringing some good specimens of Bechuana arms to barter for muskets and ammunition. He made me a present of some Bechuana beer, and a sort of fermented porridge; this, he said, he considered as a gift, but he expected that I, in return, would give him some gunpowder. This is the usual style of presents in Southern Africa.

In the afternoon I exchanged a musket for nine very handsome assagais, a battle-ax, and two shields of buffalo hide. I also exchanged some assagais for ammunition, and obtained other articles of native manufacture in payment for cutting the arms of two or three of the nobility, and rubbing medicine into the incise to enable them to shoot well. While performing this absurd ceremony, in which the Bechuanas have unbounded faith, I held before the eyes of the initiated sportsman prints of each of the game quadrupeds of the country ; at the same time anointing him with the medicine (which was common turpentine), and looking him most seriously in the face, I said, in his own language. "Slay the game well; let the course of thy bullet be through the hearts of the wild beasts, thine hand and heart be strong against the lion, against the great elephant, against the rhinoceros, against the buffalo," &c.

On the 8th we marched at sunrise, and, trekking steadily along, arrived on the 8th at the drift on the Limpopo where, on the former occasion, I had crossed the river. The game was very abundant in our course, but Carey and Present were rarely successful in killing, and I was obliged, at length, weak as I was, to take the field, as we were sadly in want of flesh. On the 13th. We made the banks of the Ngotwani. u|> which we proceeded for several days; but, finding that there was scarcely any water in it, and that it would be impossible to reach Sichely's country by this route, I determined to retrace my steps. We accordingly marched for the Limpopo, which I fell in with once more on the 23rd, having killed a noble old lion in my way.

We trekked up along the banks of the river for the Mariqua, and a little before sundown fell in with two enormous herds of buffaloes, one of which, consisting chiefly of bulls, stood under the shady trees on one side of the bank, while the other, composed chiefly of cows and calves, stood on the opposite side, a little higher up the river. In all there were at least three hundred. Thinking it probable that if I hunted them I might kill some old bull with a head perhaps worthy of my collection, I ordered my men to outspan, and, having saddled steeds, gave chase to the herd of bulls, accompanied by Booi and my dogs. After a short burst they took through the river, whereby I lost sight of an old bull which carried the finest head in the herd. My dogs, however, brought a cow to bay as they crossed the river, which I shot standing in the water, but not before she had killed a particularly favorite bulldog named Pompey.

On finding that he was attacked, the lion at first made a most determined bolt for it, followed by all the dogs at a racing pace; and when they came up with him he would not bay, but continued his course down the bank of the river, keeping close in beside the reeds, growling terribly at the dogs, which kept up an incessant angry barking. The bank of the river was intersected by deep water-courses, and, the ground being extremely slippery from the rain which had fallen during the night, I was unable to overtake him until he came to bay in a patch of lofty dense reeds which grew on the lower bank, immediately adjacent to the river's margin. I had brought out eleven of my dogs, and before I could come up three of them were killed. On reaching the spot I found it impossible to obtain the smallest glimpse of the lion, although the ground favored me, I having the upper bank to stand upon; so, dismounting from my horse, I tried to guess, from his horrid growling, his exact position, and fired several shots on chance, but none of these hit him. I then commenced pelting him with lumps of earth and sticks, there being no stones at hand. This had the effect of making him shift his position, but he still kept in the densest part of the reeds, where I could do nothing with him.

Presently my followers came up, who, as a matter of course, at once established themselves safely in the tops of thorn-trees. After about ten minutes' bullying, the lion seemed to consider his quarters too hot for him, and suddenly made a rush to escape from his persecutors, continuing his course down along the edge of the river. The dogs, however, again gave him chase, and soon brought him to bay in another dense patch of reeds, just as bad as the last. Out of this in a few minutes I managed to start him, when he bolted up the river, and came to bay in a narrow strip of reeds. Here he lay so close that for a long time I could not ascertain his whereabouts; at length, however, he made a charge among the dogs, and, coming forward, took up a position near the outside of the reeds, where for the first time I was enabled to give him a shot.

The lion then sprang up, and, facing about, dashed through the reeds and plunged into the river, across which he swam, dyeing the waters with his blood; one black dog, named "Schwart," alone pursued him. A huge crocodile, attracted by the blood, followed in their wake, but fortunately did not take my dog, which I much feared he would do. Present fired at the lion as he swam, and missed him; both my barrels were empty. Before, however, the lion could make the opposite bank, I had one loaded without patch, and just as his feet gained the ground I made a fine shot at his neck, and turned him over dead on the spot. Present, Carollus, and Adonis then swam in and brought him through. We landed him by an old hippopotamus foot-path, and, the day being damp and cold, we kindled a fire, beside which, we skinned him. While this was going forward I had a painful duty to perform, viz., to load one barrel, and blow out Rascality's brains, whom the lion had utterly disabled in his after-quarters. Thus ended this protracted and all but unsuccessful hunt; for when I at length managed to shoot him, the dogs were quite tired of it, and, the reeds being green, I could not have set them on fire to force him out.

On the 27th we reached the junction of the Mariqua with the Limpopo, when we once more bade farewell to the latter, and held up the northern bank of the Mariqua. This fine little river averages here about five or six yards in width, and meanders along in a very serpentine course through a very broad open vley, its banks being in many places destitute of cover, excepting reeds, and in others is densely clad with groves of thorn and willow trees, &c. Here I found reitbuck, which do not frequent the Limpopo in those parts which I have visited. The country looked fresh and green, and all the usual varieties of game were abundant. Elephants had been frequenting the district some months previously, but had now deserted it. About fifty miles to the south and east a very bold and rocky extensive blue mountain chain towered in grand relief above the intervening level forest. The length of this mountain chain seemed to be about a hundred miles, its course about northeast, and it gradually became loftier and more rugged toward the northeastern extremity. I believe the Limpopo rises somewhere to the east of this chain, and I felt a strong desire to follow it to its source, but under existing circumstances this measure was not advisable. On the march we passed a small village of Bakalahari, which was surrounded with heaps of bones and skulls of game.

Next day we marched about eight miles up the river, and outspanned in a wide open vley. On the march I shot one sassayby, and wounded two black rhinoceroses. In the afternoon I rode up the edge of the river with Ruyter in quest of reitbuck, of which I saw several small troops, but did not kill any, not getting a chance of the old bucks, which I hunted for their heads. I, however, shot one enormous crocodile, which we discovered fast asleep on the grassy bank of the river. He got two balls, one in the brains and the other behind the shoulder; yet, nevertheless, in the struggles of death he managed to roll into the water and disappeared. I was extremely surprised to see so enormous a crocodile in so small a stream; his length was considerably greater than the width of the river at the spot where I shot him.

Marched again at sunrise, and I and Ruyter rode ahead to seek reitbuck. I detected one of these squatting beside the river to shun observation, and shot him dead on the spot. He proved to be an old buck; but both of his horns being broken in fighting, I did not keep the head. A little after this, two packs of wild dogs kept trotting and cantering slowly along before us, one on either side of the river; we had started them from two pallahs, which they had caught and were consuming. More reitbuck were seen, and presently an old buck, carrying unusually fine horns, started up before us in company with four does. By taking up a position in a hollow in the vley, and sending Ruyter to drive them toward me, I had the satisfaction to succeed in bowling over this fine old buck, which proved to be a princely specimen. I shot him running, and broke his back.

On the 31st, as I was riding along the river's bank, about two miles below the spot where some days before I had fired at a large crocodile, I came upon a similar reptile lying asleep on the opposite side, which I shot dead on the spot, putting the ball through the spine close into the back of the head. On receiving the ball, he only made a slight convulsive movement, and then remained still and motionless as if still asleep, not having in the slightest degree altered his position a copious stream of blood issued from the wound, and colored the shallow water in which he lay. Having crossed the river at a drift about a mile below, I rode up to inspect this hideous monster of the river, which, to my surprise, I found to be the same one at which on the 28th, I had fired, and, as I supposed, killed. He bore the marks of both my bullets, one of which had fractured a part of his skull. The crocodile was a very old fellow, and a fine specimen, its length being upward of twelve feet. I resolved, therefore, to preserve the skin, and with this intention, in the forenoon, marched down six men, who were occupied until sundown in the novel work of flaying the crocodile.

A few days after this, just as Swint had milked the cows, and was driving them from the wooded peninsula in which we lay, athwart the open ground, to graze with my other cattle in the forest beyond, he beheld four majestic lions walk slowly across the vley, a few hundred yards below my camp, and disappear over the river's bank at a favorite drinking-place. These mighty monarchs of the waste had been holding a prolonged repast over the carcasses of some zebras killed by Present, and had now come down to the river to slake their thirst. This being reported, I instantly saddled up two horses, and, directing my boys to lead after me as quickly as possible my small remaining pack of sore-footed dogs, I rode forth, accompanied by Carey carrying a spare gun, to give battle to the four grim lions. As I rode out of the peninsula, they showed themselves on the bank of the river, and, guessing that their first move would be a disgraceful retreat, I determined to ride so as to make them think that I had not observed them, until I should be able to cut off their retreat from the river, across the open vley, to the endless forest beyond. That point being gained, I knew that they, still doubtful of my having observed them, would hold their ground on the river's bank until my dogs came up, when I could more advantageously make the attack.

I now sat in my saddle, anxiously awaiting the arrival of the dogs, and, while thus momentarily disengaged, was much struck with the majestic and truly appalling appearance which these four lions exhibited They were all full-grown, immense males; and I felt, I must confess, a little nervous, and very uncertain as to what might be the issue of the attack. When the dogs came up I rode right in toward the lions. They sprang to their feet and trotted slowly down along the bank of the river, once or twice halting and facing about for half a minute. Immediately below them there was a small determined bend in the stream, forming a sort of peninsula. Into this bend they disappeared, and next moment I was upon them with my dogs. They had taken shelter in a dense angle of the peninsula, well sheltered by high trees and reeds. Into this retreat the dogs at once boldly followed them, making a loud barking, which was instantly followed by the terrible voices of the lions, which turned about and charged to the edge of the cover. Next moment, however, I heard them plunge into the river, when I sprang from my horse, and, running to the top of the bank, saw three of them ascending the opposite bank, the dogs following. One of them bounded away across the open plain at top speed; but the other two, finding themselves followed by the dogs, immediately turned to bay. It was now my turn; so, taking them coolly right and left with my little rifle, I made the most glorious double shot that a sportsman's heart could desire, disabling them both in the shoulder before they were even aware of my position. Then snatching my other gun from Carey, who that moment had ridden up to my assistance, I finished the first lion with a shot about the heart, and brought the second to a standstill by disabling him in his hind quarters. He quickly crept into a dense, wide, dark green bush, in which for a long time it was impossible to obtain a glimpse of him.

We followed up the banks of the river for several days with the usual allowance of sport. On the 16th we came suddenly upon an immense old bull muchocho roiling in mud. He sprang to his feet immediately he saw me, and, charging up the bank, so frightened our horses, that before I could get my rifle from my after-rider he was past us. I then gave him chase, and, after a hard gallop of about a mile, sprang from my horse and gave him a good shot behind the shoulder. At this moment a cow rhinoceros of the same species, with her calf, charged out of some wait-a-bit thorn cover, and stood right in my path. Observing that she carried an unusually long horn, I turned my attention from the bull to her, and, after a very long and severe chase, dropped her at the sixth shot. I carried one of my rifles, which gave me much trouble, that not being the tool required for this sort of work, where quick loading is Indispensable.

After breakfast I sent men to cut off the h]ead of this rhinoceros, and proceeded with Ruyter to take up the spoor of the bull wounded in the morning. We found that he was very severely hit, and, having followed the spoor for about a mile through very dense thorn cover, he suddenly rustled out of the bushes close ahead of us, accompanied by a whole host of rhinoceros birds. I mounted my horse and gave him chase, and in a few minutes he had received four severe shots. I managed to turn his course toward camp, when I ceased firing, as he seemed to be nearly done up, and Ruyter and I rode slowly behind him, occasionally shouting to guide his course. Presently, however, Chukuroo ceased taking any notice of us, and held leisurely on for the river, into a shallow part of which he walked, and after panting there and turning about for a quarter of an hour, he fell over and expired. This was a remarkably fine old bull, and from his dentition it was not improbable that a hundred summers had seen him roaming a peaceful denizen of the forests and open glades along the fair banks of the secluded Mariqua.

During our march on the 19th we had to cross a range of very rocky hills, covered with large loose stones, and all hands were required to be actively employed for about an hour in clearing them out of the way to permit the wagons to pass. The work went on fast and furious, and the quantity of stones cleared was immense. At length we reached the spot where we were obliged to bid adieu to the Mariqua, and hold a westerly course across the country for Sichely. At sundown we halted under a lofty mountain, the highest in the district, called "Lynche a Cheny," or the Monkey's Mountain.

On the forenoon of the 26th I rode forth to hunt, accompanied by Ruyter; we held west, skirting the wooded stony mountains. The natives had here many years before waged successful war with elephants, four of whose skulls I found. Presently I came across two sassaybies, one of which I knocked over; but while I was loading he regained his legs and made off. We crossed a level stretch of forest, holding a northerly course for an opposite range of green, well-wooded hills and valleys. Here I came upon a troop of six fine old bull buffaloes, into which I stalked, and wounded one princely fellow very severely behind the shoulder, bringing blood from his mouth; he, however, made off with his comrades, and, the ground being very rough, we failed to overtake him. They held for the Ngotwani. After following the spoor for a couple of miles, we dropped it, as it led right away from camp.

Returning from this chase, we had an adventure with another old bull buffalo, which shows the extreme danger of hunting buffaloes without dogs. We started him in a green hollow among the hills, and, his course inclining for camp, I gave him chase. He crossed the level broad strath and made for the opposite densely wooded range of mountains. Along the base of these we followed him, sometimes in view, sometimes on the poor, keeping the old fellow at a pace which made him pant. At length, finding himself much distressed, had recourse to a singular stratagem. Doubling round some thick bushes which obscured him from our view, he found himself beside a small pool of rain water, just deep enough to cover his body; into this he walked, and, facing about, lay gently down and awaited our oncoming, with nothing but his old gray face and massive horns above the water, and these concealed from view by rank overhanging herbage.

Our attention was entirely engrossed with the spoor, and thus we rode boldly on until within a few feet of him, when, springing to his feet, he made a desperate charge after Ruyter, uttering a low, stifled roar peculiar to buffaloes (somewhat similar to the growl of a lion), and hurled horse and rider to the earth with fearful violence. His horn laid the poor horse's haunch open to the bone, making the most fearful rugged wound. In an instant Ruyter regained his feet and ran for his life, which the buffalo observing, gave chase, but most fortunately came down with a tremendous somersault in the mud, his feet slipping from under him thus the Bushman escaped certain destruction. The buffalo rose much discomfited, and, the wounded horse first catching his eye, he went a second time after him, but he got out of the way. At this moment I managed to send one of my patent pacificating pills into his shoulder, when he instantly quitted the field of action, and sought shelter in the dense cover on the mountain side, whither I deemed it imprudent to follow him.

On the 28th we marched at sunrise, when one of my wagon-drivers chose to turn his wagon too short, in opposition to my orders, whereby it was very nearly upset, for which I flogged him with a jambok, and then knocked him down. This man's name was Adonis he was a determined old sinner, on whom words had no effect. Our course lay through a wide, well-wooded strath, beautifully varied with open glades. As we proceeded, fresh spoor of buffalo and care leopard became abundant, and about breakfast-time, as we were crossing an elevated slope in the vicinity of the Ngotwani, I had the felicity to detect a magnificent herd of the latter browsing in the middle of the strath about half a mile to our left.

As I had enjoyed very little sport with camelopard either in this or the last expedition, my time and attention having always been engrossed with elephants, I resolved to avail myself of this opportunity, and accordingly, having caught a couple of my mares, I rode for them, accompanied by Booi as after-rider. I had directed my men to outspan, and my intention was, if possible, to hunt one of the camelopards to my camp; but in this I failed. On disturbing the herd they separated into two divisions, one of which took right away down the wind, being a tail-on-end chase from my camp the finest bull went with this division, and him I followed. After a sharp burst of about a mile, I headed and laid him low with two shots behind the shoulder. Having cut off his tail, we were returning to camp, and had proceeded about halfway, when we came upon the other division of the herd.

When I came up I was within twenty yards of the lions before I was aware of their proximity. Observing me, they sprang to their feet, and, growling sulkily, trotted up the mountain side. I only saw one of them at first, and ran forward for a shot. Having ascended the steep a short distance, the lion halted to have a look, giving me a fine broadside, when I shot him through the heart. On receiving the ball he bounded forward, and was instantly obscured by the trees. I advanced cautiously, and next moment the other lion sprang up with a growl, and marched with an air of most consummate independence up the mountain side. I imagined that this lion was the one I had fired at, and sent two more shots at him, both of which were too high; after which he disappeared over a ridge immediately above. On proceeding to inspect the spot where the lion had been lying, I found that there were two beds, consequently that there must have been two lions, and I conjectured that I had killed one of them. In case, however, he should be only wounded, I deemed it prudent to ride down to the wagons, which were then passing below me, to obtain some dogs to pioneer. Having procured these, I and Ruyter returned to the spot, and found the lion lying dead on the mountain side. We proceeded to skin him, and returned to the wagons with the spoils. The other decamped; the dogs could not find him. Both of these were first-rate old lions, but the one that escaped was the larger of the two. In the afternoon I rode on to Sichely; kraal on the Rouloubeng, having directed my men to follow with the wagons.

On arriving at the station, I found that Mr. Livingstone had left that morning to visit a tribe to the east of the Limpopo. I waited upon Mrs. Livingstone, who regaled with me with tea and bread and butter, and gave me all the news. I remained a week in the station, and on the 12th I inspanned. At sundown we halted near the Pass of God, intending to hunt sable antelope, having seen a small troop of them in the month of May on a steep mountain side, beneath which I formed my camp.

CHAPTER XXXIII

Next morning I rode through the Pass of God and held west, accompanied by two after-riders. I rode to within a couple of miles of the Kouloubeng, and returned close in under the mountain chain to the south of the pass. I went forth on foot, accompanied by Ruyter, and ascended the mountain immediately above my camp to seek for sable antelope. I had the satisfaction to discover the spoor of three bucks on a piece of rocky table-ground on the highest summit of the range, and soon after I started a princely old buck from his lair. He was lying in long grass in a sandy spot behind a bush, within eighty yards of me. Starting from his mountain bed, this gem of beauty rattled up a rocky slope beside which he had been lying, and, halting for a moment, looked back to see what had disturbed him, when I sent a bullet through his ribs, and, as ho disappeared over the ridge, lodged another in his vitals. Having loaded, I followed on the spoor, and soon observed him within a hundred and fifty yards of me, standing in a green hollow far below, whisking his tail, and evidently severely wounded. A strong breeze which was then blowing was against me, as it shook a young tree of which I wished to avail myself for a rest. I nevertheless managed to make a fine shot, and sent a bullet through the center of his shoulder, bringing him down on his face, and laming him. The potaquaine disappeared down the wooded mountain side over a rocky ridge, but no rude fears agitated my breast; I had lamed him, and that was enough if stalking should fail, there were dogs at my wagons that could very soon bring him to bay.

On the 15th I was occupied during the morning in stuffing the head of the sable antelope, after which I rode forth with two after-riders, and, holding a northerly course, skirted the range of hills beneath which we were encamped. I soon reached a gorge in the hills, through which I rode, and at its upper extremity discovered springs of water forming a little stream. In a basin in the hill side opposite this little stream I observed a rattling old buck roan antelope or bastard gemsbok standing under the shade of some young trees, the sun being extremely powerful. I first endeavored to stalk in upon him, but, finding that the ground would not admit of that, I laid a plot for him. Guessing from the lay of the land what course he was most likely to take, I instructed Ruyter to give me about twenty minutes to steal forward, and then to endeavor to move him toward me. Before, however, I could gain the point I wished, an eddy in the breeze apprised the roan antelope of my proximity, when he instantly started to pass a shoulder of the mountain opposite which I already was. As I was screened by some thorn-trees, I made a run to save the day. When the buck halted, I likewise halted; and when he ran, I also ran; thus, when he halted the second time, and looked down to see what had disturbed him, I had got within two hundred yards, and was standing in position, with my rifle steady on a branch of a thorn-tree.

In the morning I rode forth with the Bushman, and, holding a southwesterly course, examined the mountain ranges and several fine straths in that direction. At length I started a small troop of zebras, and soon after I observed a fine old buck roan antelope, which got my wind. Returning from following this buck, I shot a steinbok; this shot at the steinbok started a troop of seven or eight old bull buffaloes, which Ruyter had found, from the summit of a rocky hillock. I followed, when the invariable rhinoceros birds started them, and I galloped on in their wake.

Presently they halted to look behind them, and I at the same instant sprang from my mare and lay down in the grass. My mare commenced eating the grass and whisking her tail, which the buffaloes observing, and fancying that she was some species of game, made of their minds that it was all right, and, coming forward a few steps, tools up a position under a wide shady tree, not evincing any further signs of fear. Thus I was enabled to take my time and select the finest head in the troop. After about twenty minutes spent in studying the set of the heads. I shot one princely old bull, when they all made off. Following on their spoor for a short distance, I found my bull lying dying beneath a thorn-tree, and his comrades standing near him. As the old bull died, he roared loudly, as buffaloes are wont to do. His comrades came forward and walked round him, smelling the blood, when I wounded two more, and a little after a third, which the natives discovered on the following day. On returning to camp I dispatched men for the head of the buffalo and a supply of meat.

Next day, while exploring a fine mountainous tract of country to the southwest, I suddenly found myself in my old wagon-spoor of '45, within a short distance of the bold gorge in the mountains in which my oxen had been chased by lions. In this fine pass two streams of water meet it is a first-rate district for game when the country has not been ransacked by Griqua hunters. I immediately found the spoor of a troop of buffaloes it led me into a rich, green, and well-wooded glen in the hills, through which one of the afore-mentioned streams flowed. The wind was as foul as it could blow, and this troop got my wind. Returning from spooring them, however, I very soon fell in with another troop, reposing under dense shade in the same glen. I crept in within thirty yards of them, and there lay for upward of an hour, endeavoring to select the finest head. The buffalo which I wanted was lying down, his body screened by stout thorn branches.

I pushed on the wagons as rapidly as I could, considering that the country was almost destitute of water, my cattle consequently being in a desperate condition; and in the afternoon of the 13th I reached the Hart River, where I outspanned within a quarter of a mile of the town or kraal of the Batlapis. The river was greatly swollen and quite impassable, the rain having been very heavy in certain parts of the country. Shortly after we arrived old Mahura, with a party, made his appearance, and came down to greet me across the river, and beg for some coffee.

In the morning, by Mahura's request, I inspanned and crossed the Hart stream, and encamped on its southern bank. In the course of the day I obtained ten karosses in barter from the tribe, and one very good spotted cat as a present from the chief. I also obtained a large sack of Kaffir corn in barter for beads, and milk was pressed upon us to any amount. A few fine oxen were offered for barter, but I did not require them, preferring to purchase karosses. Mahura favored me with a visit morning and evening, remaining at the wagons about three hours on each occasion, drinking coffee to an immense extent, and pestering me with requests for various articles of which he stood in need.

On the 16th I deemed it high time to be getting under way, being quite sick of the presence of Mahura and his retinue, who came down to my wagons, and remained there for the greater part of the day, merely to eat and drink and pester me, not bringing any articles of any value for barter, and asking absurdly high prices. Accordingly, at an early hour, I ordered my men to count my cattle and inspan, and in about an hour we were on the move. Old Mahura was coming down to drink coffee, and met us as we were going past the town. He was evidently vexed at my sudden departure. I presented him with some coffee, sugar, and other articles equivalent in value to the kaross which he had given me, and took leave of him. In the afternoon we marched about six or seven miles nearer to the Vaal, and halted in the hollow where nearly ten months before I had coursed an old blue wildebeest with dogs.

Considerable delay was caused next day along the line of march by young oxen, which could not be persuaded to trek, although flogged until their sides and flanks were red with gore. About four hours after the sun rose we reached the fount beside a few acres of bush, where we outspanned. Our march was across boundless open country. We saw a good deal of game, blue and black wildebeest, blesbok, springbok, and a fine troop of about thirty hartebeests. In the afternoon I again marched, and at nightfall we encamped on the bank of the fair Vaal River. It was considerably swollen, heavy rains having lately fallen; but, being upon the ebb, I deemed it well not to take the drift until the morrow, when, having arranged two trektows, we commenced crossing the Vaal, one wagon at a time, with twenty oxen, and in about two hours my three heavily-laden wagons were brought through in safety.

On the 24th our morning's march brought us into the district where in the commencement of last winter I had seen such overwhelming swarms of blesboks Boers were encamped on the opposite side of the river. I outspanned beside some shady thorn-trees; lions' spoor was seen on the line of march. In the afternoon I lost my march, being obliged to halt soon after I inspanned to correct a bush of the iron axle-tree wagon, which was loose.

The 25th was a cloudy morning, with a cool breeze. Our morning's march brought us to a forsaken Boer encampment, around which lay the remains of the different varieties of game frequenting the district. We halted for breakfast beside several acres of thorn-cover on the bank of the river.

As we were breakfasting on the 24th by the banks of the river, a trader from the Pari (a district near Cape Town), of French extraction, passed us with his two wagons laden with merchandise. He took a cup of tea with me and gave me the news of the colony. Observing the skull of an old bull buffalo fastened on one of my traps, he asked me if it was the head of an elephant. Another Boer had asked me a few days since if a crocodile's heal, which was tied up at the back of Carollus's wagon, belonged to an elephant. In the afternoon, as we were inspanning, we were visited by a rebel Boer of very large proportions. This man told us plainly that the Boers did not consider themselves as conquered, and that they intended to try it once again.

We had now reached that point in our line of march where we were to take leave of the Vet River. I rode ahead of the wagons to hunt, and after proceeding about a mile, found myself out of the country of sweet grass, and entering upon bare and boundless open plains, thinly clad with sour pasturage, the favorite haunt and continual residence of innumerable herds of black wildebeest, blesbok, and springbok. As I rode on, large troops of these excellent, sport-yielding antelopes gratified my eyes in every direction. I had been long away from them, far, far in the dense forest regions of the far interior, and now I gazed once more upon them with a lively feeling of pleasure and intense interest which no words can describe.

On the 28th I rode in a northwesterly course, and gave chase to a noble herd of about two hundred black wildebeest. These being very wild, I yacked them on the Boer principle, and, taking a double family shot at about three hundred yards, when the dust had blown past one fine bull was found to have bitten the dust this was very near camp, so I dispatched Ruyter for men and a pack-ox to bring the gnoo to camp. I held on in a westerly course, and found the game extremely shy, owing to the high winds.

In the afternoon I inspanned and marched, there being very little grass here for my cattle, and danger of the oxen taking a horrible and very fatal illness, called by the Boers "snot sickness," which cattle are very liable to from pasturing on ground frequented by black wildebeests. The sky to the north and west looked very threatening, and, before we had proceeded far, black masses of clouds came rolling up toward us, and vivid flashes of forked lightning, accompanied by appalling peals of thunder, proclaimed the approach of a storm. In a few minutes it was upon us, the rain falling in torrents. We held for a rocky coppice or hill, beside which we outspanned, and in about an hour the storm had passed away vast herds of game surrounded us on every side.

Next day we marched, the country being very heavy for the bullocks, owing to the rain which had fallen. I held across the country for a range of stony hills, dotted over with dwarfish trees and bushes, on which I expected to find sweet grass for my cattle. On my way thither the plains on every side of us presented the most lively display of game, and I was tempted by the endless streams of blesboks to halt my wagons for a minute to catch and saddle steeds and give them chase They proved extremely shy, and in about four hours I rode to seek my wagons, having bagged a gnoo and a brace of blesboks.

While following the game, one of my after-riders started an ostrich from her nest, which she had scooped in the sand : it was about seven feet in diameter, and contained thirty-four fine fresh eggs. I left Ruyter in charge of the nest, the eggs being in danger from jackals and vultures, and particularly from the ostrich herself, who would return in our absence and break every one of them. Having reached my camp, I dispatched two men with leather sacks to fetch them.

On the 14th, with much difficulty, we got over the cable by which the raft was worked, and the Boers, by way of experiment, loaded her up with a party of Bechuana Caffres, and endeavored to cross the river. There was a small boat attached to the float. When they had got about half way across, the water rose partially over the float, when a panic came over both the

Boers and Bechuanas, and a rush was made into the little boat. A capsize was the consequence; and at the same moment, the rope which attached the boat to the float parted. The unfortunate men were then swept away down the rapid current; and of twenty seven men who were on board of the punt, four only escaped. Two of those who were drowned were Boers. After this accident I directed ray men, who were in an isolated position on the opposite side of the river, to inspan and remove down to Norwal's boat, below Alleman's Drift, where I met them with the cap-tent wagon; and at sundown next day we had safely ferried over the other two wagons, and encamped once more on British territory.

The ferrying was a very laborious proceeding, each wagon having to be off-loaded, and then taken to pieces, and so brought over, bit by bit; the oxen and horses, &c., swam the river. My wagons were now all safely across; so, after loading them, we marched on the 18th, about 10 A.M. At sundown we entered the town of Colesberg, and drew up opposite to the old barracks, having been absent exactly twelve months.

As my wagons advanced into the town, the news of our arrival spread like wildfire, and multitudes both of men and good-looking young women rushed to see the old elephant hunter, who had been mourned as dead. We were soon surrounded by nearly one half of the population, who mobbed-us until night setting in dispersed them to their homes.

During my stay in Colesberg I had much pleasure in meeting my friend Mr. Oswell, of the Honorable East India Company's Service. He was then en route for the far interior, intending to penetrate the Kalihari in a northwesterly direction, and visit the lake of boats. This was an expedition which I myself had often thought of making, but a limited finance, and my fancy for collecting objects of natural history, led me to incline my course to the more verdant forests of the East, where I deemed I could more certainly first collect, and then export, the precious spoils of the elephant. Mr. Oswell being in want of draught oxen, I permitted him to select as many as he required from my extensive stock, with which he shortly set out, in company with Mr. Murray, on his interesting journey of discovery. I was occupied in Colesberg till the 12th of April, when I marched to "Cuil Vonteyn," a farm belonging to a Mrs. Van Blerk, which I reached in about three hours; the country all karroo, herds of springboks feeding in sight of the house. Here I found nine heavily-laden wagons drawn up, which I had hired and laden up to transport my collection of hunting trophies to the sea. When I entered Colesberg I had almost made up my mind to make another shooting expedition into the interior; but a combination of circumstances induced me at length to leave Africa for a season, and revisit my native land.

Having thus resolved to leave the colony, I directed my march toward Port Elizabeth, by way of Graff Reinett, crossing the bold mountain range of Snewberg. On the 10th of May I reached the shores of the ocean, which Ruyter and others of my followers, now beholding for the first time, gazed upon with wonder and with awe. On the 19th I took my passage for Old England in the bark "Augusta." My valuable collection of trophies and my Cape wagon, weighing all together upward of thirty tons, were then carefully shipped, and on the 7th of June I set sail (my little Bushman accompanying me) for my native land, after a sojourn of nearly five years in the wild hunting grounds of Southern Africa.

Printed in Great Britain
by Amazon